The Educational Technology Reviews Series

Number ten
Using Programmed Instruction

Educational Technology Publications
Englewood Cliffs, New Jersey 07632

V

Library of Congress Cataloging in Publication Data
Main entry under title:

Using programmed instruction.

(Educational technology reviews series, no. 10)
Articles selected from Educational technology.
1. Programmed instruction—Addresses, essays,
lectures. I. Educational technology. II. Series.
[LB1028.5.U75]   371.39'442   72-12692
ISBN 0-87778-058-7

Printed in the United States of America.

First Printing: January, 1973.

ABOUT THIS BOOK

This volume contains articles published in recent issues of *Educational Technology* Magazine. The articles were selected from among a larger number of works dealing with the topic of this volume which have been published by the Magazine. The articles herein appeared originally in *Educational Technology* within the past five years.

This volume is to be revised periodically, according to developments in the field, as reflected in the pages of *Educational Technology*.

CONTENTS

A Technology of Performance Problem Solving

J. H. Harless

The question raised in this special section of **ET** implies that PI is some "thing"; second, that this "medium" had its heyday and is no longer with us (like the Edsel, bathtub gin, or the slate tablet). It is no longer possible to speak of PI as **a** thing (unless we agree to talk about it as **one** of the possible product-types of a process).

The process of computer programming produces instructions to the computer, a piece of software. The thing generated by the process of automobile assembly is an automobile. The "thing" produced by the PROCESS of instructional programming is BEHAVIOR CHANGE—**not** a text of frames or a roll of tape for a teaching machine.

There are at least three distinct levels of meaning to the phrase:

1. PI as a unit of instruction, a single product.
2. PI as a process of producing validated learning **systems**.
3. PI as the father of a technology for addressing and solving performance deficiencies.

Programmed instruction at all three levels is alive and well.

A decade ago, when the ballyhoo about programmed instruction began, the first level of meaning was current. That is, PI was defined as a product, a piece of software having certain common characteristics: subject matter broken down into small steps; provision for overt responding to stimulus elements in physical units or "frames"; some tactic for giving the student immediate confirmation of his response; and the steps arranged into a "logical" sequence. Some persons added: validated-according-to-behavioral-objectives (although few bothered to systematically derive the objectives or worry about their value).

PI still exists in product form—in greater quantities than ever. However, the previous "rules" have been ridiculed by subsequent research and experience. That is, there are numerous examples of PI products which violate the above characteristics. No longer are the products bound by a physical format like the frame—or even a written text. There are excellent programs which do not require a single overt response by the student. Sequence and size of steps are determined according to well-demonstrated paradigms rather than loose guides

J. H. Harless is president of the J. H. Harless Company, Falls Church, Virginia.

A MODEL FOR THE ANALYSIS AND DESIGN OF EFFECTIVE LEARNING SYSTEMS

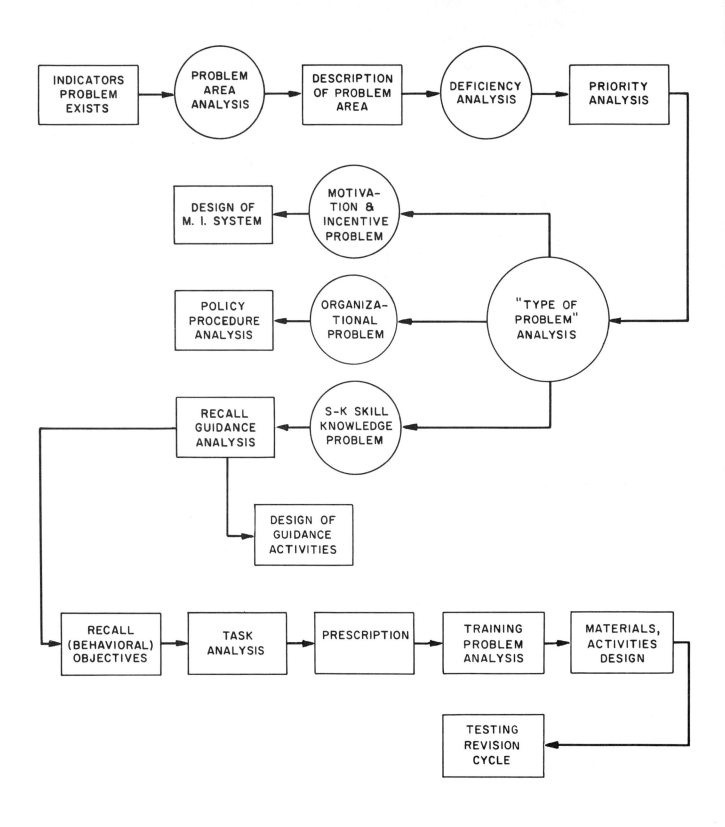

like "logical sequence" and "smallest meaningful steps."

The sub-technology for producing **physical** teaching sequences has grown and expanded into computer assisted instruction, programmed films and tapes, "programmed lectures," etc. However, this growth in product variety precipitated a much more interesting ascendance in the meaning of "programmed instruction."

At the second level of meaning, PI is a **process** for producing LEARNING SYSTEMS. By definition, a system is a process; that is, all pertinent factors and components are studied in relation to all other. The product of a system analysis is a functioning body of components which complement each other and play individual roles. One of the roles in a **learning** system may be a programmed **text** in the product sense; however, the system may contain other media and activities in a programmed **relationship**. A learning system designed to teach some performance area or the other, for example, might contain the following components:

- A PI text teaching the verbal facilitating elements of the area, such as the overall steps, error recognition, covert discriminations, etc.;
- A programmed film designed to demonstrate the performance area to a higher level of stimulation;
- A trainee guide (like a cookbook) designed to facilitate the trainee's practice;
- Precisely designed feedback documents for a live instructor to use in monitoring and aiding the trainee's gain in proficiency; and
- Programmed model practice jobs to maximize transfer.

The point is that all activities are programmed. There is a defensible selection criterion and sequence rationale for the media and activities in the learning system. Too, the product of the instructional programming process is behavior change (manual performance in this example).

In short, the second level of meaning of programmed instruction implies the process of determining the most cost/beneficial combination and sequence of instructional strategies for a given area, for a given trainee population.

There is a growing group of individuals and organizations who were fathered by the learning system "phase" of PI development. These people prefer the designations Behavior Engineer or Educational Technologist, rather than the more limiting title of "programmer." To be sure, today's Behavior Engineer is skilled in the development of programmed material and learning systems; but his concern is much broader. The Behavior Engineer starts with few assumptions—not even that a training or educational deficiency exists in a given group of people. He certainly does not assume that a PI text or a learning system will be prepared.

I suggest (see **Figure 1**) that there are at least the following major phases in a performance problem-solving process undertaken by the Behavior Engineer.

1. The Behavior Engineer narrows the area of concern through a process of describing and verifying that "some deficiency" exists by ferreting out symptoms or problem-indicators.

2. He performs a systematic derivation of a "model of mastery" in the domain indicated by the first step. That is, before any given performance area or subject matter body is treated, he must describe in detail what **non**-deficiency performance is.

3. He compares actual performance to the mastery model. The product of this involved analysis is a description of deficiencies. The first three steps, therefore, make up an "object generating" sub-system.

4. He hypothesizes and checks possible **causes** of each deficiency. That is, some deficiencies are due to a lack of skill/knowledge on the part of the performers. Some are due to a lack of motivation/incentive/feedback given. A surprising number of times neither of the above is at fault; often the criterion performance is not achieved because the organization prevents or hinders correct performance: operational inefficiencies, poor scheduling, ill-defined organizational goals, missing or improper equipment, workload imbalance, etc. I submit that one of the most common errors committed by programmers, managers and educators is that all deficiencies can be remedied by training or "educating."

5. He designs and prepares the appropriate system for solving each type of deficiency. A learning system solves don't-know-how-to problems. Behavior management systems solve can-do-but-won't-do deficiencies. Organizational or operational changes are required to remedy non-training, non-motivational problems.

6. He validates, revises and implements remedy-systems.

Perhaps I am calling for an absurd jump for the phrase "programmed instruction" to encompass the last level. Nevertheless, that is "what is happening to programmed instruction." At least, this is the context in which the first two meanings must be set if we are indeed to have an educational revolution.

In summary,

1. PI has grown in meaning from a product to a process and perhaps to a technology of performance problem solving.

2. The products of the process have changed and encompass virtually every medium. □

The Criterion Problem in Programmed Instruction

Robert K. Branson

Experimental psychology has offered to educators three panaceas: intelligence and aptitude testing, programmed instruction and the instructional systems approach. Each started in the laboratory, was tried out in specific school situations and was heralded with enthusiasm by researchers and hucksters alike. The same developmental course was followed by all three: success in the military, success in industry, and a minimum degree of success in the schools.

Psychological testing

Psychological testing procedures have been used in the schools longer than either programmed instruction or the systems approach. Tests have been legislated as a part of regular school programs and as screening procedures for college admissions. There is currently a feeling that testing has been utilized to its fullest feasible extent in

Robert K. Branson is with Deterline Associates, Los Altos, California.

schools; yet the positive results reported in the literature are disappointingly meager.

The original correlational approach was replaced by a considerably more sophisticated technique of factor analysis. Despite the amount of effort expended, the value of statistical prediction in the schools remains limited to predicting academic success for elementary students.

Recent efforts to identify predictors of academic success and non-academic success (tests which will predict grades or other achievements) have been disappointing, considering the amount of time and effort previously spent on the problem and the sophisticated statistical evidence which can now be applied.[1,2] Even relatively successful testing programs are restricted to predictions for groups, not individuals.

While the schools may view testing's lack of success as something that might have been expected, psychologists have continued to strive for more accurate predictions. Why should procedures that have worked so well in the military and in industry fail to achieve similar results in academic settings? A typical answer is that the military and industry are concerned with **training**, that **education** is fundamentally different from training, and further, that the true purpose of education cannot be formalized by precise specifications, as can training.

Programmed instruction

Programmed instruction in machine and book form achieved an impressive list of successes in the Air Force. DuPont and other companies had excellent results with their programmed materials. As evidence accumulated, there was great hope that the technique would be successful in the schools.

Isolated classes tried programmed texts in specific course content areas, with generally favorable results. Rarely did the program do worse than traditional methods when the same criterion test was used. Since most indicators have been highly encouraging, why hasn't programmed instruction virtually taken over from other methods?

Teachers were reported to oppose programmed materials of the fear of being replaced. Administrators were blamed because they lacked the courage to try new methods. Publishers still are being blamed for not dropping traditional materials and promoting programmed materials exclusively.[3]

The systems approach

The systems approach resulted in startling improvements in managment and planning and in operations that were difficult to imagine when the technique was first used. Military, scientific and industrial users of the systems approach have all reaped impressive benefits from its applications. The story repeats itself. Empirically developed procedures work extremely well in a variety of similar situations and flounder **when applied to the problems of the schools.**

Adequate educational criteria

Each of these has a fundamental requirement that must be satisfied before significant results can be achieved: There must be **adequate criteria.** The specifications for adequate criteria have been carefully researched and repeatedly presented in the literature. While adequate criteria for psychological tests differ statistically from the requirements of the systems approach and programmed instruction, they are basically similar.

Adequate criteria can be stated in behavioral terms such that independent observers can identify the presence, absence or degree of the prescribed behavior in the target population using appropriate measuring devices. Adequate criterion behavior can be described in terms of a subject matter or a co-ordinated skill. E. K. Strong demonstrated that one only needs to identify the gross behavior in a target population; it is not necessary to formalize a definition or description, only to identify the **people** who have it.[4]

So long as we continue to emphasize the development of better and better programmed materials, while avoiding the overall criterion problem, we can expect the same things to happen to programmed instruction and the systems approach that has happened to testing. Gradually, the technical problems and limited usefulness of the technique will relegate it to a position of second-class citizenship, rather than the dominant place in instruction that it should occupy.

Fair comparisons of various instructional methods can only be made when alternative means for reaching identical criteria are tested in rigorous experimental style. Vague and spurious benefits that have historically been claimed for traditional methods, when tested against programmed methods, could then be proven or discounted. All expected instructional benefits should be specified **a priori**, and measures for them applied after instruction. If they have real benefits, the data should confirm them.

Grading systems approximating the normal curve are not acceptable criteria for comparison of methods of instruction. Conversely, measured achievement of specific levels of knowledge or skill is an acceptable criterion, since each person in the class has the opportunity to meet the prescribed specifications, regardless of how well or poorly his classmates do. Criterion referenced measures of performance should be used almost exclusively to evaluate instruction and students.

Proximate and ultimate criteria

In order to formalize criteria so that they become a part of the system for improving instruction, care must be taken in discriminating between proximate and ultimate criteria. Ultimate criteria represent the long-term effects that we expect from the total educational experience. A learner satisfies ultimate criteria when at some remote point in time he exhibits appropriate behavior which resulted from **specified** prior experience.

Current educational experiences are presumed, on the basis of impressionistic data, to contribute to the satisfaction of ultimate criteria. Yet, if one identifies appropriate behavior in an adult and attempts to trace its origins to specific school experiences, there is virtually no reliable data to support such connections. Further, if one identifies a specific school experience, then tries to project the influence it will have on remote behavior, again there is little, if any, acceptable data. Caplan has gone so far as to question our ability to prove statistically the main effects of any currently used educational or instructional variable.[5]

Proximate criteria can be stated clearly in behavioral terms, and represent the immediate measurable effects of instruction presumed to be necessary prerequisites for ultimate criteria. Successive proximate criteria should be the interim steps to the satisfaction of an ultimate criterion. Each proximate criterion relates directly to a demonstrable aspect of one or more ultimate criteria.

An ultimate criterion might well imply **why** a given subject matter or skill is to be taught; the proximate criteria subordinate to it enable us to determine **whether** the material was learned.

Testing, programmed instruction and the systems approach

Each of these techniques has a significant role in education. The systems approach, properly applied, enables us to select a mission, to define ultimate criteria, to derive proximate criteria, and to use the measured results of the system to revise its own operations.[6,7]

Psychological testing and performance evaluation techniques enable us to determine whether and to what degree learners possess the behavior that was specified. The measurement of subtle behavior and the assessment of performance is a highly developed and continuously improving discipline.[8,9]

Programmed instruction, in its generic sense, provides the methodology through which learners can satisfy **proximate criteria**. There are three tests which must be satisfied if instruction is properly to be classified as **programmed:**

1. The intents (proximate criteria) must be stated in behavioral terms such that learner outcomes can be independently verified.

2. There must be a provision for interim feedback to the learner of his own progress.

3. The utility of the materials or processes must be established through use with the target population, and the materials must be evaluated on the basis of data generated in the tryout.

Presumably, all forms of instruction could be modified to fit the programmed model. Generally, one cannot obtain highly effective or efficient instruction unless the materials and procedures are designed for use by **individual students** rather than groups.

The future

The future of programmed instruction as a methodology seems to be limited by the degree to which there is application of the systems approach and appropriate measuring techniques. The advantages of programmed instruction can never be fully established until all instruction is measured on the basis of learner outcomes, rather than the time allocated for instruction.

Recent innovations, such as team teaching, have been much more fully accepted, with faddish swiftness, and solely as a matter of faith, even though there is virtually no competent data establishing team teaching as a useful technique.

Serious researchers have invented and developed in the past fifteen years such innovations as individualized instruction, computer based and computer assisted instruction, only to find each of them separately and all of them collectively classified as not feasible for public schools. The absence of criteria for evaluation and the lack of empirically based instructional techniques leaves us with a simple conclusion: The only possible approach to education is what we are doing now.

Would our current approach be feasible if we were starting from scratch? Perhaps that is why there are so many laymen who feel qualified to criticize the schools. □

References

1. Lloyd G. Humphreys. The Fleeting Nature of the Prediction of College Academic Success. **Journal of Educational Psychology, 59,** 1968, pp. 375-380.
2. James M. Richards, Jr., J. H. Holland & S. W. Lutz. Prediction of Student Accomplishment in College. **Journal of Educational Psychology, 58,** 1967, pp. 343-355.
3. T. F. Gilbert. Some Issues in Mathetics: I. Saying What A Subject Matter Is. **NSPI Journal, 8,** 2, 1969, pp. 4-19.
4. E. K. Strong. **Vocational Interests of Men and Women.** Palo Alto: Stanford University Press, 1943.
5. Stanley W. Caplan. Does School Make a Difference? In **Fostering and Reinforcing Innovative Behavior in Selected School Personnel.** Albuquerque: Southwestern Cooperative Educational Laboratory, 1967.
6. Robert K. Branson. The Systems Approach: An Introduction. In **Proceedings, Sixth Annual Community College President's Institute,** Ann Arbor: Midwest Community College Leadership Foundation, 1966.
7. Robert M. Gagne. **Psychological Principles in System Development.** New York: Holt, Rinehart and Winston, 1966, Chapter 12 and 13.
8. **Loc. Cit.**
9. E. J. Webb, D. T. Campbell, R. D. Schwartz & Lee Sechrest. **Unobtrusive Measures.** Chicago: Rand McNally, 1966.

Needed: High Quality in Programmed Materials

Allen D. Calvin
Contributing Editor

The first requirement for the acceptance of programmed materials is that they be of the highest quality. This sounds so obvious that it does not appear to need saying. However, we must remember that for years educators were sold materials, such as the Dick and Jane type of books, that did not work. Educators, therefore, began to believe that one set of materials were just as "good" or "bad" as another. The idea that there were materials that could actually **teach** was completely foreign to many educators. Instead, they would look at the "illustrations" or the "binding," and never bother with the fundamental question "do these materials teach?" It never occurred to them that there could be such materials.

Further, the term "programmed materials" has no meaning. It is a term like "high fidelity" or "sports car." It is quite obvious that many audio systems sold as "high fidelity" are actually of extremely "low fidelity." Thus, people will often use one of these so-called "high fidelity" sets and say they can't see anything so exciting about "high fidelity." The same is true of our other example of the "sports car." There is, after all, a considerable difference between driving a Detroit "sports car" and a Lotus. But, to the uninitiated, a "sports car" is a "sports car" is a "sports car" . . .

Because you call materials "programmed" doesn't mean anything. Very often, materials were called "programmed" which, in fact, were "antiprogrammed." These materials were produced and put on the market, and when educators refused to enthusiastically purchase them, the distributors complained bitterly about the "lack of willingness of educators to accept innovative materials." Actually, once educators learned that there was such a thing as programmed materials that actually did teach, the reception was overwhelmingly enthusiastic. At the present time, BRL materials have been both state adopted and city adopted throughout the country. For example, a million of our mathematics books have been purchased by the State of California for next year, and the City of New York will use over a million of our reading books. "Lack of willingness to accept innovative materials"?

The second crucial factor in the acceptance of programmed materials is provision for support services. The conventional distributor who attempted to market programmed materials often tried to market them in the same way as he did other textbooks. Since the other textbooks were not designed to teach in the sense of programmed textbooks, they were often just dumped in the schools. In such instances, failure was assured.

Programmed materials have become the vehicle for individualizing instruction and thereby dramatically changing the structure of the schools.

It is apparent to us that programmed materials will be the dominant method of instruction by the end of this decade. As study after study comes in demonstrating the effectiveness of high-quality programmed materials, the public is demanding more rapid expansion.

We sincerely hope that more and more educational technology companies will resist the siren lure of irrelevant hardware and join with us in helping to individualize the school systems of America. If they do so, then they too will find, as we have, that the combination of high quality programmed materials plus appropriate support systems creates an approach which is welcomed with open arms by administrators, parents and students. □

Programmed Instruction in the Soviet Union

Introduction

T. C. Helvey
Contributing Editor

In many scientific and non-scientific reports, one still finds in the historical introductions the cliche "Already the old Greeks have. . . ." Today, in the reports in the field of cybernetics, especially in cybernetic pedagogy, one has to modify this by stating that "Already the Russians have. . . ." because they surely have; I always read their reports with appreciation and envy.

Of course, a simple analysis reveals the reason why the Russians are ahead of the United States in this, and in some other fields: they educate in colleges and universities three times more scientists and engineers than the Americans, and the rigor and depth of their instruction is at least equivalent to that of ours. It is natural that from such a rich technological human pool many excellent men will emerge.

Although I admit that science and its achievements are "international," nevertheless emotionally I would like to see the United States in the lead. This does not counteract my belief that science and its achievements should be universal property for the betterment of mankind, and the best instrument of peace. Scientific and engineering accomplishments do spread through political and language barriers (in spite of the immature secrecy of some individuals and "classification" by governments). They are spread in the professional literature and at international meetings and societies, such as the recently formed World Organization for General Systems and Cybernetics. It is unfortunate that the international information transmission through the existing channels is inadequate.

This is why very few persons in the Western hemisphere are familiar with the pioneering work of L. N. Landa in the field of automation in pedagogy. He is director of the Programmed Instruction Laboratory of the Academy of Psychological Sciences in Moscow. If one looks into the development and achievements of Professor Landa, one becomes aware that he is not only promoting the profession by his own efforts but is a powerful force in motivating others to do the same. Of course, he is endeared to me by the fact that he is a cybernetician, and advances what I have been preaching for years, namely that in studying education one cannot learn "methods" of instruction or students' behavior in learning, by themselves. Because the student-teacher environment is a singular system, with rich feedback loops, restricted communication channels and considerable noise in all parts of the system, and which furthermore is complex enough to have a trend of self-organization, it is **cybernetic** and will yield best results if treated as such.

This does not mean that I am in agreement with all of Landa's statements. But cybernetics and pedagogy are not like politics; thus, the fundamentals are not based on dogma. Consequently, in a controversy, defeat is just as welcome and acceptable as success.

I am grateful to Landa (and to the publisher of this magazine) for the article which illuminates excellently the scope of the interest in Russia for automated instruction and its cybernetic aspects. It will be a most important time for those of us who are unfortunately incompetent in the Russian language when Landa's books will be translated into English.*

---

*Two books by L. N. Landa, in English, are scheduled for publication during the coming year by Educational Technology Publications.

Introduction

Felix F. Kopstein
Contributing Editor

Though the admission may be uncomfortable, it is none the less true that the American community tends to have a parochial view of educational technology. Perhaps because few of us read any language but English with ease, we are deterred from the study of many foreign scientific and technological journals. Of course, this does not explain why such journals from the non-United States English-speaking world are not read very much either. Surely we have learned by now that no nation, regardless of its size or wealth or power, has a "monopoly on brains." Our foreign colleagues seem to appreciate this point. The existing parochialism is a unilateral one, since foreign technical journals are studded with references to American work.

In particular, the USSR responded with avidity to the notion of programmed instruction as it began to be reported in the United States during the late fifties and early sixties. However, from the beginning, there appears to have been a marked difference.

While American thought, with the exception of Crowder, was by and large founded on the "atheoretical" principles of operant conditioning, or on a variety of extant learning theories, the Russian approach derived heavily from **cybernetics**. From the beginning, also, one of the outstanding exponents of a melding in instructional technology of psychology and cybernetics has been Prof. L. N. Landa. His 1966 book, "Algorithmization and Learning," is clearly discernible as a major intellectual influence in much European—particularly East European—work. While so far no English translation has been available, one is now in preparation. Its appearance will make Prof. Landa's stimulating and original thinking accessible to a monolingual English readership.

The article which follows is Prof. Landa's account of the genesis, evolution and present status of programmed instruction in the USSR. Prof. Landa is now preparing a second article for **ET** readers, reporting in some depth on his own work.

Programmed Instruction in the Soviet Union

L. N. Landa

Since 1962, programmed instruction has begun to develop systematically in the USSR. In contrast to the United States, where it arose as a result of a purely psychological analysis of the learning process and at first was merely a supplement to certain psychological theories of applied instruction, programmed instruction in the Soviet Union began from the very start to develop on the basis of a wider, cybernetic* approach to the process of instruction and to examining it as a particular instance in the control process. This approach was set forth by the author of the present article in two lectures[1] (at a conference on the philosophical problems of cybernetics at the Soviet Academy of Sciences and at the Soviet State Committee for the Coordination of Scientific Research Projects), after which the Ministry of Higher and Intermediate Special Education in the USSR and the Ministry of Education of the RSFSR reached the decision on the advisability of developing programmed instruction projects in the universities, schools and technical institutions, and on providing government support for the development of these projects.

---

*"Cybernetics is the science which studies the communication and the processes of control in living organisms and machines." — N. Wiener, **Cybernetics**, 1948. "Cybernetics describes an intelligent activity or event which can be expressed in algorithms. Algorithms, in turn, refer to a system of instructions which describes unambiguously and accurately an interaction which is equivalent to a given type of flux of intelligence and a subsequent, controlled activity. The development of cybernetics aims, among other things, at the design and reproduction of functions which are peculiar to intelligent organisms."—T. C. Helvey.

1. The basic positions of these lectures are reflected in the article by the author of this article, "On the Cybernetic Approach to the Theory of Instruction," in 1961 and 1962. (O Kiberneticeskom Podxode k Teorii Obucenija) Problems of Philosophy No. 9, 1962 (Voprosy Filosofii). There is an English translation: JPRS 17, 896, 1 March, 1963. OTS 63-21233. U.S. Department of Commerce, Office of Technical Services, Building T-30, Ohio Drive & Independence Ave. S.W., Washington, D.C.

Of course, a cybernetic approach to the learning process did not exclude the psychological and pedagogical approaches. Moreover, it proceeded from the fact that, in learning, common patterns of control take the form of directing the mental activity and behavior of students; it is in connection with this fact that effective control in learning is only possible on the basis of knowing about and taking into account the psychological and pedagogical patterns. However, the significance of the cybernetic approach to instruction lay in the fact that specific psychological and pedagogical patterns of learning and instruction were examined from a more general, cybernetic point of view. Thanks to this, there opened up the possibilities of optimizing instructional control based on applying the achievements of a general theory of control and the sciences connected with it (mathematical logic, information theory, algorithm theory, regulating theory and the like) to this type of control. If instruction represents a particular aspect of the control process, then, first the general patterns of control learned from cybernetics and general methods of its optimization are applicable to it; secondly, it requires studying the specific forms and patterns of this aspect of control which have been conditioned by the specific character of its object. Such an approach opened the way in the USSR for the intensive development of projects in regions of an essentially new scientific direction—cybernetic pedagogy (or pedagogical cybernetics) and set a whole series of new and interesting problems before these new trends. Projects have developed along these lines simultaneously in several countries, including the United States. [See "Cybernetic Pedagogy," by T. C. Helvey, **Educational Technology,** September, 1969.]

It must be said that the cybernetic approach to instruction and the interest in programmed instruction did not arise by chance in the Soviet Union. It was prepared for by the logic of developing several strictly psychological and pedagogical ideas and approaches which, with the appearance of cybernetics, were interpreted cybernetically and therefore began to develop as psychological-cybernetic ideas. Among these ideas, it is necessary above all to draw attention to the idea of controlling the formation of students' thought processes with the help of special directions, some of which, as it turned out, can be interpreted as algorithmic-type and others as heuristic-type. The interpreting of these directions in terms of the algorithm theory and the theory of heuristic process opened the way in the Soviet Union for a new scientific field,[2] which has received the appellation of "algorithmization of instruction" (algoritmizaciia v obucenii). This trend, which originally had worked out the problem of instructing students in common methods of thought, acquired a more general significance and began, with the help of algorithms, to work out not only the problem of forming reasoning in students, but also other mental processes, as well as every possible form of behavior. Moreover, it became clear that it was possible to describe algorithmically not only the activities of the students, but also the work of the teacher, which permitted the interpretation of programmed instruction as algorithmized instruction (such an interpretation has been developed in a number of papers and articles in the Federal Republic of Germany). What serves as a basis for such an interpretation is the fact that the construction of a defined program of instruction necessarily assumes the preliminary formulation of an instructional algorithm, while it does not necessarily assume the instructing of students in algorithms in the course of carrying out this program.[3]

Research projects on the applicability of the algorithmization idea to instruction are connected with other tendencies in scientific work being developed in the Soviet Union and receiving the

2. The first works on this problem were published by the author of this article in 1961 and 1962: "Teaching Students Methods of Rational Thinking and the Problem of Algor-

ithms" (Obucenie Ucajuscixsja Metodam Racional'nogo Myslenija i Problema Algoritmov), **Problems of Psychology,** 1961, No. 1. (Voprosy Psixologii); "An Experiment in Applying Mathematical Logic and Information Theory to Several Teaching Problems" **Problems of Psychology,** 1962, No. 2 (Opyt Primenenija Matematiceskoj Logiki i Teorii Informacii k Nekotorym Problemam Obucenija, "Voprosy Psixologii." Research on this problem has been summarized in the monograph "Algorithmization in Teaching," Moscow: "Prosvescenie", 1966 (Algoritmizacija v Obucenii). Research on the problem of teaching students directions of an heuristic-type (on the material of solving geometric problems by proofs) was completed in 1954 and was reflected in a dissertation which was defended in 1955 (c.f. "On the Forming in Students of a Common Method of Reasoning when Solving Problems" /O Formirovanii u Ucascixsja Obscego Metoda Rassuzdenij pri Resenii Zadac/Autoreference—dissertation, Moscow, 1955). Results of this research were also published in the article: "On the Forming in Students of a Common Method of Thinking when Solving Problems" (O Formirovanii u Ucascixsja Obscego Metoda Myslenija pri Resenii Zadac) Problems of Psychology (Problemy Psixologii) 1959 No. 3. The special work of the author of "Das Verhaltnis . . ." has been devoted to the problem of the correlation of algorithmic and heuristic processes: "Das Verhaltnis zwischen heuristischen und algorithmischen Prozessen und einige Probleme ihrer Herausbildung durch programmierter Unterricht," "Wissenschaftliche Zeitschrift des padagogischen Instituts Gustrow," Jahrgang 1966/67; Sondernummer.

3. For a more detailed understanding of the "algorithm of teaching" and "teaching algorithm" see the author's brochure, "Algorithms and Programmed Instruction," Moscow, 1966 (Algoritmy i Programmirovannoe Obucenie). There is an English translation, "Programmed Learning and Language Laboratory," edited by K. Burg, London, Longmans, 1969, pp. 57-135.

name, "Theory of Stage-by-Stage Forming of Mental Activities" (Prof. L. Ja. Gal'perin and his co-workers[4]).

What this theory says in effect is that mental activity can be effectively molded only when it goes through a series of stages in the process of its formation. These are: (1) the preliminary familiarization with the activity; (2) material or materialized activity, when the trainee carries out the activity in an external material form; (3) the external speech stage, when all elements of the activity are presented in the form of external or expressed speech (oral or written); and (4) the stage of speech "about oneself," when the activity is carried out in the form of a pronouncement about oneself.

The theory of stage-by-stage formation of mental activities and the algorithmic approach have in common the fact that they both require the operation-by-operation analysis of the students' thought processes and their operation-by-operation formation. The difference between them lies in the fact that a single action is the subject of the stage-by-stage theory (the stages of its forming and its parameters), while the subject of algorithmic theory as applied to learning is the connection between the actions themselves, their interdependencies and their structures, which provide the determination of sufficiently complicated intellectual and other problems, and serve as the basis of formation of other common methods of thought in students.

If the theory of forming thought processes by stages was a purely psychological theory, the theory of algorithmization was a psycho-cybernetic theory which made possible the development of the idea of cybernetic pedagogy and led to programmed instruction on a somewhat different theoretical basis from what took place in the United States in the work of Skinner and his school (it is not possible here to analyze Skinner's theory and the approaches described in the present article). Nevertheless, a series of the most general principles about programmed instruction theory—principles of activity, contingent re-inforcement, operant conditioning, individualization have coincided, so that it became possible to develop the approaches characterized above within the framework of programmed instruction.

Such was the theoretical situation at the moment when the expediency of beginning studies on programmed instruction in our country was recognized.

A series of organizational measures were taken to carry out the accepted resolutions on developing studies on programmed instruction. An interdepartmental council was formed to deal with the question of programmed instruction, under the auspices of the Ministry of Higher and Secondary Specialized Education of the USSR. Its functions were to coordinate throughout the country studies on programmed instruction. Similar councils were created in some of the other ministries and departments. In the Council on Cybernetics of the ANSSSR (The Academy of Sciences of the USSR), a commission on programmed instruction was created, and in the Pedagogical Society of the RSFSR, it was a section of technical methods and programmed instruction. An important step was taken in creating scientific research laboratories for programmed instruction. Such laboratories were created in the Institute of Psychology at the Academy of Pedogogical Sciences at Moscow State University, at the Moscow Institute of Energy and somewhat later at a series of other institutes and universities.

Articles on programmed instruction published in 1962-1963 in the general press and in scientific journal aroused an interest in this new direction in many teachers from educational institutions of every type—universities, technical schools, secondary schools and educational institutions for professional and technical education. Not only specialists in psychology and pedagogy began to study programmed instruction, but also student-teachers and engineers—and they were the majority—who often had not the required psychological and pedagogical background. It is natural that the theoretical level of several articles and selections appearing at the time was not always sufficiently high. The distinguishing feature of that period in the development of programmed instruction was the popular interest in teaching machines. In a short time, many types of teaching machines were manufactured, beginning with the simplest perforated mechanisms (perforated cards and cassettes) and ending with automated types. It was not uncommon that machines were created earlier than the programs, and that the latter then "caught up" with the machines. During this period, great attention was paid to the problem of programmed-automated control of students' knowledge. This is natural to the degree that control: 1) is a highly labor-consuming part of teaching, and 2) creating equipment for control is easier than for teaching.

A great interest in programmed instruction was expressed in the organization of a series of conferences on programmed instruction and on the

---

4. See for example L.Ja. Gal'perin: "The Development of Research on the Forming of Mental Activities" (Razvitie Issledovanij po Formirovaniju Umstvennyx Dejstvij) in the collection "Psychological Science in the USSR (Psixologiceskaja Nauka v SSSR) Vol. I Academy of Psychological Sciences of the RSFSR, Moscow, 1959; L.Ja. Gal'perin "Basic Results of Research on the Problem of 'Forming Mental Activities and Concepts'" (Osnovnye Resul'Taty Issledovanij po Probleme "Formirovanie Umstvennyx Dejstvij i Ponjatij"), Moscow, 1965.

application of technical methods to the educational process. These conferences took place in Moscow as well as in a number of other cities—Leningrad, Kiev, Minsk, Kishinev, Sverdlovsk, Kransnojarsk, and so on. The more heavily attended were those conducted in Moscow by the Ministry of Higher and Secondary Specialized Education in the USSR, and also by the Pedagogical Society of the RSFSR, attracting each time more than a thousand participants.

As the greater number of teachers interested in programmed instruction have mastered the theory of programmed instruction, have created experimental programs or teaching machines and have tested them in practice, the second period in the development of programmed instruction has begun, which is characterized by more profound interest of teachers of various disciplines in the general psychological-pedagogical aspect of programmed instruction, and their more profound working out of the theoretical problems of programmed instruction. The majority of teachers have begun to understand that machines in themselves cannot resolve the problems of radically increasing the effectiveness of instruction; that for instruction (with or without the help of machines) effective programs of instruction are needed, and the latter cannot be drawn up without a profound knowledge of psychology and pedagogy. Mathematicians, physicists, biologists, chemists, engineers and teachers are turning to psychology and pedagogy, which was not the case before. This shows a positive effect, not only on the increase of their own pedagogical qualifications, but also on the development of psychology and pedagogy themselves, including the theory of programmed instruction, since the representatives of a series of precise sciences have introduced the methods of the precise sciences into pedagogical psychology, and they have begun to investigate the problems of instruction and the application of precise methods.

In this period, the construction of mathematical and cybernetic models of the processes of learning and instruction is attracting a great deal of attention, as are attempts to describe the various psychological manifestations in the precise language of mathematics, mathematical logic and the theory of control. The different aspects of the process of learning and instruction (including programmed instruction) are the object of a precise scientific analysis, which leads to the differentiation of the problems of research in this field and to a considerable expansion of the subjects of scientific studies.

This is easy to prove, when comparing the problems of conferences taking place in 1963-1964 and reflected in the book, "Application of Technical Methods and Programmed Instruction in Se-condary and Specialized Schools and in Universities" (Primenenie Texniceskix Sredstv i Programmirovannogo Obucenija v Srednej, Special'noj i Vysej Skole)[5], and in the agenda of the Fifth All Russian Conference on the Application of Technical Methods and Programmed Instruction (1969) as reflected in the material of this conference.[6]

Thus, in the book "Application of Technical Methods" (1965), all reports were combined in the following groups (according to the problems) which found expression in the sections of this book:

1. Problems of the theory, organization and experience of applying technical methods and programmed instruction.
2. Methods of programmed instruction in the process of teaching natural sciences.
3. Methods of programmed instruction in the process of teaching the humanities and musical disciplines.
4. Methods of applying technical methods and programmed instruction to the various types of sport.
5. Teaching apparatuses and the method of using visual aids.

At the 1969 conference, 20 symposia worked on the following problems:

Symposium 1. Mathematical and logical methods of investigating the process and structuring of instruction.

Symposium 2. The development of thinking by means of programmed instruction. The formation of algorithmic and heuristic processes.

Symposium 3. The problem of applying programmed instruction to special areas of instruction (medicine).

Symposium 4. Principles, rules and methods of putting together instruction programs.

Symposium 5. Problems of the didactic and economical effectiveness of programmed instruction. Criteria and methods of evaluating it. Methods of experimenting with programmed instruction.

Symposium 6. The role and place of programmed instruction in the educational process. The combining of programmed instruction with other forms of educational projects. Methods of putting into practice programmed studies.

5. "Primenenie Texniceskix Sredstv i Programmirovannogo Obucenija v Srednej, Special'noj i Vysej Skole," ed. V. M. Taranov, Moscow, "Sovetskoe Radio," 1965.

6. "Pjataja Vserossijskaja Konferencija po Primeneniju Texniceskix Sredstv i Programmirovannomu Obuceniju," Simposiumy Nos. 1-20 (The subject matter of each symposium is published in a separate book.) Editors in charge are—L. N. Landa (Symposia 1-15) and N. M. Saxmaev (Symposia 16-20) Moscow, Pedagogiceskogo Obscestva, RSFSR, 1969.

Symposium 7. Methods and criteria for evaluating the knowledge, ability and skills of students under programmed instruction.

Symposium 8. The possibilities of constructive and selective answers under programmed instruction.

Symposium 9. Calculating of individual peculiarities of students when constructing teaching programs and when carrying out programmed instruction.

Symposium 10. The problem of applying programmed instruction to specialized fields of teaching (music).

Symposium 11. Ways of applying programmed instruction to forming technical and professional skills and abilities connected with production.

Symposium 12. Adaptive and informational-logical possibilities of teaching equipment and the direction of their expansion. Psychological-didactic requirements for teaching machines and the problem of communication between pupil and machine.

Symposium 13. Spheres, methods and effectiveness of applying teaching and controlling equipment.

Symposium 14. Problems of using electronic computers in teaching.

Symposium 15. Technical problems of constructing teaching equipment.

Symposium 16. Didactic problems of using visual and audio appliances in the educational process.

Symposium 17. The areas of application and the functional role of static screen appliances in the educational process.

Symposium 18. Areas of application and methodology of using educational films.

Symposium 19. Television and instruction.

Symposium 20. Effective ways of applying audio appliances to teaching.

In this short article, there are not the possibilities of describing the contents of the symposia and giving an analysis of the basic directions in research as well as the results of this research.

Let us, however, consider several problems of putting programmed instruction into practice.

At the present time, teachers of several hundred universities, schools and technical institutes as well as those from educational institutions in the systems of professional and technical education are studying problems of programmed instruction. Teachers studying programmed instruction have worked out teaching programs in many academic subjects (mathematics, physics, chemistry, native and foreign languages, engineering, biology, medicine, economics, and so on). In certain cases, whole academic courses are programmed; in others, only separate divisions. Printed (for the most part, manuscripts done on mimeographs) teaching programs are verified experimentally and are used in studies by their author or by a collective of the faculty with whom the author works. In some universities, programmed studies according to subject have already been systematically carried out for the duration of several years; in others, they have a basically experimental character. The degree of application of programmed instruction in one or another educational institution depends most of all on the availability of teachers there who are interested in this new method and are capable of working out teaching programs. Teaching programs are formed either according to a linear or ramified system, although the majority of existing programs are linear.

Programmed instruction is carried out either with the help of machines or without machines, with only the use of programmed appliances. There often occur combined forms; teaching is carried out without machines, but control is established with the help of machines.

In many institutions, a great deal of attention is paid to combining programmed instruction with traditional forms of educational projects, and this combination is in different forms. Accordingly, the importance of programmed instruction varies.

The teaching machines in use can be separated into three classes:

1. Machines for individual use (of low adaptability or highly adaptable).
2. Automated classes with a centralized control panel.
3. Teaching complexes based on computers. Several machines, (like the "lastocka," "mincanka" and the automated class "accord" and a few others) transmit serially.

Machines are used to fulfill different functions, for example:

Individualizing teaching under conditions where there is a huge auditorium;

Daily consultations and consultations before examinations;

Independent work with teaching programs outside of regular school time;

Application of simultaneous control within the framework of one subject;

Daily control and autocontrol;

Control at stages of instruction and at the examination.

At the present time, a great deal of attention is given to working out an automated information system of a university on the basis of computers. Among the problems raised here, the following may be indicated:

The working out and adjusting of the educational plan, of schedules, semester graphs, etc.;

Assessment and control of daily and semester progress of the students;

Analysis of teachers' filling of a calendar plan;

Direction of the course of teachers' scientific research and of students' scientific work projects;

Direction of economic activities of a university;

Accumulation and distribution of reference and informational materials (composition of student-body, teachers, graduate students, availability of empty auditoriums and so on).

The creation of automated informational systems at universities requires the solving of a series of theoretical and technical problems and the use of new methods to resolve pedagogical and technical problems. Thus, to solve the task of optimizing educational plans, methods of interconnected planning are used to optimize teaching processes —methods of algorithmic analysis of the educational activity of teachers and students, and also methods for optimizing algorithms of teaching on the basis of applying mathematical logic, information theory and also psychological and didactic data.

A great deal of attention is paid to creating teaching complexes based on computers which must, for example, solve the following problems:

Realization of teaching programs of varying degrees of complexity;

Simultaneously teaching a large number of students with an individualizing of the actual process of teaching;

Gathering and processing of statistical information on the course of teaching, with the purpose of an operational change in the sequence of the teaching process, the improvement of teaching programs and so on; and

To inform teachers at an appointed time of the progress of the teaching process.

Along with work on applying computers, work on creating centralized adaptive teaching equipment solving a variety of problems without the application of computers is being carried out.

As for the effectiveness of applying programmed instruction, the majority of teachers studying programmed instruction remark on its indubitable effectiveness, although concrete facts concerning efficacy are the most disparate (from an insignificant rise in progress to a rise in progress by 1½ to 2 times and a saving of time by 30%-50%). Such a contradiction of facts is completely natural, since the effectiveness of teaching depends on a series of factors (content of instruction, quality of programs, character and degree of perfection of applied technical methods, etc.), which are different in different instances.

On the whole, programmed instruction in the Soviet Union wins more and more supporters, and studies on programmed instruction are showing considerable development. ☐

This paper was translated into English by Virginia Bennett, for **Educational Technology**.

Contingency Management and Educational Technology

Jerome P. Lysaught
Contributing Editor

To many of us who have attempted, over a considerable number of years, to blend the principles of reinforcement theory with the technology of media to effect predictable learning outcomes, the developing concepts of contingency management provide more than a new approach for arranging operant conditioning. Contingency management may, indeed, represent an important link in the *rapprochement* between various insights on human behavior that have all too often in the past been construed as representing opposing points of view. We may find ourselves, like the blind men of Hindustan, to have been proclaiming the nature of the whole while grasping only one part of the puzzle of human learning.

For example, reinforcement theory has quite forcefully drawn our attention to the importance of the individual learner, the necessity for developing unambiguous stimuli, and the desirability of immediate differential feedback to reinforce correct responses and to extinguish incorrect efforts. We can indicate this emphasis with a simple diagram that includes the elements of the learning process as seen from this point of view.

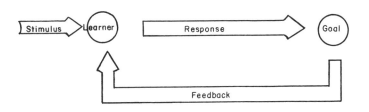

Of course, we know that human learning situations involve more complexity than this. Stimuli can sometimes be provocative to one individual and not to another. Responses may or may not result from the presence of a "stimulus." Goals may or may not be attractive to a learner, and feedback cannot always be phrased simply in a yes-no or right-wrong context. Hopefully, we long ago determined that the early quarrels over the relative effectiveness of a short versus a long stimulus, an overt versus a covert response, or a linear versus a branching feedback pattern, were directed at the form rather than the substance of the approach—just as surely as was the question of whether a book or a mechanical page turner was an inherently superior method of presentation.

Unfortunately, these neat bits of paraphernalia served to take us away from some of the vital questions about which we had very inadequate answers. For example, a reinforcer, by definition, is anything which tends to ensure the repetition of a response. What are the reinforcers for human learning behavior? Are these universals, or are there actually alternative events or outcomes that might be positive for one individual affected by the same reinforcers over time, and in varying circumstances?

Perhaps not all the "truths" about human behavior are bound up in the formularies of reinforcement. The Gestalt psychologists have suggested that one view of human learning behavior involves the concept of an individual life space. In such a system, one might hypothesize a slightly variant diagram to illustrate the learning process. It could be shown in this way:

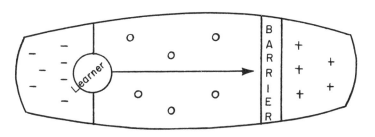

Here the learner is attempting to move from a negative (or neutral, or less positive) valence to a positive (neutral, or less negative) valence. Such movement is through a field which involves friction and entropy, and generally across some barrier, before it can successfully attain the desired goal. The "barrier" can include learning prerequisite skills, developing mastery of motor manipulation, etc.

A comparison of the two models raises some imperative questions for the educational technologist. How do we know that the goals the student perceives in a learning situation possess a positive valence for him? How do we know that his present situation is "uncomfortable" enough to cause him to seek change behaviors? What do we know about the barriers for the individual?

Let me suggest what some of these conditions may mean in a real life situation. The disadvantaged learner may not see any reason to learn a set of job skills if he knows that there is no opportunity ladder beyond the entering task requirements for a janitorial assistant. The mere fact that we may be able to develop highly specific behavioral objectives may not be any guarantee that the student wants to perform them or sees any advantage in doing so. Indeed, well developed objectives may help to convince the learner that he wants no part of them. (And I *do* feel that that is a positive contribution.)

Likewise, what we educators assume as states of need leading to learning change behavior—that is, initial states of negative, neutral, or low positive valence, may not be perceived by the learner in any such light. Without going into any of the complex socio-economic-cultural problems that lie behind the manifestations, it is quite obvious that many people are quite content with welfare payments if the only real alternative is a low-paying job. The differential in money is not a sufficient inducement, and the feelings that some persons may have about the relative moral and ethical profundities just may not be at all important to many individuals.

Indeed, if we step a little further from our habitual nest in learning psychology to ask what the social and industrial psychologists might tell us about the reinforcers that exist in the real world, we may actually be astonished. The rather simple assumption that human beings like to "learn" and that new learnings in themselves are reinforcing events is subject to a great deal of construction. If we define learning as behavioral change, then we must recognize that there are states of human existence which call for marked variations in the structure of reinforcers.

Maslow, for example, has generated a widely-accepted view of a pyramid or continuum of motivation. It suggests that for each individual there is a priority of needs whose general direction is predictable. But personal levels of satiety make speed and movement difficult to predict. He suggests that there is an imperative of needs from the survival requirements through security, belongingness and esteem needs to those of self-actualization. As soon as one's personal needs to belong are filled, for example, then further increments of belongingness fail to serve as reinforcers. One can only be motivated to change through adding "esteem filling" rewards. Herzberg suggests that this interpretation can be complicated by the fact that some "reinforcers" only prevent frustration and negative behavior while others serve as positive motivators. In any event, basal needs must be satisfied before one can proceed to other motivators or reinforcers.

This analysis suggests that we might consider an enlargement of the goal area of learning behavior as shown below:

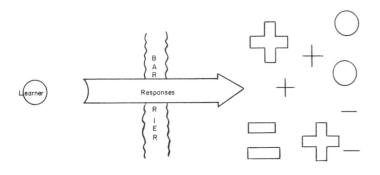

The response generated by the student might be rewarded by any one of several events. To differing individuals, however, some of the subsequent rewards may actually be neutral, or mildly or heavily negative, or mildly or heavily positive. And it is precisely this variation in reinforcing qualities due to individual need levels (commingled with personal perceptions) that remains one of the most important unresolved problems in all learning.

Precisely because much of the experimental work in contingency management has revolved around the arrangement of learner-selected rewards with experimenter-controlled requirements and durations, we have hope that we can determine what is important to the learner—so important that it can serve as an inducement for action and change in behavior—and what the sequencing of reinforcing events might be that can produce more prolonged, vigorous and successful learning.

If we add to this the possibility (which is closely related to both reinforcement theory and the social-psychological learning models) of encouraging learner-centered instruction in terms of goal selection, instructional sequencing and feedback frequency, we may actually cut to the heart of human learning. We ought to be able to analyze the learning behavior of human beings better than that of other organisms—simply because man is self-reflexive, as Korzybski points out, and he is also capable of "time-binding," so that he can help us analyze and interpret the routes taken to learning.

What is the relevance in all this to technology? The crux of any real attempt to make learning into a science is accurate observation and measurement. We will have made some real progress once we dismiss our *a priori* conclusions about reinforcement and other instructional variables, but we are still faced with the problem of developing a system for presenting stimuli, responses and reinforcers in such a way that we can reproduce them, analyze them and develop worthwhile probability statements from them.

Rather than looking at educational technology as a varied collection of projectors, audio-visual devices and electronic gadgets, we should be considering them from the standpoint of their capacity to present stimuli, record responses and trace individual learners through a progression of steps toward an instructional goal. Viewed in this way, a highly sophisticated computer system may be essential to further research on learning—simply because we must deal with the complex logic of the human student.

Contingency management is, perhaps, the most significant reminder of this fact that we have today. Just as reinforcement theory stemmed from countless observations of organisms under controlled conditions, so the theory of reinforcers must proceed from controlled observations of human learners in essentially free conditions. Given time and technology equal to the task, we may determine the conditions under which certain kinds of contingencies will increase the rate and accuracy of learning. But before we can move to controlling learning through these reinforcers, there is no way of circumventing the prior necessities of the scientific method—*observation and measurement.*

In the past, technology has not been an unmixed blessing for American education. We have gone through our fads and our foibles, sometimes believing that a new piece of hardware could in itself solve the problem of learning. Certainly since the time of the hornbook, technology has helped. But there is the point! Technology is only as good as the purposes to which it is put and the control that is exercised over it. With contingency management, and with learner-centered instruction, we are raising significant new questions about the learning process. Technology has already played a part even in raising these questions. Until we had simple, low-cost television taping, for example, we could hardly experiment with how we might use such a recording device for analyzing individual learning styles. The challenge now, however, is not to adapt learning methods to the technology, but to use the technology to discover more about learning.

For many years, a small group of advocates has argued that the greatest benefit from programmed instruction was its capacity for use as a research tool. While others sped on to developing one- or two-dimensional learning programs, a few people kept to the task of seeing what the process itself might uncover in terms of basic learning processes. Contingency management deserves far more than to be exploited now as a gimmick or a stunt. It deserves serious inquiry, strengthened through the application of sophisticated technology, because it may contain the means for determining what *does* make a person want to learn and want to change his behavior. From past experience, we can surmise that the fad will come and that surface enthusiasm will develop. Beyond all this, however, there is real hope that basic research will be conducted to advance the knowledge of human learning processes. □

Up the Programmer: How to Stop PI from Boring Learners and Strangling Results

Dudley Post

Everywhere new technology falls short of its promise, short of having the major economic impact predicted. Sometimes—as with computer assisted instruction—the cost of delivery is just too high. Sometimes all the pieces have not been invented, e.g., the electric car. Or, perhaps, the social mechanism/innovations are missing, as with planned communities and metropolitan government.

Programmed instruction is another in the list, for while the concept of programmed writing may be the soundest innovation ever in the educational materials field, its product—programmed instruction (PI)—is being held back by a needlessly narrow theory. Every person who still believes in the undeviating application of prescribed rules of programmed instruction, who believes in strict logic, consistent small frame size, metered response frequency, the 90/90 criterion and other dogma, and who considers these rules/principles the guts of the method, should count himself guilty for the meager acceptance of "pure" PI in the public schools and the aversion of so many learners who have tried it.

The most important long-run contribution of PI (and of performance contracting as well) will probably turn out to be *the assumption that learning is the responsibility of materials, that the author can, to a great extent, control and engineer quality and quantity of learning and is, by extension, accountable for the results,* which is a complete reversal of the teacher-student, author-learner rules. Other lasting contributions of PI are the importance of success and reinforcement, behavioral objectives as a starting and ending point, and building in learner involvement. But such principles have been lost in the scramble to evolve a technology based on the programming technique, when in fact the technique should be subordinate to the underlying principles. This is why arguments over the relative merit of linear vs. branched vs. Crowder PI are misleading and pointless, the real issue being "Is the technique used an effective embodiment (implementation) of learning principles?" The separate schools of PI are legitimately different from one another, as each has different priorities. Branched PI believes errors are instructive; linear, that success and reinforcement are more important. Branched likes to save time by skipping at the learner's discretion, while linear believes there cannot be too many sequencing decisions. In practice, of course,

Dudley Post is currently a Manpower Planner with the Boston Model Cities Program.

these views need not be incompatible, but legitimately different applications of sound learning principles. It is inevitable, of course, that all successful rules and principles will become part of every programmer's tool kit.

Programmed instruction has enjoyed nominal growth since its initial spurt in the early sixties. But its limited acceptance is not all due to those traditional apologists, the difficulty of client education, the high cost per learner hour, or the shortage of trained programmers, the slumping economy. The computer industry has overcome these same obstacles in much more severe form. No, the limitations of PI are more inherent in the technique than they are in administration, yet the limitations show little sign of being admitted, much less corrected. The fact is that programmed instruction is hampered by a narrow theory of learning which, in turn, leads to narrow results.

The PI ballgame is dominated by the linear and the branching players—with adjunct advocates on the sidelines dashing in for an occasional play. Each faction defends its theory as both the correct and the sole bearer of truth. Yet, it is not unreasonable that twenty more factions of PI could appear, and all major ways people learn would still be far from represented.

I apprenticed under two programmers: one, who was used to writing programs for newly literate Spanish-speaking hospital workers, believed in short frames, one-word responses, in simple programs with lots of feedback and *never* too much information. The greatest crime was a program that was too difficult. My other mentor had learned his trade writing bank management programs, and he believed in large frames with multiple responses and frequent blank line, open-ended responses. The greatest crime to him was a boring program. Yet, both felt his was *the* way to write PI, because each had experienced success with his way. Both my mentors were right, but they were only right for their respective learner populations, which were quite different. Variety and interest were rightfully central to bright bankers, while success through repetition was the proper concern of the hospital workers. This shows both the great strength of PI and a reason for its weakness as a technique. Its strength is the principle of adapting materials to the learner population and taking responsibility for their success. Its weakness has constantly been premature overgeneralization; because repetitive reinforcement and constant success and tiny frame size worked with animals, it was expanded to people and indeed basically worked with slow learners. But to assert this as *the* technique for all learners is both unsound and at times absurd.

The worst offender has been Skinner himself, or whatever yo-yo first claimed that conditioned response (CR) explained all learning, an absurd notion for anyone who has learned a sport or to write an original paragraph. CR has led to a rigid overemphasis on frame construction and metronomic responses of consistent size and format, which PI has prided itself on, but is increasingly confined by. The other mainstream of theory—the intrinsic/Crowder/scrambled/branched PI—is based also on sound but incomplete principles. Learners,

this theory asserts, can learn from mistakes and at different rates; some learners even need exposure to different amounts of the same topic. This is a major amendment to the CR litany, yet it too is overasserted as *the* way to program instruction. Given the range of learners and subjects, not to mention the crude state of the art, no major technique should be looked at as either all-inclusive or irrelevant.

The best specific example of a naive, premature, constricting application based on incomplete theory is the 90/90 criterion, which says that 90 percent of all learners must answer 90 percent of the responses correctly for a program to be acceptable. This standard was almost arbitrarily established by the Air Force on the perfectly sound notion that success is a better motivator than failure. But, like so many good ideas, when pushed too far it becomes useless and even destructive. For while people need success, they also need challenge, and the two are a direct trade-off. Studies have repeatedly found that people set themselves an average 60 to 70 percent chance of success in game situations. The range may be higher for learning situations, especially if job-related; but certainly for all but the most insecure or slowest learner, being repeatedly 90 percent correct is not success but boredom.

One of the problems programmed instruction set out to overcome was the failure and discouragement of so many learners, particularly poor ones, with new subject matter. This led to the maxim that success (defined as a correct response) was a good thing and, therefore, the more success the better. But this is a limited view of success. If I asked someone to name the current U.S. President, he would take no pride in saying Richard Nixon; but if I asked him to name all U.S. Presidents, he would be rightly self-congratulatory if he could. Similarly, a learner is not satisfied by being right if it's no challenge, regardless of the newness of the subject matter. And a 90/90 program rolls on like the New Jersey Turnpike, with errors as frequent stoplights on the same road. It becomes soon apparent to the most dense learner that this thing is rigged, it's made so *anyone* gets the right answer. There can be scant satisfaction after that, save for the deluded author who thinks he has *programmed in* a feeling of success. Again, because success worked with slow learners, it was inappropriately expanded to all learners, whereas in truth challenge is most people's kick, not facile, contrived, effortless success.

This can be said another way by looking at the complement of success—mistakes. There are only five kinds of mistakes in PI, those due to:

1. Carelessness
2. Under-cuing
3. Misleading, poorly written frames (unintentionally difficult)
4. Assuming knowledge the learner lacks
5. Too difficult (intentionally).

Carelessness cannot be eliminated and can only be partially controlled by the programmer; 2 and 4 are poor programming and are the only valid reasons for the

90/90 criterion. These three kinds of mistakes should rightfully be excised from PI land. But programmers also try to eliminate number 5-type mistakes, and this is wrong. Intentionally difficult frames represent challenge and, therefore, the possibility of meaningful success, and should be consciously written *into* programs, not written out. Perhaps in the final stage of revision, after 90/90 has been reached, frames should be removed or deliberately made more difficult, to bring the rate down to 70/90 or 80/90—depending on learner population.

Better than one restrictive standard appropriate to failures and slow learners would be some *set* of several standards, such as 100/60, 80/70, and 80/80, which could serve any target population *as called for*. And if 100/60 proved too easy, say, for a program to train door-to-door salesmen accustomed to one-in-ten odds, a 100/10 standard should be unflinchingly applied. It is subjective learner success the programmer should seek, not compliance with a superannuated rule. The key is motivation, and this is created by challenge, by stimulation, as well as by success. To put the burden all on success is naive and limiting.

A just slightly less important example of over-applying a narrow rule rather than the principle behind it is the ruthless efficiency of PI writing. The strict format, intentional repetition, objectivity and scant imagination of programming's tundra is legendary (but not unique, as textbook users know). What PI writer has not heard someone say, "I learned a lot from that program, but I'll never take another one."

Mass writing in any field inevitably yields some mediocre products, but contrasted with the average newspaper column, PI is as much fun as the Dewey Decimal User's Guide. Programmers assume that the learning principles alone are powerful and complete enough to do the job and, therefore, the writer should purge any personal style. But this policy leads to suboptimization of the most blatant kind. The writer should be dedicated to holding the learner's attention for the length of the program, and only secondarily working to keep the number of words (and hence learning time) to a minimum—because without the learner's concentration either learning time or the error rate will wander up. Excessive efficiency does not pay off, in terms of learner attitude or even objective measures, when it sacrifices appealing diversions, "irrelevant" ideas, "excessive" examples, anecdotes, historical detail or humor. Whatever makes the material livelier, more appealing, more self-motivating, better written is justified up to some limit, say 30 percent of total frames. PI, after all, grew out of a partial answer to the question "By what principles do people learn?" Yet, given that the principles of PI are not a complete learning theory, it makes just as much sense to approach the matter from the other end and ask: "What do people choose to learn from? What do they enjoy learning from successfully?" Imitate *that* form and its principles, be it good journalism or *Laugh-In*. *Sesame Street* is quite right in modeling its style after what the kids prefer to watch, enjoy and learn from—TV commercials. Commercials are expensively produced and condition the pace and expectations of children, so that

any educational medium must compete with these trained expectations. The same is true but less obvious in print. Programmed instruction is competing with everything else the learner has read, and if its interest, pace and style fail to match his conditioned expectations, motivation is lost. No learner gives a handicap to a program because it is educational and, therefore, "good" for him.

There is nothing new about this point. Scientific innovations involving people often maximize a single objective measure of performance at the expense of people's needs, which are harder to measure. Scientific management multiplied worker productivity by helping men to work more intelligently, but went too far in streamlining motions and job organization, and as a result trampled all over the need for variety and challenge, for self-control, each worker's unique pace and style, his unique way of doing the job. It is often said of industrial engineers that they can design a job for maximum efficiency over one hour, but not over 500 hours, because they ignore this human factor. Highway designers straightened out roads to improve safety, but got carried away—and soon drivers were going to sleep on interminable stretches. So now designers *build in curves and variety*; driving time may be slightly longer, but more people want to use the road, and accidents are down. Speed, then, should not be the sole criterion for a highway or a program. For an hour, or maybe four or five hours with highly motivated learners, one can get by with a boring program. But after that the risk of "accidents" goes up, and the learner is likely never to return to such a road.

Perhaps the only solution is to measure subjective reaction and thereby make it a part of objective performance. Perhaps the weight given the subjective side should even increase with longer programs, where motivation becomes more important. Subjective performance has been ignored partly for that catch-all excuse—it is hard to measure. Yet it is a mistake to think learner acceptance is not crucial to PI, just because it is not the learner who makes the purchase decision. As the high schools and universities are being loudly told by their students, without relevant (motivating) subjects, they tune out. John Holt long ago told us his third graders learned nothing unless they were interested in the topic at hand. The same is partially true at the smaller level of PI—putting an obligation on the writer to at least be concerned with minimizing tune-out. If one takes seriously the principle that failure to learn is the material's fault, then failure to be motivated is the material's fault as well.

While it may appear I am condemning programmed instruction, that is not my intent. The point is that credit should go where credit is due. The *concepts* behind PI are far more innovative and powerful than current *practice*. Like performance contracting, the real innovation is probably *accountability*—the idea that the materials rather than the learner are responsible for success. Yet it is the *form* which has been oversold as the real innovation. Setting behavioral objectives and analyzing subject matter rigorously accounts for a majority of the learner time saved by PI, and this is not a new concept or technique but merely a standard of quality and writing procedure. *Revision cycles* and *validation* with learners account for its effectiveness, more than the responses and sequencing.

Someday, after the last conceivable .002 percent of marginal efficiency has been squeezed from programming, some mischievous non-educator will discover that the most effective program is one the learner prefers, just as the best program writers are people who enjoy writing programs. Someday the subjective element will be rediscovered—that creative people with adequate resources make more effective teaching materials than uncreative PI companies, that *Sesame Street's* success is due to mixing entertainment and learning, and that perhaps efforts are best put into making arresting, high-impact, attention-grabbing products and working backwards from that objective rather than forwards from dozens of out-of-date micro-measures of what has worked and assembling them into a scientific and logical, but unpalatable, program.

Conclusion

Programmed instruction sells more to industry and military than to schools, not just because the former are more cost conscious and the latter group-paced, but because increasingly students have a choice over how they learn, if not over what they learn also. Business and military still rely on authority—but this is passing, just as it has already passed in the schools: employees will not always learn their job from an unmotivating or boring medium. Programming must keep up with its customers' expectations, not just by becoming "appealing," but by re-examining the limited theory which may guarantee its rejection by a generation bred on the non-linear, involving electronic media. It is all too easy to put off such a re-examination because the paying customer is so rarely the end user of PI. However, the learner's needs cannot be ignored indefinitely. Ask any college president. ☐

Dear Machine: Don't Call Us, We'll Call You!

John Taylor Canfield

"... students are human beings first and students second. As people they want to be seen, listened to and understood. As students they want meaningful information and skills to process a vast store of experiences and the practical ability to earn a living."

-Norman A. Newberg*

Students have many concerns, running the gamut from worrying about getting a job and getting a date to "getting their heads together" on such questions as Who am I? To whom do I belong? Over what do I have power? and Why do I feel the way I do? Until now, for the most part, schools have dealt formally with the question of getting a job, informally with getting a date, and hardly at all with the questions of identity, interrelationships and personal power.

This lack of attention to the human concerns of students has contributed to alienation, hostility and violence in our schools, on our campuses and in our streets. As students, critics and reformers push from all sides for change within our schools, we, as educators, must address ourselves to the emotional and psychological needs, along with the intellectual and vocational needs of the students.

Educators and psychologists across the country are beginning to devote time, energy and money to the development of affective curriculum materials and processes to fulfill these needs. In California, for example, Uvaldo Palomares and Harold Bessell have completed materials of the *Human Development Program* (HDP) for use in preschool settings and the early elementary grades. Sitting in the "magic circle," the children and their teacher verbally explore themselves and others each day through group interaction and activities related to specific affective learning goals.

Sample "magic circle" topics are: "It made me feel good when . . . I made someone feel bad when I . . . Something I do very well is . . . The thing I like

---

*Newberg, Norman. Education for Student Concerns: Courses in Communications and Urban Affairs. In Alschuler, Alfred (Ed.) *Educational Opportunity Forum: Psychological Humanistic Education.* Albany, New York: The State Department of Education, Division of Higher Education, Fall, 1969, I:4, p. 24.

John Taylor Canfield is with the Center for Humanistic Education, University of Massachusetts.

best is . . . ." In preschool and kindergarten, the children participate in "Mastery" sessions which are specifically designed to provide them with desired positive feedback, to enhance their feelings about their ability to manipulate their environment and thus build their self-esteem.

In addition to the development of self-esteem, the HDP materials are designed to enhance the student in the following areas: self-awareness, considerateness, eagerness, effectiveness, flexibility, interpersonal comprehension, sensitivity to others, spontaneity, stability and tolerance.

Science Research Associates and Argus Communications have also developed programs aimed at the affective development of children in grades K-3. SRA's *Focus on the Self Development Program* while less structured than the *Human Development Program,* strives to achieve similar goals through the use of records, filmstrips and guided group discussion. Argus' *Hello People,* with its emphasis on self-concept and multi-ethnic social interaction, help the child learn to cope with today's complex society.

Combined Motivation Education Systems is publishing a *Curriculum for a Developing Self,* a K-12 project which Harold C. Wells and I developed. This is an experimental curriculum which enables students to maximize their full potential by focusing on six processes of human growth: learning to accept oneself, developing a better relationship with reality, becoming one's natural and creative self, viewing life in its broad perspective, expanding autonomous behavior, and developing a kinship with mankind.

Hoping to increase students' long term operant behavior—those things that a person does voluntarily on the basis of stable internal cues—Alfred S. Alschuler and his associates have recently published material representing course strategies used by the Harvard Achievement Motivation Development Project. Concentrating on grades 6-10, this material focuses on developing achievement imagery, decision making and realistic goal-setting through the use of feedback.

Sparingly, and with caution, city school boards, foundations and the government are funding curriculum development, action projects, Title III centers and university research programs to further the development and implementation of strategies that deal with humanistic concerns within the affective domain. Terry Borton, author of *Reach, Touch and Teach: Student Concerns and Process Education,* has been appointed director of the Office of Affective Education in Philadelphia. Dr. Borton and his group are developing curricula, training teachers and performing evaluative studies in new affective education techniques.

William Glasser, author of *Schools Without Failure,* is directing work at the Education Training Center in Los Angeles. Dr. Glasser's thesis is: every child has two basic needs—the need for love and the need for self-worth. Through the use of the "class meeting," Dr. Glasser trains teachers to help students satisfy these two basic needs through involvement, relevance and responsibility.

The Ford Foundation has provided a three-year grant of $500,000 to Gerald Weinstein, director of the Center for Humanistic Education at the University of Massachusetts and to George Brown at the University of California at Santa Barbara to develop a data bank of humanistic exercises, develop and disseminate humanistic curricula, train teachers and evaluate the results.

Will these efforts bring change in the classroom? Certainly, the teacher's traditional role as the know-it-all dispenser of information through classroom lectures must be altered. New ways must be found to enhance self-concepts, clarify values, facilitate "magic circles," conduct "classroom meetings," and assist students in the processing of their emotional concerns. The experience of the past five years with methods provided by educational technology indicates that these new ways of educating are desirable. Turning much of traditional subject matter instruction over to technological aids such as teaching machines, audiovisual devices, programmed materials and simulation games does allow teachers to focus on areas requiring sensitive human interaction.

The introduction into the learning environment of effective technological hard- and soft-ware has demonstrably minimized the need for suppressive discipline in the classroom. A humanizing aspect of technology that accounts for reduction in misbehavior is found in the ability to provide opportunities for children to progress with their own interests at their own rate and on their own level of competence. In addition, the step-by-step successes of programmed instruction tend to eliminate the frustration of failure, thereby enhancing the student's self-concept.

A programmed reading course developed by M.W. Sullivan and associates and published by Behavioral Research Laboratories has effectively helped over a million children learn to read at an average of better than double the usual progress. Many children, by using these materials, have taught themselves to read at the fifth and sixth grade levels by the end of the first grade. These impressive results are less startling when one realizes that using similar materials, along with the techniques of contingency management, Lloyd Homme and his associates have taught three-year-olds to read at the fifth grade level!

The introduction of Individually Prescribed Instruction, computer assisted instruction, programmed materials and "Sesame Street" into the home and classroom provides a greater opportunity for students to actualize their own cognitive learning styles and to determine their own paths to growth. Likewise, these technology-based techniques allow teachers to concentrate their attention on the personally *human* concerns of their students. Released from the tasks of maintaining classroom discipline, imparting factual information and supervising repetitive drill, they can now facilitate group meetings in which students discuss their hopes, fears, dreams and anxieties. Teachers can help students in their struggle to resolve value issues and conflicts and to overcome feelings of alienation, powerlessness and self-doubt. Teachers can help students set meaningful goals, order their priorities and make important personal and social decisions.

This may sound idealistic (and I believe it is), for

"Have you noticed how school is eating into the best years of our lives?"

how are teachers to be prepared to handle these altered roles? An examination of current teacher education practices leads me to believe that an extensive reorganization of preservice and inservice teacher education is required.

Currently, teachers are not being trained to respond effectively to the concerns of their students. That is, teacher education focuses primarily on the subject matter content and the "how to" aspects of teaching the academic disciplines. This narrow concentration of teacher training is found in two recent educational "innovations": the "new" curricula and the MAT Program. Both of these are hardly more than bigger and better ways to teach *subject matter*. The new curricula include the PSSC physics program, the CBA and CHEMS chem-study programs, the GCMP and SMSG math programs and the BSCS biology approach. The Master of Arts in Teaching (MAT) Program, which has been praised as "the new way to train teachers," again places the emphasis on the academic disciplines rather than on humanistic process and concerns of students. As a result, one receives an MAT *in* social studies, English, mathematics, biology, French, etc.

In addition to this increased concentration on courses in the academic disciplines, schools of education also require the adherence to an archaic educational philosophy representing a society and a culture that no longer exist. Educational psychology courses continue to focus on the medical-model of individual pathology and abstract learning theories which have questionable relevance to practical application in the classroom.

It is safe to conclude, I believe, that traditional education courses and practice teaching do not sufficiently equip teachers for the humanistic side of

education. Educated in a lock-step manner, teachers continue to teach in a similar fashion.

The results of this training are that teachers generally ignore the variety of needs, desires and motivations of students, and classrooms become constrictive and demotivating. As a consequence, constructive student energy is re-channeled from emotional growth and development to the frustration and rebellion prevalent on today's high school and college campuses.

While it may be important to learn to run movie projectors, understand set theory and cut out Easter bunnies, more basic learnings should be included and emphasized—such as how to discern the basic dynamics present in a group, how to run a class meeting in Dr. Glasser's sense, how to deal with their own and their students' emotions, how to facilitate and nurture creativity, how to help students discover meaningful and productive interests, how to set and achieve their goals, how to creatively solve problems and how to constructively manage conflict.

It is becoming apparent, however, that a prime factor in the development of a student's potential goes beyond the skills listed above. This key factor is the teacher's attitude toward his pupils. The teacher must not only believe in the unlimited potential of each of his students, but he must actively convey this belief to them. The teacher's belief in the student increases the student's belief in himself. The following statement from a teacher after sensitivity training illustrates this point.

> The youngster who really made me understand this was Eddie. I asked him one day why he thought he was doing so much better than he was last year. He gave meaning to my whole new orientation. "It's because I like myself now when I'm with you," he said.*

A way to help teachers obtain this nurturing capability is to have them experience the development of their own potential with a group of peers in a workshop setting. There are many workshop methods such as sensitivity training, psychodrama, Gestalt therapy and encounter groups, which effectively help people to actualize their personal and interpersonal potential. However, largely due to the sensationalism of the popular press and the guarded conservatism of many educators, these methods have been considered too threatening to gain access into many schools. With this conservatism in mind, I would like to describe a relatively nonthreatening program which seems to have been effective with many kinds of teachers.

Based on the desire to facilitate the development of the attitudes and skills necessary to create comprehensive learning environments, a group of psychologists and educators at Combined Motivation Education Systems in Rosemont, Illinois, have designed programs which permit and encourage personalized educational experience to identify and develop the unused personal strengths and potentialities of the participants.

*Shostrom, Everett L. *Man the Manipulator.* New York: Bantam Books, 1968, p. 118.

The Combined Motivation Education Systems program is based on the premise that people accomplish the most when they are doing what they want to do—when they are operating under their *want* system rather than their *should* system. The program assumes that everybody is already motivated intrinsically (from within), and that pressure from the outside reduces, rather than increases, one's motivation to achieve. A student will act on his internal motivation more forcibly when supported, rather than pressured, by the teacher.

All too often, educators confuse the verbs *motivate* and *manipulate*. Motivation comes from within; manipulation, from without. Only when internal motivation is operating at its optimum level can maximum growth and development take place. This brings me to the title-theme of this article.

We must provide responsive environments in our schools with which the learner can interact as frequently as he desires. That environment ideally includes cognitive and affective responders—teaching devices and human beings (sensitive human beings who can respond to the emotional and behavioral concerns that students bring with them).

Both people and machines must be able to respond to the student's concerns when he raises them, and not in a preconceived lock-step design promulgated by a curriculum specialist from some downtown office. Learning is based on need, not order. Ordering is what the student does with learning after he has experienced it. Therefore, learning environments must be created to respond to students' needs wherever and in whatever sequence they may arise. Students must be given the right to say, "Dear Machine (and teacher): Don't call us; we'll call you." □

References

Alschuler, Alfred (Ed.) *Educational Opportunity Forum: Psychological Humanistic Education.* Albany, New York: The State Department of Education, Division of Higher Education, Fall 1969, I:4.

Alschuler, Alfred, Diane Tabor & James McIntyre. *Teacher Achievement Motivation and Achievement Motivation Materials.* Middletown, Connecticut: Education Ventures.

Borton, Terry. *Reach, Touch and Teach: Student Concerns and Process Education.* New York: McGraw-Hill, 1970.

Fantini, Mario & Gerald Weinstein. *Making Urban Schools Work.* New York: Holt, Rinehart and Winston, 1968.

Focus on Self-Development, Stage One: Awareness. Chicago, Illinois: Science Research Associates, Inc.

Glasser, William. *Schools Without Failure.* New York: Harper and Row, 1969.

Hello People. Chicago, Illinois: Argus Communications.

Human Development Program. San Diego, Calif.: Human Development Training Institute.

Raths, Louis E., Merrill Harmin & Sidney B. Simon. *Values and Teaching: Working with Values in the Classroom.* Columbus: Charles E. Merrill Publishing Company, 1966.

Wells, Harold C. & John T. Canfield. *Curriculum for a Developing Self.* Rosemont, Illinois: Combined Motivation Education Systems.

Some Real and Spurious Problems of a Programmed Course in Music Ear-Training

Leo Horacek and Gerald Lefkoff

The authors are involved in a course of instruction that is entirely programmed, and which has built into it about as much flexibility in work and in grading as could possibly exist in a system which requires grades at the end of each semester. Since it is so throughly programmed and so flexible, it might be expected to show the problems that are likely to occur in programming of music ear-training. A brief description of some of these problems and of possible solutions constitutes the subject of this article.

As a preliminary, it should be said that music ear-training is in some ways a rather atypical college course, and that there are some rather unusual problems with the course. First, there is actually a rather large number of quite different learnings which are involved. Students learn to identify various kinds of tonal patterns by ear, to write in notation tonal patterns heard, and to reproduce these patterns by voice. While musicians typically think of these skills as closely related, the behaviors are actually quite distinct, having only in common various musical patterns as stimuli or responses. The musical patterns are of at least three quite separate types: rhythmic, melodic or harmonic; and while these often appear together in music, each involves unique characteristics.

Further complications result from the great disparity of backgrounds that students have—some coming to college with almost no learning in this area, some with a great deal. Students differ greatly also in what appear to be either innate or very early learned perceptual skills necessary to much of the work. As a result of this, they typically move at very different rates, and ultimately arrive at widely differing levels of achievement.

The varied nature of the tasks expected of the students and of the personal competencies of each student creates a need for extended practice and drill in each area, which can be varied as needed for each student. The program of study devised by the authors to fill this need is a four-semester course of study, in which the organization by semester may be selected for each student, with provision for unlimited repetition of or return to any lesson or section, using tape recorded and printed materials.

It is apparent that programmed instruction, with its high flexibility of scheduling and great potentiality

Leo Horacek is professor of music at West Virginia University. **Gerald Lefkoff** is associate professor of music at West Virginia University.

for individualization, is ideal for the solution of most of the problems mentioned above. The experience of the authors is that, to a very large degree, programmed instruction lives up to its promise in this regard. It was found, however, that along with the very desirable effects, the individualization and flexibility resulted in a number of problems, most of which were not foreseen. Some of these are real but are subject to amelioration; others are real and apparently incurable, and must simply be lived with for the sake of the values of programmed instruction. Other problems are only apparent, spurious problems, perhaps blessings in disguise—often actually advantages which are irritating because they require change of method or thinking.

One set of problems connected with the flexibility and individualization in the program involves the way the course differs from conventional course organization. Typical concerns are: 1) since the student may choose what units he will work on, some students may never come into contact with certain important aspects of music theory; 2) two students with the same grade may have covered different materials; 3) semester organization may be different for different students; and 4) a student with real aptitude may accomplish the minimum objectives of the course without much effort, thus learning less than he might have under conventional instruction.

To a small extent, some of these are real problems, which can be cured without sacrificing the desirable aspects of the course. For example, where there are units that students might avoid, the system of grades and incentives can be altered to make these units more attractive. For the most part, however, it is apparent that such problems are not problems at all. A flexible, individualized program is often uncomfortable for a teacher because it eliminates the confident feeling that he is doing his job well by putting the student through time-honored processes. The student is uncomfortable because a failure to produce or achieve is made quickly evident, and because he must bear responsibility for his own planning and achievement. Either may be disconcerted by the absence of a fixed syllabus and a day-to-day schedule. But the aspect of the program involved in each of these problems is capable of contributing significantly to the progress of every student, and must be considered advantages rather than problems.

Another set of problems is likely to arise from the concerns of teaching faculty in other subject matter areas involved in the development of the student. A program which is innovative in either content or method is likely to produce a kind of generation gap. Where the students have not been put through the same educational processes which have been standard in the past, there often seems to be an important frame of reference missing. Here, too, we must conclude that such conditions are normal results of progress in thought, and that while they do produce temporary difficulties in communication, they are not real problems.

There are a number of quite real problems which arise from the individual, self-governing nature of the student's work. Most important of these is the difficulty of providing incentive. Students are so accustomed to working for a teacher who guides, prods and praises that often they have very little capacity for doing prolonged work on their own. While the reinforcement in each frame in programmed instruction can apparently provide what is necessary to make learning take place, it often does not result in sufficient incentive to make the student report to the listening lab, to make him terminate a conversation and turn to his work, or to turn his eyes from entertaining contemplation of the student in the next booth to the examination of the printed materials of the course.

A second problem resulting from the individuality of the work is that students are often reluctant to make their own decisions regarding the organization of their work. Determination of just what unit or segment of the semester's work to take up next involves a decision of a type students are rarely expected to make in any level of education.

A third problem is that many students get lonesome. Some students are apparently so accustomed to working in a group that extended work done completely alone seems to disconcert them.

Each of these three problems results from what might be considered a failure in the student's previous education. The ability to work alone, to organize one's own work and to work for distant goals would be desirable ends of education. We wish that we could report that by tossing pupils into a programmed course of study, the sink-or-swim principle would remedy these conditions. Unfortunately, the usual result is that most students do not acquire these desirable qualities, and some simply fail—unless something is done to help these conditions.

In the course of instruction in which the authors are involved, three kinds of remedies have been invoked to help these problems.

1. Advisors are provided whose duty is to keep in close touch with a number of students, to give guidance regarding the course of study, to provide incentive through praise where appropriate, and generally to give those students that need it a feeling of working for someone other than themselves. There has been some difficulty in determining just what level of staff personnel is most appropriate for this purpose. In the authors' program, there have been tried at various times regular teachers of the subject matter, graduate assistants of various degrees of training, and undergraduates who have been through the course. Each has advantages, but it has been found that well-trained permanent staff members are best for the purpose.

2. The grading system has been devised to provide incentive in the form of grades or scores which contribute to the semester's grade. It is apparent that some sections of the work are likely to be more attractive than others, some more difficult than others. It is also apparent that some students are very successful and earn scores that provide very substantial incentive, and that some students do very poorly and find little incentive to move on to further work. In conventional instruction, the good teacher can often solve such problems with sensitive handling of each student. In the

authors' program, a system was devised whereby points toward the grade are earned which reflect any achievement and serve to constantly reward progress even of the most minimal kind, and which will encourage students to tackle the most difficult tasks. Also, there were many revisions of the material itself, most of which were for the purpose of providing for regular recognized progress for every student. The results of these revisions were to break up difficult material to make for easier achievement, and to organize each lesson so that it contained easy learnings to provide means of accomplishment for the poor student and challenging learnings for the good student.

3. In its inception, the program permitted complete freedom by the students regarding their attendance in the lab and in the organization of their work times. Later, this student independence was lessened in setting up certain attendance requirements for their work. This seemed necessary in part because most of the student's other courses have fixed attendance times, and it was an almost irresistible temptation for the student to postpone work in music theory when he was crowded for time. While it was felt at the time that this represented a retreat from the objective of providing maximum flexibility in instruction, there seemed to be no real decrease in the flexibility for the work of each student. □

The Reinforcement Principle of Behavior and the Human Adult

D.T. Hoffman

Reinforcement may be a bit of food for a hungry animal, water for a thirsty one, the sight of mother for the human infant, or, for the infant duckling, the sight of whatever object on which its affection was stamped during the process of "imprinting." In a hundred thousand cages over the past 35 years, a million rats, pigeons and other small animals have shown that the rate of pecking a key on the wall of a cage or pressing a bar protruding above the food cup is highly dependent on the reinforcement which the animal receives. The generality of the principle was demonstrated when the same results were obtained with chimpanzees, human infants and other primates. Whatever actions immediately precede reinforcement undergo an increased likelihood of recurrence. When the experimenter arranges it so that each depression of the bar or peck on the key will be followed by food, the rate of those actions increases; when food no longer comes, it declines. How long it takes for the bar-pressing to stop entirely depends on the reinforcement schedule set up by the experimenter. (In some experiments, animals do not receive reinforcements after every "response.") The consequences of the animal's action—whether reinforcement or nonreinforcement—produce reliable changes in his subsequent behavior. Each reinforcement strengthens the immediately preceding action, and behavior is thus controlled by its consequences.

By "consequence" is meant whatever happens immediately after; there may be a logical connection, or, the reinforcing event may be an accidental occurrence that would have happened even if the behavior had not occurred.

The question arises whether this reinforcement behavior principle also applies to the behavior of a man. Is a human adult also likely to repeat any action followed by a satisfying (reinforcing) event, even when the person *knows* that there could only have been an accidental and entirely fortuitous relationship between his behavior and the "reinforcement"? Suppose that as I sit here at my typewriter, my son comes into the room shouting, "Hey! I got an 'A' in Math!" and that just prior to his coming in, I had made a typing error. It is obvious to me that, as pleasing as it is to have my little boy bearing such good news and looking so happy,

D.T. Hoffman is associate professor of psychology at the University of Bridgeport, Connecticut.

neither my writing the paragraph, nor my making that mistake, could conceivably be the cause of his performance in arithmetic. If my behavior had anything at all to do with the happy event, that behavior occurred a long time ago. Maybe I helped by providing him with comfort and security, with the conditions essential to physical health, maybe by giving him his own room, and turning the television set off during the evening. Whatever it was I might have done, it certainly was not the paragraph or the error. Am I to believe that those behaviors could have been strengthened and made more likely to recur because my son burst into the room with good news when he did? A baby's behavior, a white rat's, or a dog's may have been demonstrated to follow this principle of automatic behavioral control by reinforcement consequence. But does it apply to me?

There are strong opinions on both sides. Some writers claim that the ability to be *un*affected by "consequences" which bear no logical relation to behavior is the very mark of human-ness. Man, they say, is rational, human—not a beast, and not a machine. On the other side of the issue, it is said that man will be harmed by falsely trying to elevate himself above animal and machine. Only by acceptance of our beast-like or machine-like characteristics can we hope to exert control over them. Those who oppose conceiving of man's behavior as controllable by reinforcement are concerned lest man lose his "humanity" or be subject to domination by others. Those who accept the possibility that behavior obeys knowable laws are concerned lest important facts be overlooked. They see an analogy between opposition to the concept of laws of behavior, and opposition, in the 17th Century, to Galileo's contention that the earth was not in the center of the universe. However much Galileo's opponents *wanted* the earth to be the focal point of all things, however much they *believed* in the earth's central position in the grand design, the actual relation of the earth to other heavenly bodies was unaltered by their refusal to look into the telescope. Similarly, if man's behavior is controlled by its immediate consequences, wishing it were not so, however sincerely, will not change the process.

Yet common sense suggests that the adult human is vastly different from the white rat. According to common sense, I may have an increased likelihood of doing things which seem to be *logically* and *causally* related to the event, such as making sure that my children have an adequate diet and a quiet time to study. But it seems ridiculous to imagine that I will be a less adequate typist or have a stronger tendency to write on a certain topic because my son is a good student and announces it while I happen to be at the typewriter.

One trouble with this reasoning is that common sense has been notably defective in the past. Since maggots always appear on spoiled meat, it seemed obvious that the maggots came from the meat. But when meat was placed in a jar with a cover made of fine screen which kept flies and maggots out, but let odors escape, maggots appeared on the screen, but not on the meat. However, when Leeuwenhoek, as the result of this and of his observations using the newly invented microscope, asserted that the spontaneous generation of living matter from nonliving matter is an impossibility, he was believed to have lost hold of his common sense. It still seems obvious that heavy objects fall faster than light ones, and indeed they do when there is friction, as in the case of a feather wafting through the air, or of objects whose fall is impeded by a parachute, but most people do not realize that it is friction that produces the observed differences, and that on the moon (a near vacuum) a four-pound piece of lead and a feather would touch ground at the identical instant. Or, for another example, to some people today, and to all peoples of a dark past, it is common sense that the male has nothing to do with the conception of a child.

Common sense is dispelled by a process we designate with the term "science," but it is a mistake to think of science in too restrictive a sense. The methods of science are logic and observation, and no individual would survive for long if he did not possess some ability to use these methods. Our ancestor who noted the correlation between sexual behavior and pregnancy and advanced the theory that the two were causally related acted in the best of scientific traditions. It has been said that many of yesterday's scientific discoveries are today's accepted common sense views of the world. It once was common sense that a thunderstorm was caused by the wrath of God, yet today's conceptions of thunderstorms, even for the poorly educated, rarely include angry gods. That the blood circulates through veins and arteries is common sense today, but when Harvey postulated the existence of the then unseen capillaries, he was subjected to ostracism and ridicule. The history of science is replete with similar examples. Therefore, we cannot be comfortable about what today seems logical or obvious. We need the careful methods of observation and hypothesis-testing that characterize scientific research to tell us what our common sense views should be. Whether the reinforcement principle holds for the adult as it does for the infant is a scientific problem. The answer will be provided by further research.

In the meantime, we must remain uncertain. Perhaps man's ability to "think" is also his ability to allow events that happen *now* to strengthen behaviors that happened in the past, that unlike the infant and the beast, the human adult is *not* merely the automatic product of the fortuitous "consequences" of his acts. Or, there may be many occasions when the human adult *is* controlled, or partially controlled, in the automatic manner of the white rat. If he were not, he might have great difficulty adapting to the myriad conditions which make up his natural environment. If it were necessary for us to stop and cogitate at every turn, if the bulk of our behavior were not handled in a fairly automatic way, including the "automatic repetition of reinforced acts," we might be less, not more, flexible in our dealing with nature.

As we come to understand the processes of nature which control us, whatever they turn out to be, we may ourselves learn to control, indirectly, if not through conscious will, some of the behavior which we would like to change. After all, we are not, in truth, very happy about much of human behavior. War, racism, crime, drug addiction, alcoholism, automobile accidents, economic recessions, air pollution and overpopulation all represent behaviors we would like to change but have not found a way to influence effectively. There are many others which may seem less urgent but which combine to reduce severely the quality of human experience, for example, stuttering, vandalism, not attending in class, bad teaching, poor performance on the job, psychosomatic illness, laziness and the generation gap. To learn more about what affects behavior increases the likelihood that we will be able to solve the problems which those undesired behaviors produce and to develop alternative behaviors which can be substituted for them. A start in this direction would seem to involve acceptance of the *possibility* that man's actions, even those of the intelligent human adult, may, at least in part, be an extralogical, automatic matter, which can be controlled only indirectly, through understanding of the natural laws of behavior.

We should be receptive to scientific understanding of human behavior, just as we have learned to become receptive to changes in our conceptions of the physical universe and to the technological changes which have resulted from these changed conceptions. There is strong evidence that the human adult and the rat behave similarly under certain similar conditions. While we may not like to think of ourselves as rat-like, we should evaluate the evidence, rather than draw our conclusions on the basis of superstition and prejudice. We can be comforted in the knowledge that science is a most human of ventures; no rat ever followed the logic of a syllogism, or built a computer. Does the rat really represent so great a threat to us in intellectual accomplishment that we must defensively deny whatever useful similarities permit our learning from caged *Rattus rattus* instead of from caged *Homo sapiens?*

The hoped-for outcome of behavioral science is the improvement of the human condition. How those who have undertaken to engage in first-line fighting for psychological knowledge go about it, the apparatus they use, the species they use (in the impossibility, or undesirability, of subjecting humans to the controlled conditions of laboratory research), their experimental designs and research tactics are hard to evaluate. The layman might do a better job, or at least not feel so "out of it," the more scientific training he has had, which is a sound reason for increasing the emphasis on behavioral science at lower educational levels. But some gap always exists between the scientist himself and his ultimate audience, particularly during that long trial and error period in which new theoretical approaches are being groped for, tentatively formulated and subjected to their first early testing.

Like an expectant father, we sometimes find it hard to wait passively in the anteroom during the birth process. As well we might. We are, after all, called upon to pay the bills. And we are very eager for promising offspring of scientific investigations. But it is a mistake to think of science as a secret, mysterious process conducted in dark recesses of university corridors and laboratories. To conceive of science in such a way is to be unaware of its basically public nature. The scientist works not in a vacuum, but in a social milieu. The hallmark of his professional competence is his ability to communicate his procedures and findings to others. The responsible public neither rejects nor accepts out of hand, but listens, learns and inevitably, but not precipitously, on the basis of careful attention to the evidence from all sides, makes tentative evaluations.

It seems that the time for responsible lay evaluation of the reinforcement principle and its possible application to human behavior has not yet come. This is still a wait-and-listen time; research findings accumulated so far, while consistent with the principle, do not provide overwhelming evidence that reinforcement underlies all human behavior, nor is it clear to what behaviors it is likely, or not likely, to apply. What seems to be the case, at this point, is that the reinforcement principle provides a usable basis for setting up guidelines for effective behavior management in certain situations, for example, in schools and other institutions. Perhaps, it will turn out that as Newton's physics was incorporated by later physical theories, the reinforcement principle may prove to be a rather crude approximation to an as-yet-undreamed-of more adequate formulation of the laws of human behavior. But right now, it works in some situations, and all that is really essential is that scientists and educators and others be permitted to continue to explore possibilities of putting the principle to use. Perhaps, in the course of this work, other discoveries will be made. Perhaps the golden age of humanity will come, not in spite of, but because of, our acceptance of the demonstrated application of the principle of reinforcement, even its possible application to the behavior of the human adult. □

Premature Instruction

George L. Geis

A key motto of the Now Generation, "do your own thing," may seem like an invention to those under thirty, but it appears to be only a rediscovery to those who have been around a bit longer. Everyday observations as well as data from psychological laboratories lead to the conclusion that one repeats those actions that have been rewarded in the past. In this way we each acquire a unique set of habits. So, in a sense, people have always been doing their own thing. Furthermore, we know from human and infra-human studies that it is not necessary for the reward to regularly follow the activity. An irregular schedule of reward, far from weakening the behavior, tends to *strengthen* it even further. Extrapolating from the laboratory to the complex and chaotic everyday world this fact alone may help explain why we do our own thing so often, even when it is inappropriate to do so.

We all have heard stories (possibly apocryphal) of medical cases in which a person in poor health is referred first to one specialist and then to another, each one claiming that the cause of the illness lies in *his* area of expertise. If a patient with a chest pain is sent to a cardiac specialist, the chances of the "cause" being a heart condition are high. If he should take a wrong turn in the professional building and end up in an allergist's office, the chest pains may be traced to the high pollen count. If he should have the misfortune to bungle into a psychiatrist's office his discomfort may be explained in terms of an overabundance of, or a glaring deficiency in, mother love.

Often the specialist is a solution in search of a problem. The heavy investment in building up one's expertise in an area, and the history of reward for the exercise of those skills, may lead to the misapplication of them. (In the above example, the problem might not even have been a medical one, and *my* medical solution would be inappropriate. The poor patient may simply have been sleeping on a bad mattress.)

In instruction, as in medicine, the professional does his own thing. Teachers teach; programmed instruction specialists develop programs; and centers to improve instruction insist on making such improvements. The instructional specialist, whatever his area or particular set of skills are, may see all problems as susceptible to instructional solutions.

In this essay, teachers and instructional designers are seen as agents of behavior change. Their function is to guide, elicit, modify and create behaviors. There are a great number of people similarly oriented, who consciously or unconsciously, intentionally or inadvertently, spend their professional lives attempting to change others' behavior: for example, architects, advertisers, psychotherapists, writers of guide books or cook books, and financial advisors. Teachers represent one subset of the class: "behavior change agents."

The behavior change agent is, of course, only one factor in the modification of another's activities. In addition, a person's immediate social and non-social environment, his history, his current motivational states and the like, act to produce his behavior at any moment.

It is naive and arrogant for one professionally involved in changing behavior to assume that he (or he and his colleagues) can manage to produce all kinds of modification in another person's behavior. It is especially impertinent (as well as self-defeating) for a person in instruction to assume that *all* behavioral changes sought can be brought about through teaching.

This essay originally began as a prescription for more effective design and development of instruction. In the preparation of such a prescription, it became evident that the conditions under which the prescription was to be used should be defined. Even the most effective medical treatment is at least useless and sometimes harmful when applied to the wrong patient. Similarly, a description of more effective ways of designing instruction could be worse than no description at all, if the procedures are applied indiscriminately.

Therefore, an attempt will be made to delimit the kinds of problems to which an instructional solution might be applied, i.e., it presents an analysis of the conditions under which it is appropriate to begin an instructional solution to a problem.

The analysis involves two activities: Verifying the existence of a problem and determining whether an instructional solution is appropriate. In approaching the matter this abstractly, it is necessary to set aside for the moment the real chronology of events. Typically an instructor comes to the attention of instructional designers with a "problem;" the instructor assumes *that* he must teach and *what* he must teach. This paper will approach the subject differently.[1] It purposely does not take into account existing instructional institutions or personnel and the demands to support them.

Step I. Establishing the Need for a Consequence

In a world which had no tradition of education and educational institutions, an instructional designer might begin by examining the environment for needs or problems. Some of these might be alleviated through the development and use of instruction.

Presumably all teaching is aimed at providing people with the ability to do things so that they can affect their environment in certain ways. The output of instruction is not merely the skills and knowledge that people acquire but a supply of people who act upon the world to produce certain effects (including effects upon themselves), Therefore, the proper place to start the process of generating instruction is at the end or output.

Education is a system to produce changes in the environment by developing mediators of such changes. The design of

A version of this paper was originally prepared for a conference at the Center for Learning and Development, McGill University, November 21, 1969. The author expresses his gratitude to Patricia O'Connor, K. Brethower & D. Brethower for helpful comments and criticism as the paper was developed.

GEORGE L. GEIS is assistant professor of psychology at the University of Michigan.

[1]The paper represents what is called a systems approach. Various attempts have been made to apply the systems approach to educational problems. See, for example, Csayni, Attilla, Determining Objectives: A Behavior Systems Approach, *National Society for Programmed Instruction Journal,* Feb., 1968. Carter, Launor F. The Systems Approach to Education — Mystique and Reality, *Educational Technology,* April, 1969. Task Group 6: Systems Approach to Education, *Proceedings of Project Aristotle Symposium.* National Security Industrial Assoc., Washington, D.C., 1968. Lehman, Henry, The Systems Approach to Education, *Audiovisual Instruction,* Feb., 1968. Banathy, Bela H. *Instructional Systems.* Palo Alto: Fearon Pub., 1968.

systems to produce changes in the environment ought to begin with identification of what changes are desired. A proper analysis, it is suggested, proceeds from effect, or consequence, to cause. ("Consequence" is similar to what Thomas F. Gilbert has called *accomplishment*.)

The observer, then, would begin by noting that there were certain needs not being satisfied. Broadly stated: Some things are happening which people wish would not happen and some things are not happening which people wish would happen.

Several actual examples may be useful in illustrating the application of Step I to real situations. The nursing educator brings a request to an instructional designer: improve the effectiveness of nursing education, perhaps by the use of expensive media, through teacher training, or through any of a variety of "solutions." Step I is invoked. The educator is persuaded to examine, in a joint effort with other medical educators, the desired consequences of the nurse's behavior. The consequences of nursing education (along with the education of doctors, hospital personnel, and the like) involve the production of comfortable and healthy patients. The final output of nursing education, therefore, should *not* be considered an educated nurse but a comfortable and healthy patient.

Another example involves a request to "improve language learning." In language training the emphasis is almost always on the teaching of certain behaviors to the speaker. Looking at the area of instruction from the proposed "consequences point of view," it is obvious that the end point is *not* the behavior of the speaker but the effect upon a listener. Were we training children to push a cart, it would be obvious that we would not concentrate upon formal properties of the child's pushing behavior as much as we would upon his effectiveness in moving the cart. The aim of language, in a sense, is to move the environment about, using small muscles. Appropriate questions formulated for consideration by the language teacher included: What are the desired consequences of speaking, reading and writing a language? What are the effects expected and desired, when a speaker talks to a listener?

An interesting third example involved the development of instruction for interviewers in social work agencies. A common starting point for such instruction has been either the analysis of the interview into its component parts or an analysis of the behavior of the interviewer (for example, "the interviewer should learn to be supportive"). But these are, respectively, once and twice removed from a statement of final consequences. Step I was used as a starting point. Teachers and designers started by examining the conditions (including changes in interviewee behaviors) which lead to better family relationships, to temporary support for needy clients, to referral to an appropriate social agency, and the like. Often the goal of an interview is to obtain and evaluate information from a client and then to persuade the client to take certain actions which the interviewer feels are appropriate. The consequence is presumably that the client is happier, healthier or less a threat to society than he was before the process started.[2]

It is easy to see how quickly one moves from the specific and narrow limits of a traditionally defined "job" to a broader focus of a system designed to produce a consequence. In the care of a patient, in the solving of a client's problems, and in the education of a human being it is likely that many elements (human and non-human) will be involved. Closer examination of these components is the next task, Step II.

Before going on, two notes should be added.

The language and examples used in the description of this step so far may have implied that the sole aim of education is the development of demonstrable and specific knowledge and skills.

There is often a confusion in education between two aims. On the one hand, skills and knowledge seem to be taught for their own sake, and on the other, they seem to be vehicles for the development of traits, strategies, viewpoints and attitudes which, it is hoped, extend far beyond the content area.

For example, a history course eventuates in an examination or term paper in which content specific behaviors are supposed to be demonstrated. Yet most educators, and certainly the teacher of the course, would claim that producing a way of thinking is a major purpose, perhaps the major purpose, of the course. Similarly, the scientific viewpoint as well as a knowledge of chemistry is supposed to emerge from a course in chemistry. There are changes attributable to specific content being taught on one hand, and other changes for which the content is viewed as a carrier or medium (thus, the scientific viewpoint might as well be taught in a course in physics as in chemistry.)

This is not the place to go into the murky area of transfer of training or generalization — an unhappy history which, in modern times, begins with the teaching of Latin in order to produce more rigorous thinking. The point to be made does not require a lengthy discussion or analysis. It is enough to recognize here that content is often used as a medium for teaching general patterns of behavior.

The model described here may be applied to the production of those general patterns. However, examples involving knowledge and skill are used because they seem to present the clearest instances, those that are most easily examined and clearly illustrative of the points being made.

A second comment concerns constraints on objectives. Unfortunately, as described above, the development of goal statements might suggest an elitist and conservative (in the true sense of the word) view of education. Thus, it might seem that the educator alone determines the objectives of the instructional system; also it might appear that the role of the educator (or any agent of behavior change) is to fit his students neatly into existing molds. This need not follow from what has been said.

First of all, it is feasible (and, in the author's view, necessary) to engage all members of society, students as well as teachers, in the entire process being described. All concerned members of society must have a voice in defining needs and determining which deserve attention.

The apparent conservative bias may be further reduced if one more point is added here. Changes in what exists, and the capacity to produce further changes, can be viewed as continuing major societal goals. Goals may be derived not only from examination of the present but also from extrapolation of current trends to the future. (For example, as computer hardware was designed, it could be predicted that a new group of people — computer programmers — would be needed as part

[2]For an interesting attempt at stating behavioral goals for counseling, see: Krumboltz, John D. Behavioral Goals for Counseling. *Journal of Counseling Psychology, 13,* 3, 1966, pp. 153-159 and Krumboltz, John D. *Stating the Goals of Counseling.* California Counseling and Guidance Association, Monograph Number One, 1966.

of the system.) The generating of people who are themselves flexible and who in turn generate change might well be Education's most important output. It is one that can be justified both in terms of benefits to the individual and to society.

Step II. Defining the Components Necessary to Produce the Consequences

Having made explicit the needs and desired consequences relevant to the particular inquiry, one might next do a component, or systems, design. The aim of this effort is to specify the necessary components to produce the desired consequences.

Even a rough component analysis will usually reveal a division into human and non-human components. We are becoming more aware of the enormous amount of environmental change that can result from the use of non-human components in a system.

To return to nursing education as an example, one can observe that much that has to be done to make a patient comfortable in a hospital can be taken care of by non-human components. Certain tasks that were until recently thought to be exclusively human have been reanalyzed and appropriate equipment developed. Prototypes of the automated hospital, in which human intervention is minimal, already exist.[3]

The term "non-human" may include not only machines but also infra-human organisms. Although only a start has been made on the use of other animals as components of systems, the examples are noteworthy. Pigeons have been used to guide ballistic missiles (Skinner, 1960) and to inspect items on production lines (Cummings 1956). In both cases, they have been shown to be very good workmen, from the point of view of management. (Needless to say, there are objections from fellow workers.) These examples seem strange and, at the moment, trivial. Yet they reveal important problems. Replacing a man with a machine or even the suggestion that part of his job might be replaced by a machine can lead to trouble. We have not yet had librarians and accountants destroy computers (in the way that textile workers destroyed the first power mills) although the suggestion has been made publicly. The relationship between worker and automation is still to be worked out. The replacement of a human by a pigeon seems even more outrageous to most of us. Innumerable articles have been written reassuring teachers that they will not be replaced by teaching machines. Imagine the public relations work that would have to be done if lower animals were brought on the faculty! Not only is the component analysis difficult in and of itself but also it stirs up resistance and hostility, And yet, it is necessary.

Component analysis may lead to a restructuring of the system which produces the consequences desired. That restructuring may be in terms of the development of new non-human components; at least it will involve a restructuring of human jobs. In this second step, the analyst is likely to exclude more human tasks than he includes. He is likely to strip away many activities that were thought to be essential and were traditionally included in the training (and even in the performance) of the human components in the system. In addition, an examination of the present environment, the skills needed to accomplish the goals, and the skills as they are presently being exhibited, may reveal a number of components that are functioning very well. These can be subtracted out of the list of components to be designed or selected. In short: It is not always necessary to teach or develop the elements of the design. Some amount of cutting and fitting to make optimal use of what is available seems most desirable.

The analyst emerges from Step II with a system or several alternate systems which describe the components and the activities of those components necessary to produce a desired consequence.

Step III. Defining the Human "Job"

The human activities that emerge from a component analysis can now be classified into what may be prosaically called "jobs." Indeed, this step has traditionally been called "job specification." Historically, the description of a job has not arisen from the sequence of activities just described but from an examination of the present performance of a job holder. For example, the nurse in action in a hospital is studied, and what she does is written down. These activities, including all of the superstitious behaviors as well as all the efficient ones that she engages in during a day, constitute a job description which often becomes the basis for training the next generation of nurses. If Steps I and II are carried out, the usual grouping of tasks into a job will often be found to have only traditional justification: It has just grown up; it is what people do, rather than what needs to be done.

In most academic areas, not even traditional job analyses have been performed. It would not be impossible to determine what historians do; but such a specification of their activities does not exist. The role or job of a clinical psychologist is somewhat specified, but that of an experimental psychologist is ill-defined or undefined. The activities of a good citizen, or an informed, thoughtful person remain even more mysterious.

The inexorable press of specialization has forced the analysis of job descriptions in many areas; medical education is a case in point. There are *some* general practitioners, but they are a good deal rarer than they were twenty years ago. Some medical schools, nevertheless, still teach a job which simply does not exist with the frequency that the curriculum would suggest. The country doctor, with his black bag, riding through the night in a one-horse shay, able to set broken legs and cure the colic, is a romantic figure — but hardly an appropriate model for present medical curriculum developers to consider.

Here is one more academic example. An analysis of the use by professional people of the foreign languages that they learned for their doctoral examinations reveals that most of them never read a foreign journal, never speak a foreign language, never publish in a second language. Either they should be doing so and we are failing to teach them effectively, or the requirement is an irrelevant one, at least as far as practical use of a foreign language is concerned. On the other hand, even informal observation reveals that many professional people in the academic world are required to write grant proposals for research and development. Rarely are the skills necessary for such an activity formally taught in a graduate school curriculum.

The definition of the human job often turns into the definition of multiple jobs. For example, time motion studies of dentists at work have indicated that much of what they do could be done by a dental assistant. Invoking the exclusion

---

[3]See, for example, Brown, J. H. V. & Dickson, James F. III. Instrumentation and the Delivery of Health Services. *Science, 166,* Oct. 17. 1969, pp. 334-338.

principle once again, one group of designers involved in the study have concentrated upon preparing training materials for dental assistants and teaching materials for dentists intended to persuade them to use, and equip them to use, the dental assistant effectively.

The point of this discussion is to illustrate that a job can grow in an evolutionary way out of the needs of the environment; and that probably its resemblance to traditional job categories will be slight.

It should be noted that there is often a confusion between pedagogic means and professional ends. The final task that a doctor is involved in may not require him to perform blood tests and microscopic examinations of the blood; however, for pedagogic purposes it may be necessary to teach this in order to teach something else. If what is being taught has no relevance to a job, existing or newly structured, or more broadly, to a real world activity, it must be justified in terms of its demonstrable pedagogic usefulness.

At this point, it is worth summarizing what one would have in hand if he had carried out Steps I, II and III.

1. He would have an explication of present and predicted need or a series of needs. Presumably, he would be forced to contrast his statement with other statements of needs that other people are generating, and some sort of preference scale or hierarchy would be developed.

2. An analysis and design stage would have been completed, which would reveal a system, or several systems, made up of the components necessary to achieve the ends, that is to say, to alleviate the need just described. The component analysis would reveal tasks that are, for one reason or another, to be assigned to human beings and tasks to be assigned to non-human components.

3. Presumably, the non-human tasks are of less interest to us here. They could properly be assigned to engineers (or, as suggested, to animal trainers). The human tasks would then be grouped, or factored, into jobs. The exclusion principle would be applied both in separating human from non-human jobs and in attempting to set up job hierarchies for the human components (i.e., when possible, activities that can be handled at a lower level will be excluded from a higher level).

Step IV. Specifying Performance Criteria

The degree of precision involved in each of the previous steps has not been specified. It is likely, in most cases, that it will not be high. The lack of constraints in the early stages is probably beneficial. But at some point, for a variety of reasons mentioned below, criteria for the performance of each component in the system must be spelled out in detail.

Teachers, with some justification, think of the business of test development and testing as narrowing and confining to the instructional effort, sometimes directing the attention of the student and the instructor toward trivia. They are often familiar only with paper and pencil tests and, at that, with poor examples of tests. One useful thing that may come out of the "new look" in education is greater realization of the spectrum of instruments that can be used to record, measure and objectify human behaviors. An example is simulation.

Simulation has become part of the technology of education. Although its application has been mainly to teaching, some recent examples suggest it may prove equally useful in testing.

When student doctors diagnose patients and prescribe treatment, interacting exclusively with a computer, it is only a minor tragedy if the computer as a patient fails to survive the recommended treatment, or passes away while waiting for the doctor to arrive at the correct diagnosis. Such simulated patients can be used to test not only the final behavior of the student doctor with regard to diagnosis and treatment but the sequence, or method, of inquiry he uses in arriving at those two terminal points. Teachers are being taught (and can be tested as well) in simulated classroom situations using filmed groups of students. Law students attend mock courtrooms. And sometimes science students are tested in the laboratory on techniques and experimental methodology. Expanding the range of testing techniques can help reduce antagonism to measurement and thereby increase the probability that relevant and comprehensive performance criteria will be stated.

The development of performance criteria has several benefits. Having thus made explicit and operational the behaviors represented by the shorthand of component analysis, the designer has a tool which allows him to determine the validity of his analysis so far. He can try out his criteria on master performers. If they are not able to emit some of the behaviors in the performance criteria test and yet can produce the results desired the designer should reconsider those criteria.[4] (Of course, that a master can execute a required task is no absolute guarantee that it is a necessary behavior.) The first important consequence of the creation of a performance criteria test, then, is the validation of the criteria themselves. We would expect that as he developed the performance criteria and examined the results of tests of the performance criteria on master performers (i.e., validity checking) the designer would repeatedly re-examine and revise the analysis and design emerging from Steps I, II and III.

Having developed adequate test instruments, the designer may find an alternative to instruction by using those instruments as selection devices. Somewhere there may be people who can do the things he wants done. It is often much more economical, and sensible in other ways, to select than to teach. Intelligent selection presupposes appropriate test instruments. When objective measures of performance, and of behaviors correlated with that performance, have been devised, one form of a selection instrument is available.

A third use of the performance criteria is as baselines against which the effectiveness of any treatment, instructional or non-instructional, may be measured. The simple research design of *measure-test-measure again* is a potent one regardless of whether the treatment is instructional or not (e.g., performance tests may be given to the student population previous to instruction and then afterwards to discover the effectiveness of the particular instructional treatment).

The last use of performance criteria to be mentioned here is as end points for treatments.[5] The designer of instructional material can work more effectively and efficiently if, as he constructs the map of instruction, he has the major terminal points available. Often instruction almost "falls out" of such criterion tests since what must be taught becomes obvious when one

---

[4]A classic instance of mismatch between predicted necessary behaviors and actual behaviors of master performers (in this case, successful executives) can be found in Whyte, William H., Jr. *The Organization Man,* Doubleday and Company, 1956, especially pp. 201-222.

examines the tests and the acceptable answers or performance criteria.[6] With test instruments in hand, the designer can go on to the next step of examining, selecting or developing, and trying out possible solutions.

There is a similarity between Step IV and what others, for example, Mager (1962), have said about the need to state instructional objectives. However, there is a shade of difference between the sequence of events described so far which led to the statements of performance criteria, and the more traditional sources of objectives. Generally, statements of objectives are derived in part from the unique intuition and history of, and immediate controlling circumstances surrounding, the instructional designer. Another important contributing source, of course, is *content,* a static form of knowledge usually represented by textual materials. Arising from such sources, statements of objectives are likely to be a reworking of the same implied or poorly stated objectives that the instructional system is already working toward, however inefficiently. This is not to gainsay the important advances that are being made by those pressing for statements of educational objectives in terms of learner behavior. However, in the long run a mere restatement in behavioral terms of irrelevant educational objectives will not produce a marked improvement in education.

What *is* needed is a restructuring of curricula in terms of useful, functional behaviors, not mere testable statements of irrelevant goals. Curriculum redesign too often consists of reshuffling the same old pack of cards; making the symbols on those cards clearer and brighter does not change the basic constraints of the pack. To generate new and useful curricula one must move outside, to a new source, to the terminal activities or performances themselves.

Step V. Re-Examining the Performance Environment

Following the dictum "don't do your own thing" or "don't teach unless you have to," one would next re-examine alternative ways of producing the consequences desired. (Some have already been suggested, e.g., nonhuman components whenever possible might be substituted for human components.)

Mention was made of using performance criteria for *selection.* Training or teaching can be avoided if selection can solve the problem. When adequate test material is available, different populations may be tested and, by careful selection, people who can already execute the required tasks of the redesigned system can be brought into it. In highly mobile societies such as ours the concept of moving the man to the job is, of course, feasible.

The interaction of attempts at selection and component analysis need only be pointed out. If it is possible to select people who have certain patterns of skills that are needed in the redesigned system, the "jobs" can be redefined in terms of the available population. This rearrangement or reallotment of specific tasks can reduce the residual training or teaching problem.

A second way to avoid the necessity of teaching is through close analysis of the performance environment itself. Appropriate behaviors may be available in members of that environment but for one reason or another they are not called out or supported, an observation made by many people concerned with systems for changing behavior. G. A. Rummler has suggested the terms *knowledge* (what people have) and *execution* (what people do). Gilbert (1967) has contrasted performance deficit with ignorance: can do and won't *versus* can't do. Psychologists are familiar with the distinction between acquisition and performance. Different variables may operate, or at least be differentially emphasized, during acquisition and during performance (Geis, 1966).

There are many causes of discrepancies between learning and performing. What is learned may not be rewarded in the performance environment; what is learned may be punished in the performance environment; incompatible and more rewarding behaviors may be available in the performance environment; the stimulus conditions in the performance environment may be markedly different from those that obtained during acquisition. A re-examination of several critical variables in the performance environment may lead not to a design for instruction but to a redesign of the performance environment which, when tested, may prove to be sufficient.

Changes in the physical environment always ought to be considered. Changing the signals on a control panel may dramatically change the observer's performance. Placing materials on a lower shelf may increase the chances of use. A new handle on a machine can encourage better grasping. At the other end of this continuum is the addition of checklists of instructions which guide the performance bit by bit. (It is surprising how often a checklist plus instructions in its use dissolves the original instructional problem.)

In summary, one examination of the present performance environment may lead to changes in it which will eliminate or reduce the need for instruction. The environment should be examined with a second purpose in mind: The *maintenance* of the activities of new components. The design of an instructional system without a parallel design for maintenance in the performance environment is likely to make the instruction appear ineffective. As suggested above, it has been a long time since learning psychologists believed that behavior could be stamped in, in a way analogous to branding cattle. Today there is recognition of, and concern with, the maintenance of behaviors once established. The learning environment may be used to establish behaviors but the performance environment determines whether or not those behaviors will be exhibited. When the performance environment minimally supports the learned behavior, a deterioration of that behavior is likely. Our handwriting is a good example of this. Since it is primarily directed toward us or toward a sympathetic (and, incidentally, paid) secretary, most of us can note a gradual deterioration of what was a rather good hand to a scrawl unreadable by anyone but ourselves and our translator. Support systems for both the human and nonhuman components must be considered along with the design of the instructional

---

[5]Descriptions of other uses can be found elsewhere, for example, see Gagné, Robert M. The Analysis of Instructional Objectives for the Design of Instruction. In *Teaching Machines and Programmed Learning,* II (R. Glaser, Ed.). National Education Association, 1965, pp. 21-65. And, Popham, W. James. Objectives and Instruction. In *Instructional Objectives.* A.E.R.A. Monograph Series on Curriculum Evaluation No. 3 (Ed. R. E. Stake) Rand McNally and Co., Chicago, 1969. Especially, pp. 40-43.

[6]In some cases the "solution" is even simpler: Giving the student or employee the criteria and allowing him to instruct himself in whatever way he chooses until he meets the performance standards.

system.[7] (Such a support system, for example, is the type and means of feedback for the performer. Thus: What are the effects of the consequences of performance to the performer, to his peers, to his supervisors?)

In summary, the performance environment should be examined with two questions in mind:

(1) Is it possible to change some aspects of the present environment to evoke and support desired behaviors already present in the performance population?

(2) How must the environment be changed so that the behaviors acquired through instruction will be supported once the learner leaves the instructional system?

Step VI. Considering Resources and Constraints

The re-examination of the performance environment may confirm that the design of an instructional system or component is indicated. The resources and constraints involved in the production and maintenance of such a system will now be considered. The real determinants of the success or failure of an innovation, regardless of its intrinsic worth, are such practical matters as cost and availability of personnel.

Since any change involves expenditure and reallotment of resources, it would seem appropriate, before setting up an instructional system, to ask a number of questions concerning cost. For example: What is the cost to the receiving, or terminal, system if the behavior under scrutiny simply does not occur? And then, suppose that the behavior is not taught, will the final cost, in terms of deficiency of the terminal system, be greater than the cost of producing the behavior via instruction?

"Cost" can be interpreted broadly, and the concept of cost can be applied to other areas. For example, what is the value of the behavior to the learner and to other people? If there is no demonstrable value to the learner, the job of instruction may prove to be most difficult. If there is no value to others, the innovation will not be adopted or supported elsewhere.

Another cost-relevant consideration is the life-span of the instructional innovation or of the behavior the innovation produces. The rate of change in knowledge and skills is, in our society, geometrically accelerating. How long will what is taught be useful to the learner and to others?

Needs or goals are competitive. In everyday affairs they eventually become ordered in a hierarchy. Annual Congressional debate and log-rolling results in a Federal budget and legislation which define the select group of goals for which resources will be allocated that year. Cost of an instructional system may be considered in the context of a similar hierarchy. Should support be denied to the design and implementation of other behavior change systems in order to support the one being proposed?

Repeatedly, in this paper, attention has been paid to the problems of maintenance; the consideration of maintenance is appropriate in this step. Physical maintenance of an innovative facility (e.g., of the language laboratory) may prove to be too expensive for the existing instructional system. The support costs of an innovation should be estimated before the innovation is actually developed. The cost to the instructional system of maintaining the human components is, of course, equally critical in determining whether or not the innovation will last.

The cost of maintenance by the receiving system (i.e., performance environment) of the behavior to be taught must be considered. It was pointed out in the previous step that changes in the receiving environment often reduce or eliminate the need for new instruction of the people going into that environment. If new behaviors must be trained, then it is likely that the receiving environment will have to support those behaviors and probably will have to shift support or reallocate its resources to do so. Some of the more successful training efforts involve parallel training of supervisors with the supervised. In such cases there is clear recognition that if the supervisor is not specifically trained to maintain the trainee's behavior it will soon die out; the entire training program will have been a costly failure. The cost of maintaining the learner's behavior includes, in this case, the cost of training supervisors. Another, dramatic example is milieu therapy. This approach to psychotherapy recognizes that changes in the patient must be supported by his environment outside the therapist's office. The therapy, therefore, includes planned changes in the maintenance environment as well as the patient himself. The educational innovator might take heed.

Implementation and maintenance involve the development of subsystems concurrent with the development of the major system (e.g., the instructional innovation). It is impossible to predict with complete accuracy the course of implementation, the pressures on the maintenance system once it is in effect, the changing environment in which the innovation is located, etc. If a system is not designed to be adjustive and if data on its performance are not collected and fed back into the system, it is likely to wither or be destroyed. Only passing attention can be paid here to an important principle suggested by these statements: It is crucial to the maintenance of any system that some part of its resources be devoted to obtaining feedback on the performance of the system and some part to supporting a mechanism which responds to the feedback by producing changes when so indicated. (Instruction offers a negative instance. It is often a system without adequate means of gathering data on its performance and of converting the data it does obtain into recommendations for change.)

So much for constraints. The positive side of this step is "resources." Resources in the training environment and in the terminal environment which are presently untapped can be uncovered and used. Some examples may suggest the range of the resources that the educational innovator has at hand when constructing innovations and when seeking to have innovative behaviors maintained. Housewives, enlisted to grade English compositions, have proven to be useful aides. The each-one-teach-one system is often used by skillful teachers to relieve their own time pressures (in addition, there is some evidence that the student "teacher" learns as much as, if not more than, his tutee).[8] If the actual design and production of teaching materials is beyond the traditional resources of the system, the students themselves can often be utilized as curriculum developers. Involving students in the development of teaching materials may serve double duty: The materials can be used with other stu-

---

[7]For a discussion of maintenance in the context of training, see Brethower, Karen S. Maintenance Systems: The Neglected Half of Behavior Change. In *Managing the Instructional Programming Effort.* G. A. Rummler, J. P. Yaney & A. W. Schrader (Eds.), The University of Michigan, Ann Arbor, 1967, pp. 60-72.

[8]A well-tested innovative system involving students as staff is described in Keller, F. S. Goodbye, Teacher. *Journal of Applied Behavior Analysis, 1,* No. 7, 1968, pp. 79-89.

dents and the developers learn a great deal in the process of development. The "world outside" can and should be used as a resource in the development of educational systems. As presently used most work-study programs and field trips represent only minimal and primitive use of the resources of the world beyond the campus walls.

It is unlikely at the present state of development of educational technology that detailed and accurate information can be gathered about resources and constraints. Yet some indicators of cost are available and should be used more extensively. In the past 15 or 20 years, enormous amounts of money and effort have been poured into educational innovations. Unfortunately, the life of even the best innovation is dramatically short. Evidence is mounting which indicates that an important contributor to the demise of many otherwise worthwhile educational innovations is the lack of attention paid to resources and constraints. The instructional systems designer might bear in mind these words of Machievelli (a man skilled in examining constraints and resources): "Any plan that does not carry with it its own plan for implementation is worthless as a plan and should, therefore, be abandoned."

Summary

This paper has proposed that a decision to design and develop any instructional system (as small as a chapter in a textbook, as large as a college curriculum) be deferred until six steps are carried out. It suggests that the *how* to teach problem be approached only after one has examined the questions of *when* and *what* to teach. The first concern of the instructional designer ought to be the definition and demonstration of goals and needs at the societal level. Solutions to problems that the needs present may, but do not necessarily, involve changing human behaviors. Futhermore, only some of those elements of the solution which do involve behavior change are likely to require instructional systems. Finally, no such system should be developed until an inventory of relevant constraints and available resources is constructed and a plan for maintaining learned behavior is devised.

The decision to design and develop new instruction (or "improve" the old) is to be arrived at cautiously, only after excluding all other alternatives. The instructional systems that finally do emerge from this decision process will be undeniably relevant and must, inescapably, become efficient.

To the objection that teachers are involved in *Education* and "not merely" in instruction, the paper implies an answer. Many of the behavioral changes the "educator" wishes to produce require environmental modifications far beyond the scope of classroom and teacher.

REFERENCES

Cumming, W. C. A Bird's Eye Glimpse of Men and Machines" (pp. 246-256) & Verhave, T. The Pigeon as a Quality Control Inspector (pp. 242-246). Both in *The Control of Human Behavior* (Eds. R. Ulrich, T. Stachnik & J. Mabry), Scott Foresman Co., 1956.

Geis, G. L. Retention — A Pseudo-Problem. *NSPI Journal, 5,* 2, Feb., 1966, pp. 10-13.

Gilbert, Thomas F. Praxeonomy: A Systematic Approach to Identifying Training Needs. *Management of Personnel Quarterly,* Fall, 1967, *6,* 3, pp. 20-30.

Mager, R. F. *Preparing Instructional Objectives.* Palo Alto: Fearon Publishers, 1962.

Skinner, B. F. Pigeons in a Pelican. *American Psychologist,* 1960, *15,* 28-37.

A Curriculum Is a Set of Specifications of Which of the Following: A. Stimuli, B. Responses, C. Both A and B, D. Neither A nor B

William A. Deterline

Suppose we encounter a society in which many people have for many years worked diligently and skillfully to develop curricula. Suppose also that in this society each curriculum is a set of specifications of stimuli, information, or presentations, to which large groups of students are to be subjected; that is, there are no specifications that state with precision what capabilities and competencies the students are to develop as a result of the information — just details of what the information is to consist. And suppose that there are no "real world" paths, specifying any relevance of a curriculum or components of a curriculum to anything in the real world; nothing to inform the student in detail just what the components are to be used OUT THERE. Suppose also that students are kept completely in the dark about the relevance of the curriculum to the real world, and about what is expected of them as they proceed through the curriculum. Suppose — well, the reader gets the idea.

Webster is quite accurate, of course, in defining *curriculum* as "a course or set of courses." There is no reference to relevance, performance, effectiveness, or learning — just a set of courses. That's what we call "telling it like it is."

Consider the two extreme ends of a continuum — a continuum, not a dichotomy — along which are varying degrees of emphasis on stimuli and responses. At the stimulus end of the continuum there is no concern whatever for response considerations; no one cares what the students are to do in response to the information presented or what they can do upon the completion of the instruction; attention is directed exclusively to the questions of what to tell the student, and what to show him. At this extreme we might concentrate on the development of textbooks, films, slides, demonstration kits for teachers, teachers' manuals and other presentation materials. The results of such an effort can be quite elegant, and can make significant inroads on the many problems facing schools and teachers. The emphasis is on technically accurate, interesting, clear, well-organized subject matter, on the presentation of content, on the stimulus side of teaching and learning. Obviously, all of this is important along the entire continuum, so the *stimulus* emphasis should remain the same from one end of the continuum to the other. What does vary is the attention given to the *response* aspects of learn-

WILLIAM A. DETERLINE is president of Deterline Associates.

ing. Consider the extreme right hand end of the continuum shown in Figure 1. Although we are dealing with a continuum, we have shown the importance of stimuli and response considerations at only seven points on the continuum. At the extreme right, equal emphasis is given stimuli and responses. At this extreme, the desired responses would be identified *first,* and those response specifications would facilitate the identification and selection of the content — stimuli — that are to produce the responses. In more familiar terms, the specification of the instructional objectives, in terms of the terminal performance capability of the students, provides the maximum guidance and direction for the selection and design of content presentations. At the other end of the continuum, the content is selected because it appears logically to be a relevant part of the subject matter, and the form, media, methods, examples, problems and clarification are all selected on an artistic and intuitive basis, without very much attention to the desired *change* in the students that the presentations are to produce. Traditionally, curriculum design and development has been stimulus-oriented, on the left half of the continuum shown in Figure 1. Some attention has, of course, been given to the response considerations, in the form of workbooks and tests. But as we move to the right we begin to see instructional materials and events being designed more in relation to outcomes, and the specifications of the desired outcomes provide more detailed direction for the artistic and intuitive development of content. This is what is meant by instruction that is *response-oriented.*

Where do curricula come from? Traditionally, they have been stimulus-oriented, because they have been, in effect, a body of content that has through the years come to be identified as a course, or set of courses. By their nature, curricula are stimulus-oriented. Textbooks in most cases define curricula — not vice versa. Considerable effort has been expended in many subject areas to develop well-written textbooks around which teachers can work. But specifications no more clearly drawn than textbooks and related materials are really no specifications at all. A "package" of stimulus material does not indicate what the students should be able to do after being subjected to the content and related experiences. It might be a pleasant little exercise in academic freedom to provide a textbook and related materials and say only that each teacher can develop his own course from the content. But shouldn't the curriculum specialists have more responsibility and expertise than that? Certainly no one would claim that curriculum design and development is in any way a science, or a professional activity, or an objective methodology. It is, to date, primarily an artistic endeavor, content oriented, with little or no concern for what the students should be able to do after being subjected to a specific curriculum (although "specific" is not a characteristic except in the eyes of those who feel that content arrangement and clarification is all that there is to it!)

The myths of training and educating are readily visible in curriculum design activities and their consequences. In spite of masses of data to the contrary, many curriculum projects seem to be based on the assumption that any technically accurate presentation, if interesting and attention-getting, will teach — *something or other.* Certainly a presentation must be technically accurate and interesting, but *that is not enough.* Certainly a curriculum should consist of more than technically accurate information, and more specifications than simply "Here, present this!" Curriculum design, development and implementation, like teach-

ing, and like teacher education, must eventually come to grips effectively with the problems: *what is to be taught,* and *how it is to be taught.* These problems will not be resolved, and school will not improve appreciably until *curricula become student-behavior centered* and *teaching becomes student-behavior-change oriented.*

Perhaps the most promising developments — those that might bring about some of these changes — are those underway at many of the Regional Educational Laboratories. Because a major part of their mission is to develop instructional materials and products that produce specified and measurable outcomes, the Labs have had to learn from the experience, successes and failures of programmed instruction. And what this invariably leads to is instructional objectives, interactive instruction (with continuous student activity and feedback), and thorough testing and revision of the materials and procedures until they do in fact achieve their objectives.

Perhaps this approach will be rejected by many people who are directly involved in the more traditional approaches to curriculum design. That is to be expected. The work of a lifetime, and the methods and procedures that have proven to be at least partially effective, are not likely to be discarded simply because people, from other fields, say that there is now a better way. But isn't the whole idea to try to improve education? Isn't it worth trying *anything* that even faintly looks promising? One objection to this behavior-oriented approach is that it might "dehumanize" the schools. But has the reader visited a school recently? Has he observed the conditions under which teachers and students take part in the "educational process"? Aren't schools now, under present conditions, rapidly losing the battle and becoming more "dehumanized" each year? There is nothing inherent in the behavior-oriented approach, unless foolishly applied, that "dehumanizes" instruction. And there are increasing numbers of us who feel that this approach is the most promising direction we have for "rehumanizing" education, making teaching a dignified and true profession, and offering students the quality education that they deserve.

FIGURE 1

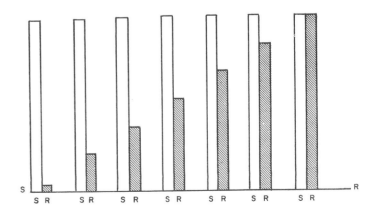

THREE ESSAYS ON OUR NEW MOVEMENT

I. A Theory of Three

Charles W. Slack
Contributing Editor

Needed: A Richer Social Microcosm

The ability of any educational system to meet the needs of the children for whom it is responsible is restricted by the type of social structure which comprises the system. In addition to learning how to read and write and do sums and take tests, children need to learn how to create and participate in their own "establishment." They need to learn about and learn to identify with a wide variety of social roles, especially those roles which involve work, play, politics or power, and affection. When one does not have an opportunity to "try on" important social roles, one becomes an inadequate, hostile-dependent creature, anxious neither to please nor to progress but only to prove that those who *are* happy or productive are wrong. Sometimes a child (or adult) will stop at nothing in order to prove that life has gypped him of being an important person: he makes a "living accusation" out of himself and dedicates his full energies toward making life miserable for those others who, unlike himself, think they have meaningful work, fun at play, political power or sufficient affection. There is one good way to state the nature of the generation gap: a person (young or old) who feels powerless, joyless, unneeded or unlovable may elect to expose the phoniness of what the rest of us call power, joy, work or love. The trouble is, to be really effective as an exposer and corrector of the faults of others requires certainly *more* role expertise than being an uncritical acceptor of things-as-they-are. Ralph Nader must know even *more* about the role of Senator, corporation president or bureaucrat than do senators or presidents or civil-servants. Whether our children choose to build or to destroy, to join or to reject, to change-from-within or to change-from-without our extant social institutions, they need experience with those institutions. I do not mean visiting the fire department on visitors' day or going to the fair. I mean finding out what it is that adults in our society do for a living on a day-to-day basis. Mechanical or hands-on experience is necessary, of course, but so is first-hand knowledge of the power and the glory, the rights and responsibilities, the decision-making and the rest of it.

In order for youngsters to feel a part of society and not just a neglected appendage, they must live *in* society and not on the fringe of it. That means that school must be a part of the larger community and must allow community participation by students and teachers.

The Inadequate Social Dyad

Our schools today are generally characterized by an *inadequate* formal social structure which does not allow each individual (student or teacher) enough choice of relevant social roles or relevant social role models. Our traditional, limited, two-role educational dyad of student and teacher is at fault. To correct this situation and to open up the school to the wider community, a theory—Triad Theory—is respectfully submitted.

Triad Theory proposes a three-role grouping to replace the inadequate student-teacher dyad. Triads, or three-role groups, have a number of contributions to make toward improving the quality of education at all levels. In understanding what is meant by the concept of *triad*, however, it is necessary to realize that the term refers to three separate social roles and not to three people. In a dyad *or* triad, there may be (and, educationally speaking, there *should* be) more than one person to represent each role.

Role Reversal

Before we get into triads, we must, in all fairness, state that even within the limits of the professional student-teacher dyad, it is possible for a school to be more or less flexible, more or less rich in regard to the allowable role relationships. Let us first examine two propositions of dyadic role theory as they apply to the excellence of schools.

First proposition:
Each student must develop a relationship with two or more teachers in order for the teacher role to have any meaning (distinct from meaning an individual person who happens to be called teacher).

Now this does *not* mean that there must be two teachers to each classroom and thus twice the budget. It *does* mean that students should have solid relationships with several different teachers. Teachers should move from group to group and students should meet with different teachers. It means that, if possible, no single teacher should dominate a student's learning for more than a short period—say a few months. Furthermore, a student should not leave a teacher forever when he graduates from one grade to another. This dropping of strong-formed relationships is most odd. Life, thank God, is rarely like that.

If children are allowed *natural* role relations with teachers, the *concept of teacher* will develop over a period of months, rather than taking the student many years, as is now the case.

Second proposition:
In order to be a student, a person must have the idea that he could be a teacher if he wanted to be. Likewise, in order to be a teacher, a person must have the idea that he could be a student.

This means, of course, that all students *must* be allowed to teach and that teachers must not stop learning. However, it means more than that. It means that students and teachers must frequently reverse roles and that each student, as far as possible, must be given an opportunity to do whatever it is that the teacher does, and, to as great an extent as is feasible, receive the same or similar consequences of action, i.e., rewards and other benefits.

Whenever a youngster gets the idea that he or she could never "make it" as a teacher, could never become what the teacher is, then that youngster drops out of school. He or she drops out mentally at the very moment the depressing thought enters the mind and then drops out physically at the earliest opportunity.

In order to work at *one* role in the student-teacher dyad, you must have the idea that you might work at the *other* role at least *some* day at least to *some* minimum extent. Without a minimum of such role-reciprocity, life, in any one role, is intolerable and the role is dropped. When a student drops out physically or mentally, whether by drugs, by poor attendance or merely through a closing of the senses, he or she has *dropped the role of student.* The ledger books and attendance lists may still carry him or her as a pupil, but a pupil he or she is not.

One must practice at playing the role of "other." Students or pupils do not become good teachers the first time they try on the new role. It is often agonizing for us as teachers to watch a pupil take over a group. One reason a pupil is awkward is that the pupil often presents himself, unintentionally, as a parody of ourselves as teachers. Even so, it is absolutely vital that each student become proficient in the role of teacher to at least a minimum degree—proficient enough so that he can say to himself, "I could be a teacher (of something) if I wanted to." Only then will the student "hang in there" rather than "dropping out."

The same holds for teachers. The teacher who does not, now and then, sit in the pupil's seat and genuinely learn from a pupil-turned-teacher becomes a poor teacher. When reciprocity of roles is missing, the teacher may become disillusioned and inadequate on the job, or worse, tyrannical and skeptical about all educational work. In any case, a teacher who does not play student becomes, finally, a non-teacher. The school system is full of teachers who have really dropped out—even though they go to work and collect their pay.

Triads in Education

Even with role reversal, dyads have a tendency to become static and uninteresting with time and to need "freshening up" by contact with new individuals in new roles. Thus, in addition to the principle of role reversal (which is not new) we propose the notion of *three-role* interactions to supplant two-role interactions in most educational and rehabilitative situations. (This principle has not, to my knowledge, been stated before, although I feel it is the primary observable difference between schools run according to newer free or "informal" philosophies and those run according to traditional rules.)

Examples of Three-Role Interactions

Here are some specific examples of triads in education and other areas of life:

—Primary triad: mother; father; children.
—Paraprofessional triad: teacher(s); teacher-aide(s); students.
—Visitor triad: teacher(s); students; visitor(s).
—Smokers' rehabilitation triad: smokers; ex-smokers (stopped smoking); non-smokers (never smoked).
—Weight-watchers' triad: people who need to lose weight; people who have lost weight and kept it off; people who never did need to lose weight.
—Learner's triad: those who have known the subject for a long time; those who have recently learned the subject; those who have not yet learned the subject.

Let us examine a few educational triads in depth.

The Paraprofessional Triad: teachers; paraprofessionals; pupils. In this triad, paraprofessionals should serve to bridge the gap between pupils and teachers. Thus, a pupil can say to himself, "if he (paraprofessional) can be an assistant teacher, then *I* might be one too." Of course, if the paraprofessional is, forever, *stuck* in his role and cannot ever *become teacher,* then, to that extent, the pupil will find in him an inadequate and unsatisfactory role model—in the long run both student and paraprofessional will "drop out" mentally and, finally, physically.

Visitor Triad: teachers; visitors; students. It is axiomatic of Triad Theory that every school worth the name must have a frequent stream of visitors of all kinds. The better the school, the more the visitors. The more the visitors, the better the school. A really *good* school will have one or two visitors who stay for weeks in addition to those who stay hours or days. Visitors should personify divergent roles: visitors in the role of pupils, teacher-visitors, parent-visitors and especially visitors who represent *roles in the larger community* which are not ordinarily represented inside the school walls. Direct experience with extra-curricular roles is especially important for adolescents who, in our society, may be completely devoid of all contact with men and women at work and thus may imagine erroneous ideas about the role of Establishment worker. Not that the young person can be forced into Establishment (or any other) values, but he can be exposed to them from the horse's mouth, rather than merely from teachers and mothers at home. The student must be exposed directly to laborers, managers, professionals, artists, government workers, police, poets and revolutionaries. He must be exposed to these roles *at the worksite* and from visitors to the school. Fathers do *not* do a good job of this because nepotism is frowned on in most middle-class occupations and the typical teenage male in our country today has never seen his father at work. Indeed, the most common work-role model for adolescents is the one role they are most commonly exposed to, namely, the role of theatrical entertainer or popular musician. If teenagers had as frequent exposure to, say, the role of marketing executive or computer operator, a great many would idolize those roles as well.

The absolute necessity for every school to have a steady stream of visitors brings up the following triad, which I call the Objective Learning Triad.

Objective Learning Triad: visiting subject matter

expert (not a professional teacher); "learning expert" (also not a professional teacher, but someone who "runs the show," a master-of-ceremonies); learners. In this triad, for example, the teacher might turn over the period to Sammy who then becomes "learning expert" for the day. Sammy then introduces Rod McLuhan, local bard, who then reads his stuff or does whatever Sammy wants him to do in the way of instruction as to what it means to be a poet. The rest of the group, including the teacher, become learners who interact with both Sammy and Rod.

Wider Social Relations

One of the best ways to look at the potential of triads in education is to realize that they "open up" the classroom and expand the traditional student-teacher relationship into a larger and more natural group.

Triads are more dynamic, and more interesting to observe and to join, than are dyads. The fact that triads are more exciting than dyads is due to the increased opportunity for a particular individual in a particular role to alter his role. In a triad, the individual has two possibilities for identification and movement; in a dyad, only one.

An Illustration from the Business World

In order to demonstrate the importance of introducing a third role in the educational process, we can examine an analogy from industry and government. In terms of role theory, the difference between a low-level clerk and a higher-level administrator or executive is that the clerk works only in a one-to-one or dyadic relationship with his boss, whereas the executive belongs to a triad and, thus, deals both with those above and with those below. All too often, the one-to-one relationship becomes a slave-master situation which is damaging to both parties. The triad allows each person a chance to "breathe" in his role by interacting with others.

Most classroom-teaching today is of the one-to-one variety in which the pupils are treated like clerks rather than like executives. This clerk treatment of students is not due to malice, stupidity or inadequate funds for education, but is rather an historic holdover from the past century.

The educational classroom of today, physically and socially, belongs to the 1800's. The room itself, with its identical rows of evenly spaced desks receding to the rear, is patterned after the clerks' office of the nineteenth century. The teacher faces the students in the same manner as the office-manager used to face his clerks. Each clerk (and each student) in those days had the primary functions of copying (there were no Xerox machines) and doing simple arithmetic sums (there were no office machines or computers either). The large clerking room with one Scrooge in front facing his rows of Bob Cratchits was a common sight until the beginning development of modern office machinery at the turn of this century.

At first, all clerks sat on high stools to discourage laziness (not so easy to get down). Students then were also forced to sit high. Eventually, however, only the "dunce" (he who got down and dared move around too often?) would have to sit on the old-fashioned high

stool. Others could sit lower, the "modern way," with their feet resting on the floor.

Each age has had its peculiar posture to mark the role of its clerks or scribes. At some times in history, we professional literates or scribes have sat cross-legged with clay tablets resting on our knees. As nineteenth century copy-clerks, we sat on our stools at slant-topped copy-desks so angled as to capture available sunlight from side windows. By 1935, long after the clerk's office had modernized, the public school also changed its appearance a bit. The overhead electric light was here to stay, thus allowing for flat-topped desks.

Since job training for clerks was the mainly recognized function of the public school classroom, it is no accident that the classroom imitated the clerks' office. This is what our nineteenth century middle class aspired for its children. If a child could learn to sit quietly and do sums accurately, rapidly and neatly, he could be destined to a life above ground in an office; whereas, if he could not learn these tasks (or could not be made to sit still), his fate as a child or adult might be the mines underground (where children pulled carts) or the mills (where they were not uncommonly chained to looms). No wonder that corporal punishment was frequently meted out to those who would not be quiet or who got down from their stools at the wrong time: by a whack of the ruler, a concerned teacher might save a fidgety child from a fate worse than death.

Our modern late stages of the industrial revolution certainly have their share of horrors of polution and waste, but child labor and copy-clerks, at least, are things of the past. The office machines and computers have all but replaced the clerks now, and those few who are left are called administrative assistants and are allowed to get up and walk around all they want—as long as they get their work done and in on time. In fact, getting up, walking around, and talking to others in person and over the phone are all requirements of, not detriments to, high-quality performance by modern office workers. Even the most lowly clerk-typist must not sit still all the time, but must coordinate her work with others, use the common office machines, acquire supplies and take her work to and from the boss. There is no doubt that the over-all posture of the scribe has radically altered during the past 50 years and one is hard put to find a genuine old-fashioned Bob Cratchit-type clerk anymore; yet the mind staggers to think how many such workers would be needed to run even the smallest of today's companies, were it not for the electric office and computing machines, typewriters, copy devices and other clerking machines.

One Exception

Ironically enough, the one office-worker who is "chained" to the machine today is the IBM key-punch operator. Since most office machines cannot yet read written symbols, someone must operate the typewriter-like key-punch devices which make holes in the IBM card, in order that the machines can "understand" the cards. The key-punch operator sits all day copying information onto cards using the key-punch typewriter keyboard. The key-punch room does resemble the clerks' office—or rather is a combination of clerks' office and old-fashioned sweat-shop sewing room.

The key-punch operator is not badly paid (on piece work) but few enjoy the work and most move on quickly to other jobs when given the chance. Key-punching would be a rather dismal model for the classroom; but luckily this will never come to pass, because by the time today's children are grown up, few if any key-punch machines will be left in operation. These will be as outdated as the steel-nib pen and the treadle sewing machine. The key-punch is already beginning to be replaced by machines which will read written symbols directly into the computer and by a variety of devices which collect information directly from the source, rather than routing it through the medium of the IBM card.

Edu-cultural lag

In general, the old-fashioned clerk has been re-placed by the modern office-worker. Why, then, does the classroom still resemble the old-fashioned clerks' office, rather than the modern junior-executive suite or, perhaps, more to the point, why do we continue to treat school children like Bob Cratchits?

The answer is that, as always, resultant changes in education lag behind the same changes in business and industry by 20 to 30 years (or about the time it takes the children involved to grow up and become influential decision-makers). I call this the "edu-cultural lag." Educational architecture in use today was, by-and-large, built in the fifties and is, largely, of the German-International (Bauhaus) design of the twenties and thirties. The very latest school buildings of the seventies reflect the industrial architecture of the fifties, with their skating-rink domes and non-supporting walls.

The same time-lag as holds for architecture holds for the treatment of students. In the early 1930's, John Dewey made academic headlines by getting American educators to think about unscrewing classroom chairs and desks from the floor when hardly even a drafts-man's stool had been fixed to the floor anywhere in American industry since 1910.

I know of one teacher* who has her classroom equipped with rocking chairs for the reading group, but aside from hers, I know of no classroom which provides its students with even the minimum of spring-backed reclinability afforded the average secretary in industry. I can dramatize this point by saying that the secretary to the principal would probably quit her job if she were required to sit all day in the same type of chair provided for her son or daughter. The kind of chair found in classrooms is only symbolic of an overall edu-cultural lag in the *role* played by (or forced on) the school child. Take the simple matter of the *number* of chairs provided. Today's modern office worker not only has a cushioned, spring-backed office chair for his or her own use, but probably another beside the desk for the visiting customer, client, co-worker, superior or subordi-nate. The presence of the visitor's chair is about the minimum requirement for the status of anything above

a secretary and is proof of the fact that the worker is part of a true triad, not just a master-servant dyadic relationship.

The possibility of each school child's having two chairs at his desk should not be dismissed as absurd. Although problems of space and budget might make it difficult, at least a shared private area where two or more students at a time can gather to discuss their work should always be provided.

Schedules

Another striking difference between the old-fashioned clerk and new-fashioned office worker is that the former was paced by the office manager or foreman, whereas the latter is self-paced. The classroom must keep up with this trend toward individual self-timing or we will be preparing our pupils for a work-a-day world which no longer exists. Thus educators must make much more use of self-instructional, self-pacing and individual-ized materials of all kinds. Furthermore, the student must be given the freedom and responsibility to choose his own learning materials.

Also, each pupil must be given the responsibility for *initiating assignments* and *carrying them out* to completion—*estimating the work time, revising those estimates* as he begins to get into the task and then, in the last analysis, *finishing on* (his own largely self-deter-mined) *deadline.* This is the pattern of today's industrial and business world. The employee is expected not only to *do* the work, but to establish his own time-to-completion and then to complete on his own estimated time. The teacher-paced schedules of stand-up-class-room-teaching and homework assignment do not teach sufficient responsibility for establishing one's own work rates and schedules. The nineteenth century model, where the boss set the deadlines *without* consulting the clerk, relieved the clerk of all decision-making functions and set him up for quick replacement by the Xerox machine and computer. Estimating times to completion is not easy. It requires practice and "maturity" in the sense of self-responsibility. The sooner one learns it the better. When the teacher sets the due-date for a report, the student may fail the course by being late. When he sets his own due-date, he runs the risk of failing *himself* as well as failing the course. There is a world of difference here. Quite a bit of research has proved (to industrial managers, at least) that self-set work schedules are not only more ambitious than boss-set schedules, but are more likely to be adhered to *once the individual (or group) who has set the schedule for himself becomes familiar with his own limitations.*

Summary

In a triad, as opposed to a dyad, the student has not just one boss to satisfy or one master to serve. Instead, triads place the student in a position similar to that of member of a modern work-team dealing with more than one other role. It is characteristic of the modern industrial, business and governmental worlds that workers must relate to more than one other role and thus must be more self-directed. We must have the skill to schedule our own work to meet a variety of needs and demands from others. Self-scheduling requires

*Betty Hughes, first grade teacher, Rocky Ridge Elementary School, Jefferson County School System, Alabama.

practice. Today, students are not getting enough self-scheduling practice because the old-fashioned student-teacher dyad is a hold-over from the copy-clerking office where one boss set the schedules for an entire class of copy-clerks. The office machines have all but eliminated the need for the nineteenth century institution of the clerking office and there are few such jobs available. Although the copy-clerking office is gone from business and industry, the classroom (which was modeled after it) is still with us because of our general "edu-cultural" lag. The sooner we can replace the outdated classroom and its simple (master-slave, student-teacher) dyad with some triads which are more representative of the real social and business world which our children will face, the sooner we will be able to bridge the *"generation gap"* between educational practice and real-world living. □

THREE ESSAYS ON OUR NEW MOVEMENT

II. How to Name Our Baby

Charles W. Slack

A Bad Name

By golly, when B.F. Skinner gave his very first talk at Harvard on teaching machines in 1956, or was it 1957, oh gee, I can't remember when exactly, *but I was there.* That makes 15 years or so for me as an educational revolutionary. Fifteen years...I've paid my dues... Fifteen years...I've watched Gabe Ofiesh and Sue Markle become presidents of the National Society for Programmed Instruction and stuff...watched guys make and blow millions (on paper) in Wall Street educational technocracy booms...watched the different movements come and go. I am an old soldier, I am; and I'm worried about the future of Informal Education. Informal Education is my new hope. It sends new life throughout these old hacked-up, battle-scarred bones of mine. I love Informal Education and that's what makes me scared. I love the concept. Every time I see it in action, it turns me on. I wish I had gone to a school like that. I wish my children could go to such schools. Informal Education is an absolutely wonderful idea, the best thing for young minds and bodies since the child labor laws. However, ominous note, there is trouble ahead for Our New Movement. The image is bad. The name is wrong. BAD NAME! SLOPPY.

The name "Informal Education" sounds loose, noisy, chaotic, left-wing, unplanned, untamed, undisciplined and, by gosh, downright *unstructured.* I mean,

can we afford to have a movement whose name sounds like *recess*...like *vacation*? There is definitely a weekend, summertime-holiday, fourth-of-July, anything-you-want, hot-dogs-and-ice-cream, comic-books-and-ring-o-leary-o sound to the very word "informal."

It brings to mind kids yelling and running around, kids not knowing where their seats are, kids who lost their rubbers, kids who forgot their homework (or, God forbid, teachers who forgot to give them any). It makes you think of sincere lib-gal teachers, very young, fresh from Wellesley or Briar Cliff, all pants-suits and owlish horn-rims, brimming over with expansive ideas but not exactly knowing how to, well, how to keep things under *control.* It makes you think of long and dirty hair on male teacher-aides with ratty old sneakers and torn-fringe jeans and a look in the eye that says they've done more than just read about drugs. It is positively scarey, "informal" is. What about "setting limits?" What about "the rights of others?" I mean a little chaos is all right, but a constant racket *all* the time! Who's in charge here? I can't hear myself think.

And another thing, the name "informal" will just get us an even *further* decrease in funds from a conservative Office of Education (What about Law-in-order? That certainly doesn't mix with Informality) and get us even more newspaper columns on stop-the-beat-nik-educators-before-they-turn-our-children-into-Godless-dropouts from the pens of Max Rafferty and William Buckley. Even now, it sounds left-wing, does "informal." Almost before it even gets off the boat from England "Informal Education" has a bad name with the right-wingers.

So what! Who cares about them? Well, I do, for one. Not about them *personally,* but I do care about the kids who happen to be under the right-wing educators. You don't choose your educators when you are a kid, you just *get* them. I happen to believe that children with right-wing principals, children with conservative, up-tight, out-of-it, scaredy-cat, *old* administrators have just as much right to Our New Movement and the rest of the best and latest that education has to offer as do children with liberal, hip, aware, open, out-front, *young* principals with beards, beads and bell-bottoms. Take *backlash,* for example! Wouldn't it be sad if the upshot of Our New Movement—this wonderful, freedom-loving, joy-producing movement—was that all the conservative, up-tight principals scheduled *out* the free periods, screwed the desks back onto the floor in rows and made everybody wear crew-cuts, just because they were afraid the local hard-hat PTA would call them "unstructured" if they didn't. Well, I've seen it happen before and *more than once*, by golly! Movement—before it's too late, change the image. Keep the concept but...get a new name!

Can a Theorist Help?

I think so. One way an educational theorist (especially a discursive one like I am) can help the movement is to suggest how to pick a name. I can't actually *pick* the name, since I have no power to get a name across, being just an educational theorist and not a politician...or a popularist. Not a powerhouse. Even so, I can state the rules by which a name should be chosen or rejected. Then, if someone reading this *is* a powerhouse (say, Gabe Ofiesh or Susan Markle is reading this; say, even Joe Harless is reading this), then these people could follow the theory and establish the movement with a new name which would get things going faster. I predict that the right name might save us all ten years or more and allow the movement to reach two or three million kids it wouldn't reach otherwise and make them happy. And the *wrong* name? What harm does that do?

Terrible Names

Educational movements of the last decade have been hampered by absolutely *awful* vocabularies: "teaching machines," "intrinsic programming," "programmed instruction," "operant conditioning," "behavioral objectives," "contingency management," "systems approach," "linear programming," "rul-eg," "pro-mod," "frame-up," "schedules of reinforcement," "mathetics," "chaining," "discrimination," and on and *on.*

Doesn't it make you wince a bit when you think that there really turned out to be no *teaching machines?* But we were all a part of the *"teaching machine movement."* We all had *teaching machines* companies, and the companies all "went public" or "sold out" to Xerox. We were all rich (on paper) from *teaching machines.* Yes, indeedy, there was a teaching machine *movement* all right. Only thing was there were just no teaching machines . . . Ahem, folks, Mr. and Mrs. PTA, Office of Education, Sol Linowitz, U.S. Industries, Norm Crowder, Encyclopaedia Britannica Salesmen, Loeb Rhodes, Jerry McDonnell, Carl Sontheimer . . . Ahem, I'm sorry to have to announce to you that a mistake was made and there are no teaching machines. Actually, I hate to admit it, but we all wasted the ten best years of our lives *believing* in teaching machines, hoping that if we believed *hard* enough, if we really *thought* teaching machines, that, somehow, it all would come true and there *would* be teaching machines. However, truth be known, nobody actually *did* ever, well, really *invent* a teaching machine. I hate to say it folks, but Skinner made a boo-boo. I mean there was a *box* with a slit in the lid and a roll of paper went inside the box but it didn't actually *turn* too good and it never actually *taught* anybody anything. It just sort of sat there and got *looked at* by the faithful grad students who came up to visit the lab. It was . . . maybe it was supposed to be a *symbol* and not really *do* anything . . . a kind of mechanical Ark. A *tiny Torah on rollers* in a stainless steel Ark—with a slit in the lid so's you could only read one verse at a time. But it was not a teaching machine . . . Skinner just called it that . . . it was a paper-roll-holding-box-with-a-slit-in-the-lid . . . tell the truth . . . that's *all* it was.

Then there were all those projectors with buttons of all kinds so the film could go backwards and forwards and up and down but *these* weren't teaching machines, either. They were just projectors with extra buttons. Anyhow, it doesn't matter what you call them now, because nobody even looks at them anymore. The ones that aren't jammed or button-broke are all over on the shelf gathering dust in the AV department. Except, of course, the light blue . . . or was it green . . . plastic Grolier ones. Remember how the Grolier Salesman said that B.F. Skinner had invented this wonderful machine that was guaranteed to raise your kid's grades and get Dumb Dora into Radcliffe. Well, these are all in the attic now. In case you forgot, they are next to the DuMont circular-screen TV, right behind Grandma's paper maché clothes dummy.

Then there was "Programmed Instruction." Programmed Instruction was the Torah-rolls that were supposed to go *into* the teaching machine but didn't, so we cut them into 8½ x 11 and sold them as an *unbound* book. Later we bound the book and called it *English 2600*—presumably to stand for the 2600 years it *originally* took to advance from the Torah-scroll to the bound book.

Unlike teaching machines, programmed instruction is still around. Programmed Instruction was the Si-Fi name we gave to the funny bound and unbound workbooks, the ones where each page was divided into teeny *sub*-pages called "frames" and teeny-tiny blanks *in* the teeny-tiny sub-pages, so's you could only write in one or two words at a time. The reason for "frames" was to fit the slit in the lid of the teaching machine. When the teaching machine didn't work, we kept the frames anyhow. So then we had workbooks with teeny-tiny sub-pages. Not exactly scientific, but what *was* in the roaring sixties? I mean, we all were too busy *going public* to worry about details. Instead of calling them workbooks, we called them "Programmed Instruction" (with two m's yet). They are about the most boring workbooks ever written, but that's O.K. since most people don't buy them anyhow because they have this inhuman sounding name "Programmed Instruction."

Then there was "Operant Conditioning" (which I won't describe) which sounds like something you do to leather but isn't. Then there was "Contingency Management," which I also won't describe but which sounds like an economist talking about saving for a rainy day. Or how about this one? "SYSTEMS APPROACH." Wow! Systems Approach has the ring of really *big money.* Trouble is, old SA rings of money *lost,* rather than money gained. Wasn't Systems Approach the reason Lockheed Aircraft lost a $1 billion overage and never did finish building the BX-119 QB7 Weapons Transport System? Wasn't Systems Approach the reason we all lost money because we bought *all* our textbooks from Sneaky-Systems-Sam, the Systems-Textbook Pusher who "coordinated" all our textbooks so we never got the authors we wanted from the other publishers? Systems Approach was originally hailed as a "New Departure" in education. As an author, I'm glad it has departed. To me, as a writer, Systems Approach meant *work-on-a-salary-and-never-get-any-credit* for your work. I like the old-fashioned Author's Approach, where the publisher *approaches* the author and gives him an advance and a royalty and his name on the cover. Well, it doesn't matter anyhow, because Systems is on the departure. Why don't we just call it "Approach Departure?

Then there was "Behaviorism." "Behavior" always sounded like something you ought to do but didn't. To get the right idea, just stress the second syllable hard, be*have*. That's it! "Now, be*have* yourself, Johnny," or "Johnny is on his best be*hav*ior today." It took 30 years to get people to understand that when be*hav*iorists talked about "reinforcement," they didn't mean seams . . . or cement. They weren't *really* trying to say that our children were objects like bridges and buildings that needed propping up with steel TCI beams. *Now* some of us know that behaviorists were really human and warm and loving after all. Now . . . 30 years later, but how come they didn't come out and say so then?

Miss Henny Slockbower, third grade teacher for 18 years in Dothan, Wisconsin, didn't understand "reinforcement" at all. She never did. She taught third grade at Dothan, making Dothan teacher-of-the-year three times and getting an extra. Masters in Music from Dothan State (Teachers') College and 19 credits toward her doctorate before she retired and moved to St. Petersburg, Florida to raise orchids in her Floridaroom and paint by numbers, and *still* she doesn't know the meaning of "reinforcement." "Reinforce Johnny for his positive behavior." My word! Miss Henny thought that sounded like "stick a steel rod up his backbone and give him a good jolt of plus-charge ions . . . or worse!" Of course all we *insiders*, the Skinnerians, we chosen few who were *paid* to go to workshops, instead of paying like Miss Henny, we special *scientists*, me, Gabe, Susan, Tom, Joe, Mager and the rest, *we* knew reinforcement really meant "let the little sweetums go out and play if he has been good and give your brownie-points and gold stars *right away* for doing the reading," but Miss Henny didn't get it. Miss Henny didn't get it at all. So, as a result of all this behaviorist, science-fiction language, all these bad-sounding words that the insiders knew were *good* words and mechanical sounding words that the insiders knew were *really* humanistic after all, as a result of making Sweetums sound like he was a machine filled with wires and transistors and old auto parts instead of sugar and spice and everything nice, *as a result*, the behaviorists were delayed 30 years . . . and never did get to Dothan, Wisconsin . . . and probably never will.

Rescuing Our New Movement

Who cares? Well, I don't care about be*hav*iorism. Let it die, too. I just don't want that to happen to Our New Movement, that's all. Our New Movement has it all over the behaviorists as far as making kids happy and having them love the reading and learn a lot. So let's be cagey about naming this thing, Gabe. Susan Markle, listen to me. This is old Big Daddy Slack talking. Joe Harless, you know I'm usually right in the long run. I don't prevaricate like your *average* workshop work-horse, your run-of-the-mill paper-grinder. I'm not your typical "educational technologist" just out for the fee. I tell the truth and I've paid my dues. So for once, why not do what I say? It won't cost you anything. Why *not* take my advice . . . get a new name, and here is how.

How to Name Our New Baby

Don't make up some Si-Fi Super-Shok Freedom-Control name like Skinner's names. Do what the successful, old-fashioned, *peaceful* namers did. Put together two *friendly* names which have never been put together before. One name has to be the name of a *place*. Something far away and country-sounding, like Summerhill, England or Mossmanse, Mississippi. Summerhill had a marvelous reputation (except in England) for years. Summerhill was to education in the fifties what Tahiti was to art in 1910: too expensive to actually *go* there but wonderful to dream about after a hard day at the compulsory SRA reading lab. Summerhill, think of it! O.K., Gabe, find the same kind of far-away place and name *us* after it. Try someplace in Russia or China, if you want. The hard-hats won't care, they seem to *want* to imitate the enemy (remember Sputnik), but please make it peaceful this time.

Now you can't have just one name: it takes *two* names to make it. Think of what would have happened if A.S. Neill of Summerhill fame had called it "The Summerhill System!" Like "Montessori Method" (come to think of it, Montessori *does* sort of sound like a *place*, and so does *Plowden*). If Neill had called it "Summerhill System" it could have been *exported* to Hohokus, New Jersey. It would have been for *you* and *me* out here in Anthracite, Pa., and not just for the Summerhillians in Downy-On-The-Whatever. We want Our New Movement to sound like it is ready to jump the ocean at the drop of a hat. "Have system will travel." All set for the Hohokus Public Schools *right now*. Get 'em while they're hot! And *no* delays allowed for workshops next year, OE committees and peer review. None of that . . . oh-well-let's-plan-a-trip-to-England-next-year- and-then-send-postcards-to-the-teacher's-room-and-bring- back-slides-for-the-PTA. We haven't got time. The kids are getting up out of their seats, Gabe! They are leaving the building. We haven't got time. They are *dropping out*. Quick, get the New Movement going or we won't have any School left!

Since "Informal Education" already has the connotation of *unstructured* and is suffering thereby, perhaps it would be best (save us all about five or six years of toil and workshop rhetoric) if the second word in the name you pick implied structure rather than being *too* artsy and do-your-own-thingish. Not hard-nose, go-to-your-seat-immediately, *punitive* structure but structure nevertheless. I like the sound of Summerhill Structure, don't you? What a nice name. Too good to be true. Sounds like they mean the guest house and not the teaching method. Well anyhow, I have made—perhaps belabored—the point. The ball is yours, Mager, all you guys with the power and the position, Larry, the guys with the super-structure, Tosti, Homme, let's give this one a real good try. Let's be *understandable* this time. Let's use names of peaceful places you would like to visit *and* let's use their words whenever we can instead of inventing our own.

Let's not use the word "technology," however. It sounds too hard. Too much wiring of the relays. Too much machine-language and continuing computer-assisted education. No, call it an art or a *craft*—ah, maybe that's it, a "craft." Well, anyway, you'll know, Joe, Sue, Gabe. I trust you, you will come up with the right name. Get to it! □

THREE ESSAYS ON OUR NEW MOVEMENT

III. Tell It What It Is

Charles W. Slack

We are all together in a common cause. We know what we don't like in American Education today. We don't like lesson plans. We don't like up-tight teachers. We don't like stand-up instruction! *Down* with stand-*up* instruction. Down with one-teacher-facing-rows-of-faces-each-in-his-own-place-and-never-get-out-of-your-seat-or-you-will-have-to-go-to-the-principal's-office. Down with all that. We hate having to all read the exact same book, the one we didn't choose ourselves. We hate having to read the same chapter *in* the same book *on* the same day and we hate having to hand in the same report all *at* the same time.

We all know what Our New Movement *isn't*. It *isn't* marching in rows. It *isn't* having to all clap together at an assembly for a speaker *they* invited without asking us and who gave a rotten speech to boot. It *isn't* token representation on the faculty committee or faculty domination of the student council. It *isn't* being forced to take a kindergarten mid-morning nap when you aren't even tired just because the teacher was out late last night. It *isn't* most of the things educators are now doing to kids, unless by educators you mean those hip, neat people like John Holt who live in and teach in and write from far-away places like English Countryside or Redwood, Oregon, or wherever in Canada *This Magazine Is About Schools* is published.

Our New Movement *isn't* rigid. It *isn't* pedantic. It *isn't* . . . "The preoccupation with order and control or the slavish adherence to the timetable and lesson plan, the obsession with routine qua routine, the absence of noise and movement, the joylessness and repression, the universality of the formal lecture or teacher-dominated 'discussion' in which the teacher instructs an entire class as a unit, the emphasis of the verbal and the de-emphasis of the concrete, the inability of students to work on their own, or the dichotomy between work and play—none of these are necessary; all can be eliminated." Quote. Unquote. Three Cheers, a positive reinforcement and a thank you very much, Charles E. Silberman, noted author of *Crisis in the Classroom*, New York: Random House, 1970, page 207. Exactly! Right on! We are *against* all this. We hate it! We hated it when we were kidsnschool. We hated it when we were studenteaching. We hate it now that we are certificateaching. We are with you all the way, Charles E. Silberman. Tell us more about Our New Movement. Tell us more about "informal" schools.

"Schools of this sort* exist in the United States on a small, but rapidly growing, scale; they can be found in the small cities and hamlets of North Dakota," (neat! neat! a peaceful far-away place) "in medium-sized cities such as Tucson, Arizona, and Portland, Oregon, in prosperous suburbs, and in the ghettos of Philadelphia and New York.

"Such schools exist on a much wider scale in England. Their rapid growth after World War II went largely unnoticed in this country, and to a surprising degree, in England itself, until 1967, when a Parliamentary Commission, the so-called Plowden Committee, called attention to the new approach and urged its adoption by all English primary schools. The approach has a variety of labels, none of them entirely satisfactory: the 'free day,' the 'integrated day,' the 'integrated curriculum,' the 'free school,' the 'open school,' and 'informal education.' The multiplicity of labels reflects the wide range of specific school practices and organization; *there is no monolithic system or approach*."

Uh oh! Watch out! No what? *No System?* I feel it coming. The U-fear, the old *Unstructure*-fear! "Monolithic" may be bad, all right, but "system" is *good*. You sound like you think there is something wrong with "system." Damn it, Charles E. Silberman, *some* system is necessary, isn't it? How do we know what we are talking about if we don't have *some* system? (Take Middletown. "What are we talking about?" says the old Buick-driving, babbity-babbity School Board President from Middletown, Ohio, and you can tell by the way he shakes his head that his question is strictly rhetorical: he definitely does *not* want us to answer his question, "What *are* we talking about?" He merely wants us all to know how he intends to swing his vote which is, of course, the deciding, majority vote. He intends to put all his weight, by golly, FOR *structure* and FOR *a-little-discipline-around-here* and AGAINST what-ever-it-is—this undefined, maybe Commie-inspired, *thing* that this, er, *young lady* with the too-large earrings keeps bringing up at the wrong time.) See, Charles E. Silberman, the danger! You *are too* unstructured. SLOPPY! You are not getting across to the right-wingers!

"Indeed," continues Silberman, getting further and further into trouble (with the Middletown School Board and with Al Capp and with Max Rafferty) with each sentence: "The 'free day,' or 'informal education,' to use a more inclusive term, is less an approach or method" (no approach, eh) "than a set of shared attitudes" (Commie attitudes, I'll bet) "and convictions" (sounds like a conspiracy to me) "about the nature of childhood, learning and schooling" (sneaky, foreign out-of-town experts). "Advocates of informal education begin with a conception of childhood as something to be cherished" (Ah, ha! I *get* it! It's all a plot to prevent our children from growing up! Suffering baby bottles! Sneaky, teat-sucking Commies! Sap the Nation's Vigor by keeping our youth in a state of *perpetual infantility*!), "a conception that leads in turn to a concern with the quality of the school experience in its own right, not merely as preparation for later

*informal schools.

43

schooling or for later life." (KEEP THEM FROM GOING TO COLLEGE TOO, I SUPPOSE!) And on and on. Believe me, on and on and more of the same.

You see, Charles E. Silberman, when you don't say enough about *what it is*, when you don't have enough *structure* and *system* and *planning* and other such words which sound *responsible-for-other-people's-children*, for goodness' sake, then people will supply their *own* idea about *what it is*. The bad guys will supply *bad* ideas and the good guys will supply good ideas but then the bad guys will call the good guys' ideas bad names and the committee will never vote the thing in and *we* here in Montclair, New Jersey, or in Suburban Hartford, Connecticut, we will still have the *Crisis in Education* or *Blackboard Jungle* or *Teaching Machines* or *Stanford Achievement Tests* or some worse atrocity, and the only place kids will be happy will be in those far-away peaceful places like Tucson, Arizona, and Plowden, England.

No, you have got to tell them *what it is* as well as what it isn't and it *has* to be more than a "shared attitude" or any other inchoate longing and it has *got* to have a structure and it has *got* to get your kid into college and it can't just be a wishy-washy, spineless, let-em-have-fun-while-they're-young, free-for-all. *I* go for your book *as is* but *I* don't make the decisions. *They* do, and *they* won't buy it. Not the way you tell it, they won't.

Providing a Structure or Whatever You Want to Call It

So that is why I write about TRIADS these days. I am trying to provide a structure for the as-yet unstructured idea from Plowden-On-The-Summerhill. I want to give it a *theory* (oh, all right, Larry, even a *technology*), a set of guidelines. I want to satisfy the bureaucrat, the administrator, the up-tight school board which is afraid of hot-pants and free-periods every hour. I want to show them that Our New Movement can be *responsible* and *hard-nosed* and *not-let-things-get-out-of-hand*. So I phrase our structure, our system, our theory, in a language every educator, everybody who has taken Psychology One, can understand. Or, if they can't understand it, at least it will sound peaceful but not wishy-washy.

TRIADS, then is the STRUCTURE OF THE ENGLISH COUNTRYSIDE SYSTEM. TRIADS is the REDWOOD, OREGON, METHOD. TRIADS is the MOSSMANSE, MISSISSIPPI, TECHNIQUE. TRIADS is the STRUCTURE OF THE PLOWDEN PLAN. Happy Holiday, kids. Best wishes on your retirement, Miss Henny. Have a grand vacation, everybody. Bon Voyage!! □

The Decline of Pedagocentricity*

George Brabner, Jr.

It is becoming increasingly evident to observers of educational trends that the traditional role of the instructor is now changing more rapidly and profoundly than at any time in history.

This article undertakes to (1) examine the changing relationship between the instructor, the learning task and the learner in light of some recent and not so recent developments that are altering this relationship drastically, and (2) set forth a simple schema for categorizing learning situations, or environments, intra- or extra-mural, which should prove useful in analyzing instruction and in clarifying the instructor's role.

"Learning-by-Doing" and "Learning-to-Learn"

Among many concepts that have emerged in the course of the development of education in the United States there are two which are familiar to virtually every educator. The first of these, "learning-by-doing," was closely associated with progressive education, as championed by John Dewey, whereas the other, "learning-to-learn," if not actually of more recent origin, has appeared frequently in current psycho-educational literature.

In both instances, there is, of course, the very real question as to how often the concepts have been interpreted in the same way by different writers; nevertheless, each represents at least a core of related ideas that have strongly influenced American educational thought.

The ideas epitomized by the expression "learning-to-learn," whether derived from the writings of Montessori, from the more experimentally based studies of "learning sets" by Harlow, or from O.K. Moore's "responsive environment" notion, are presently in the fore of educational thinking in this country. It is the hope of many educators that the concept of "learning-to-learn," with its corresponding emphasis on self-instruction, will not suffer the same fate that has befallen Dewey's "learning-by-doing"; i.e., a gradual reduction of a once vital educational formulation to a slogan largely devoid of meaning.

Dewey's instrumentalism stressed "shared participation in the use of things," however much the learner was to become increasingly self-directed in the social milieu. With a somewhat different though surely related emphasis, the "learning-to-learn" concept has tended to stress the value of independence of action by the learner, i.e., learning to learn by oneself. This does not imply that learning must be a solitary or a social phenomenon, but that in the main it should occur independently of environmental interpreters.

Technology and the Trend Toward Self-Instruction

In recent years, a rapidly expanding educational technology combined with the powerful idea of manipulating behavior by its consequences has led to such auto-educational developments as computer assisted instruction, programmed instruction, the "talking typewriter," the contingency-managed classroom, and many others.

All of these self-instructional innovators have emphasized an active approach to learning; i.e., by "doing," or, sometimes more specifically, by "manipulating," but more importantly they all

*A term which the author has coined to designate the widespread practice of attributing overriding importance to teacher behaviors in the educational process.

George Brabner, Jr., is associate professor, college of Education, University of Delaware, Newark.

exhibit two other crucial characteristics: (1) a decreasing reliance upon, or in some instances, a complete absence of, intervention by any individual performing in the traditional role of an instructor, and (2) a subordination of the *content* of what is to be acquired to the improvement of the *process* of learning per se; e.g., careful attention is given to the sequencing of concepts to be learned or to subject matter "structure."

This "private" kind of learning is traditionally identified more with the acquisition of academic subject matter than with the acquisition of social behaviors or skills, though this need not be the case. In the public schools such learning is usually heavily dependent upon the ability to read—perhaps the most significant ability for learning how to learn—for not only as the cliché states do "we learn to read and then read to learn," i.e., in the sense of acquiring more factual knowledge or content, but we read to learn how to learn more efficiently. This is true whether we are learning how to study more efficiently, think more critically, experiment more carefully, or solve problems more effectively.

In any event, the skill of reading—where censorship has not intruded—probably represents the greatest single contribution to independence of learning and thinking ever known to man. The advent of the printed word created an intellectual emancipation for millions, resulting in a degree of freedom from interpreters of the learning environ-

ment—priest, pedagogue, or prophet—never known before. This freedom prevailed despite the efforts of governments and other institutions to control thinking by controlling what was printed.

It is interesting to note in this context that, even early in the instructional phase of "learning to read," educators stress the necessity for the pupil to acquire independent word attack skills. Such emphasis would suggest that already in the first grade in a very small skill area the schools are encouraging independence of the learner from the instructor. Without this ability to analyze unfamiliar words, the pupil must, of course, rely entirely on the instructor.

Today, through the development of ingenious servo-mechanistic devices, we are approaching the stage where we will be able to design learning environments that encourage more active participation by the learner ("learning-by-doing") and less dependence on the biased, unsystematic and often irrelevant behavior of an interpreter interposed between the child and the environment.

Rather than viewing the new educational technology from a pessimistic, deterministic, Orwellian standpoint as a development leading inevitably to the enslavement of men's minds (i.e., man *vs* machine), the position taken here is that the technology can be used to free men's minds (i.e., man *cum* machine) by providing the conditions for enabling man to learn about his world in as independent a manner and as early in life as possible.*

The Decreasing Centrality of the Instructor

In the light of a long-standing custom which accepts as self-evidential that the instructor is the "heart of the educational process," it is heretical to say, but nevertheless true, that the progressive and systematic elimination of the instructor as an intermediary between the environment and the learner must become a clear and deliberate goal of education.

A constant observance of this dictum by educators is essential, if the learner is to approximate as closely and early as possible the maximum degree of independence in thought and action which he is capable of achieving.

In point of fact, there has always been in American public school education at least token acknowledgement of the validity of this principle; e.g., in the nursery school the teacher is confronted by "separation anxiety" and "over-protected" children, and he endeavors to make the child less dependent on mother and the security props of the home environment. Later on in the curriculum, the child is encouraged to work for increasing lengths of time without having to run to the teacher's desk for help every few minutes. Still later, homework is assigned, which suggests a growing awareness that the child is capable of working on his own with, in most cases, only minimal assistance from others.

Logically, one would expect that in higher education, opportunities to learn independently would abound, with instructors serving more or less as resource people; paradoxically, there is probably no other level in the educational hierarchy at which instructor-dependence is greater than in the university. This is evidenced by the continued extensive reliance on the traditional lecture approach in the classroom.

*To paraphrase Marshall McLuhan: The button may be there, but as long as there are people who are still able and willing to think, it's not inevitable that we push it.

Fortunately, this view of the role of the instructor as interpreter, explainer, entertainer-motivator, information dispenser, sage, guru, etc., is now beginning to give way to one which sees the instructor as more typically a designer or arranger of learning environments (Moore and Anderson, 1968), an engineer or modifier of behavior, and/or a sequencer of instructional concepts or objectives (Gagné, 1962; Ferster, 1968; Keller, 1968).

A common distinction made in the scientific literature between lower animal forms and man is that the former characteristically exhibit more "stimulus bound"—hence, environmentally controlled—behavior. Man, it is contended, though more vulnerable in infancy and early childhood, achieves his unique adaptive status because of the freedom of most of his behavior from such control.

It is conceivable, however, that the precise and graduated control of the behavior of the learner initially by an instructor and then, gradually, by the learner's own modification of the learning environment (i.e., self-instruction) may provide the systematically ordered conditions for a temporary type of *response bound* behavior from which much can be gained. In fact, the very imposition of such behavior control leading to increased learning efficiency should result ultimately in greater freedom or independence in coping with the environment, as interpreters are gradually faded out.

Five General Learning Environments

The following set of five diagrams represents an attempt to depict certain general learning situations existing within and without the structure of formal education.

By reference to these five types of learning environments, one should be able to (1) discern at least the gross distinctions among learning situations and (2) at the same time understand more fully the way the instructor's role changes with respect to each situation as the conditions for learning change.

One may wish to think of the ideas expressed in the following discussion as tentative steps toward the establishment of a conceptual model for instruction within formal education, i.e., a model which suggests how the learner should move through the educational hierarchy from almost total dependence on the environment and mediators of that environment to a position of maximum independence in dealing with the environment. This continuum can also be extrapolated at either end to include pre- and post-school informal education, training, or learning experiences.

Learning Situation 1

Figure 1 shows the earliest and most primitive form of learning situation in human existence.

Figure 1

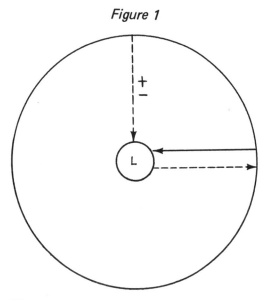

The outer circle delimits the learning environment *as encountered by the learner.* The smaller circle containing the letter L represents the learner within that environment. The dotted vertical arrow marked by a plus and minus symbol stands for the sum total of all variables within the learning environment which either facilitate or detract from

learning efficiency, e.g., temperature, anxiety-eliciting stimuli, lighting, visibility and audibility of instructional stimuli, etc.

This most basic learning situation exists in the absence of any kind of instructor or mediator in the learning environment. It typifies much of the early learning experience of infancy, where other humans are either not present or are not encountered by the infant, i.e., non-functional as mediators of the environment.

In Figure 1, which can serve to depict even an intra-uterine learning environment, the infant as learner interacts directly with the environment. This interaction is symbolized by the horizontal arrows. The dotted arrow indicates that the learning environment influences the learner more than he influences it.

He functions independently (i.e., of an "instructor") but is totally vulnerable because of insufficient neurophysiological maturation and because of the absence of instruction about the environment which will eventually enable him to cope with it.

Figure 1 could represent, of course, any individual suddenly thrust alone into an alien environment where his particular behavior repertory proves completely inadequate, e.g., a feral child, or a primitive, abruptly introduced into an advanced civilization. Note that in this situation the infant's behavior may rightly be described as somewhat "stimulus bound," i.e., control by the learner of his own responses is minimal.

If one were to draw a diagram illustrating the relationship of the mature, adult, educated learner to a non-mediated learning environment, it would be identical with Figure 1 except that the circle representing the learner might be shaded to indicate the adult's broad adaptive behavior repertory provided through education and training, both formal and informal.

Learning Situation 2

Figure 2 represents the first and probably the most common situation encountered throughout the formal education hierarchy. The larger of the two interior circles marked *I* stands for instructor. As used here, the term instructor can refer to a parent functioning in her role as a teacher in the home environment; a regular classroom instructor at any level; a foreman providing on-the-job training, etc. In short, in this and subsequent diagrams *I* designates anyone involved in an effort to optimize the conditions for learning—*including in some instances the learner himself.*

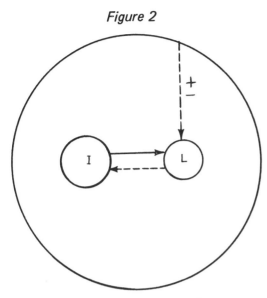

Figure 2

In Figure 2 the horizontal arrows again represent a direct interaction. This time, however, the interaction occurs principally between the instructor and the learner and is dominated by the former, hence, the solid arrow from *I* to *L*.

Figure 2 not only illustrates the most frequently occurring instructional relationship in a conventional nursery school or kindergarten, but also the most frequently occurring in the university, i.e., the classic lecture format.

In many respects the kindergarten teacher necessarily functions in the role of a mother surrogate. She must comfort the child when he is hurt, point out and discuss the dangers in the environment which the child has not yet learned to avoid, see to it that he does not over-extend himself physically, and develop the minimum level of socialization prerequisite for the acquisition of academic learning. Much, if not most, of this instruction involves talking and explaining on the part of the teacher. Most of it is teacher initiated. The extraordinary degree to which teachers rely on their own verbal behavior in instructing children has recently been pointed out in a study by Floyd (1968).

At this level in the educational hierarchy a certain amount of dependence on the instructor is understandable and appropriate, although authorities from Montessori to Moore and earlier have debated the allowable degree of dependence. Less comprehensible, of course, is the instructor-dependence intentionally or inadvertently fostered at higher levels in the hierarchy.

In Learning Situation 2, the instructor serves as the principal stimulus, or stimulus configuration, eliciting responses from the learner. It can be said that instructor involvement is maximal, here. In this situation the instructor can truly be viewed as "the heart of the educational process." Conversely, control over the learner's responses is minimal, primarily because of the absence of an adequate response recording or feedback mechanism.

Probably many current and historical figures who have acquired reputations as the greatest teachers of all time fall into this category; however, empirical evidence supporting claims of their teaching effectiveness is conspicuously absent.

Furthermore, in view of the widespread confusion concerning appropriate criteria for assessing teaching effectiveness and the dearth of evidence suggesting the superiority of any teaching method to another, it is difficult to see how the common practice of offering awards for teaching effectiveness can continue to be justified (Mitzel, 1960; Stephens, 1967).

Learning Situation 3

Figure 3 represents what is in all likelihood the most commonly structured learning situation in the elementary school.

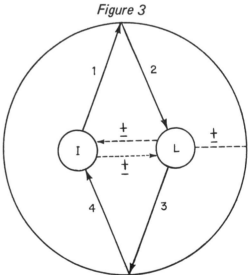

Figure 3

It differs from Learning Situations 1 and 2 primarily because the instructor now tends to rely more on the use of stimuli in the environment for eliciting responses from the learner than on his own behavior. Instructor-learner interaction still occurs but at a greatly reduced and essentially uncontrolled rate.

The dotted horizontal arrows suggest the uncontrolled nature of this interaction in that positive and negative effects on *I* and *L* may either enhance or impair the overall quality of instruction to an unknown degree.

A simple example of Learning Situation 3 would be as follows (the numbers used here correspond to those in Figure 3): (1) *I* presents a reading workbook; (2) the workbook serves as a stimulus to *L* who: (3) operates on the assigned content; (4) the results of such operations serve as stimuli or feedback to *I* who then modifies the existing task or prepares another. Learning Situation 3, unlike 1 and 2, exemplifies instructor mediation of the non-instructor portion of the learning environment. As in Learning Situation 2, instruction is mainly teacher initiated.

Learning Situation 4
Figure 4 differs significantly from Learning Situations 2 and 3 in that *I* is not present in the encountered learning environment, although *I* could be physically present in the actual setting where learning is occurring.

Figure 4

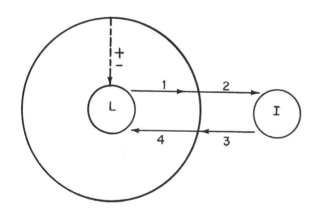

Like Learning Situation 3, the non-instructor portion of the environment becomes the principal eliciting stimulus, but unlike 2 and 3, the interaction of *L* with the learning environment is initiated by *L* and not by *I*.

Figure 4 can be illustrated by (1) a pupil interacting with the auto-educational devices of a Montessori nursery, where the teacher is viewed as a "directress" performing more of an observational than a direct instructional role, or (2) O.K. Moore's automated responsive environment, sometimes referred to as the "talking typewriter."

In the Moore environment, *L* (1) enters a booth and interacts with the "typewriter" in a free operant conditioning situation resembling that of a rat in a Skinner box; (2) the "booth assistant," or *I*, stands outside the booth and monitors *L*'s performance—*I* is invisible to *L*; (3) *I* is able to lock the keyboard or make changes in the program which (4) causes *L* to respond differentially (Moore & Anderson, 1968). Theoretically, a computer could be substituted for *I* which would not only make a continuous record of the responses of *L* but also, contingent upon the nature of *L*'s responding, make adaptive modifications in the program. In this instance, *I*, or a computer serving as *I*, mediates the learning environment, but the learning-facilitating or -inhibiting behavior of *I*, usually referred to as the "human element," is absent.

Learning Situation 5
Figure 5 represents a situation in which *L* functions in a self-instructional capacity; hence, both *I* and *L* are included in the interior circle.

Figure 5

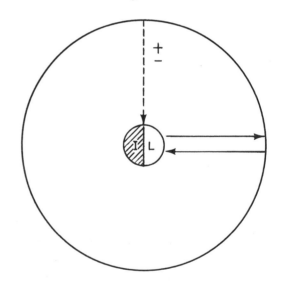

The *I* portion of the interior circle is comprised of all those behaviors acquired during the course of the individual's formal and informal education which enable him to operate on the learning environment in ways that will promote further learning independently of "mediators."

Learning Situation 5, in contrast to 4, depicts an environment which is truly auto-educational in nature; i.e., the learning that takes place is independent of the mediation of others, even the mediation that can occur in the form of a pre-structured or programmed environment.

One would expect that the mature adult learner, who has profited from his previous learning experiences—formal or informal—would be coping with his environment in this independent self-instructional manner throughout the remaining and major part of his existence. In the final analysis, it is this ability to modify and re-modify one's learning environment independently but effectively, including one's own behavior as part of the environment, that represents the ultimate objective of any democratically-conceived educational program.

Certainly, it would seem that opportunities for number 5-type learning situations should be occurring with much higher frequency in higher education than they are at present. One recent study (Jenkins & Deno, 1970) involving college students as subjects reported the following interesting findings: four groups of students were compared with respect to how well they mastered the content of the same academic task. One group was provided with behaviorally stated instructional objectives and an instructor, a second group was given the same instructional objectives but no instructor, the third group received non-behavioral objectives but no instructor, and the fourth group non-behavioral objectives and an instructor. The groups did not differ significantly from one another in achievement; however, of particular interest is the fact that both of the self-instructional groups achieved as well as the instructed groups, even when one of those groups was provided with specifically stated behavioral objectives.

Some Implied Continua

It would appear that certain continua are suggested by the foregoing discussion that would have implications for instruction. For example, instead of viewing the total formal educational process as a set of crudely ordered but discrete experiences possessing some general relatedness, one might envision as basic to any more or less continuous educational experience a continuum on which the learner proceeds from virtually complete dependence on the instructor to eventual independence, i.e., from instructor-dominated instruction to self-instruction. Looking at this continuum from the standpoint of the instructor rather than of the learner, one is talking about the extent of instructor involvement in the instructional process, i.e., from maximum to none.

An increasing awareness of the importance of environmental structuring and control based on an emerging set of behavior principles (e.g., Ferster & Perrott, 1968), as opposed to traditional pedagocentric thinking, is suggesting not only how radically the teacher's role is changing but also that systematic investigation of how that role *should* change throughout the educational hierarchy is in order.

The crucial question is not whether or not we should replace the teacher with "teaching machines," but how the teacher's role should change along the instructional continuum as his direct influence is gradually phased out. A decade ago, Stolurow (1960) made the following comment:

> The machine is the teacher's servant or aide. It is not autonomous. The teaching machine is no more likely to replace the teacher than the automatic washing machine, oven, or electric coffee pot have replaced the housewife.

This statement is no longer quite true, if under the generic term "teaching machine" we now include the concept of an automated responsive learning environment.

We are no longer thinking in terms of the discrete use of mechanical instructional *devices,* or audio-visual *aids,* that supplement what the teacher does, but in terms of whole learning environments which may be structured in a variety of ways along another dimension or continuum, i.e., from fully automated to non-automated. Perhaps distractible first-graders can acquire certain skills more rapidly and efficiently during a portion of their school day in a portion of their school environment that is fully automated.

Instead of thinking of learning environments as varying from automated to non-automated, one may prefer to think of them as varying along a continuum ranging from maximum external control of the learner's responses to minimum or no external control (i.e., self-instruction). As was indicated earlier in this article, the early imposition of control over the responses of the learner during the acquisition of long term educational objectives, with a gradual fading of control as the learner becomes more self-instructive, may result in more efficient learning; however, the same may hold true for the realization of short term instructional objectives (see Jenkins & Deno, 1968 for an excellent discussion of the distinction between instructional objectives and educational objectives.)

Above all, the viewpoint expressed here should not be confused with advocating the regimentation of the learner so that indoctrination with dogma may be more efficient and complete. No reference has been made to content in this article; the concern has only been with the process of instruction per se.

The position taken here, then, is that control over the learner's responses through control over the learning environment is a necessary developmental "crutch." The gradual elimination of this crutch eventuates in a greater freedom to learn freely.　□

References

Ferster, C.B. Individualized Instruction in a Large Introductory Psychology College Course. *The Psychological Record,* 1968, *18,* 521-532.

Ferster, C.B. & Perrott, M.C. *Behavior Principles.* New York: Appleton-Century-Crofts, 1968.

Floyd, W.D. Do Teachers Talk Too Much? *Instructor,* 1968, *78,* pp. 53 & 150.

Gagne, R.M. The Acquisition of Knowledge. *Psychological Review,* 1962, *69,* 355-365.

Jenkins, J.R. & Deno, S.L. A Model for Instructional Objectives: Responsibilities and Advantages. Unpublished research, 1968.

Jenkins, J.R. & Deno, S.L. The Effects of Instructional Objectives on Learning. Amer. Ed. Res. Association Convention, 1970.

Keller, F.S. "Good-bye Teacher . . ." *Journal of Applied Behavior Analysis,* 1968, *1,* 79-89.

Mitzel, H.E. Teacher Effectiveness. In C.W. Harris (Ed.) *Encyclopedia of Educational Research* (3rd ed.). New York: Macmillan, 1960.

Moore, O.K. & Anderson, A.R. Some Principles for the Design of *Clarifying* Educational Environments. In D. Goslin (Ed.) *Handbook of Socialization Theory and Research.* Chicago: Rand McNally, 1968.

Moore, O.K. & Anderson, A.R. The Responsive Environments Project. In Robert D. Hess & Roberta Meyer Bear (Eds.) *Early Education.* Chicago: Aldine Publishing, 1968.

Stephens, J.M. *Process of Schooling.* New York: Holt, Rinehart & Winston, 1967.

Stolurow, L.M. Automation in Special Education. *Exceptional Children,* 1960, *27,* 78-83.

A Behavior-Based Laboratory Course in Educational Psychology

Kenneth L. Collier and Richard V. Smith

The Idaho State University *Bulletin* (1965) states, "The objectives of Idaho State University are designed to insure that graduates in teacher education . . . have a broad understanding of and sensitivity to the individual learner . . . and to the conditions under which maximum learning occurs for him." Given this statement the question may arise as to the contribution that any course of instruction makes to such an objective.

In 1966 the authors set out to answer this question with regard to two courses then offered at ISU, *Educational Psychology* and *Human Growth and Development.* Three requirements were established for the outcome of the analysis:

1. the objectives of the courses must be stated;
2. these objectives must result in courses clearly unique within the college, yet consistent with college objectives; and
3. the courses should be internally consistent, i.e., the instructors should be able to demonstrate through the instructional technique the system by which course objectives are attained.

Surveys of current textbooks in educational psychology and human development, as well as discussions with colleagues, seemed to suggest that such courses should result in the students' abilities to apply general rules upon which instruction is based (educational psychology) and to understand the limits placed upon instructional objectives by the "nature" of the human being undergoing instruction (development). Based on these assumptions, the general objective of both courses was stated:

> The student is to understand a system, as parsimonious as possible, that will increase the likelihood that he will be able to produce curriculum-specified changes in the behavior of the children he teaches.

The criterion of "understanding" was the student performance of certain behavior deemed effective for instruction.

Once the general objective was established, the search began for a method of reaching the objective, while at the same time maintaining the general outcomes we had established for analysis of an education course. Our teaching of the courses had to remain consistent with the parameters of explanation that we

Kenneth L. Collier is manager, Sundance Office, Northern Wyoming Mental Health Center. **Richard V. Smith** is assistant professor of education, South Western State University, Marshall, Minnesota.

stressed within the course. By establishing the requirements and trying to meet them, we were put in the position of trying to "practice what we were preaching."

At this point it became more and more obvious that we were seriously considering an operant/respondent model and its application as the structure *and* content for the courses. Furthermore, in our efforts to increase parsimony of system for the two courses, as well as economy of instruction, we became committed to the value of subsuming the study of child development under this general model and offering one course rather than two. This resulted in a closer adherence to course analysis requirement No. 2, unique subject matter.

Our early efforts to implement the courses confirmed our orientation toward the use of the operant/respondent model for several additional reasons. If we were to increase the likelihood that our students could change pupil behavior on demand, they must learn to modify children's behavior in our course. Attempts to demonstrate such modification procedures in the formal classroom suggested that this was not a "favorable situation." What seemed to be required was a laboratory component, which in turn required that modification, or learning, be clearly demonstrable over relatively short periods of time. A wide latitude in complexity of learning from simple lever presses to concept formation and "attitude" change had to be demonstrated within the time limits of the laboratory schedules. In addition to the requirement of rapid behavior change was the necessity of accounting for the variables of which behavior is a function. The operant/respondent model seemed to fulfill these requirements quite well. Finally, there is generally no need for the use of statistical techniques, since modification is so often directly observable, or indirectly so, by comparing rates of responding through tabulation of responses over time.

For the school year 1967-68 a four-semester-hour course, *Educational Psychology*, was offered each semester. The classes were rescheduled as two one-hour sections of colloquium and one two-hour section of laboratory each week. The enrollment numbered slightly more than one hundred students. All students met together in the colloquium. Thirteen laboratory sections were scheduled, each limited to a maximum of ten students. In addition, a number of students who had completed the course the previous semester were asked to serve as proctors in the manner described by Keller (1968). The proctors received credit for their work by enrolling in a course on *Independent Problems* for one or two semester hours.

The objectives of the course were established on the basis of two general goals and the sub-objectives that would appear to lead to them.

General Goals

(1) The student would report a project in the planned modification of human behavior, and (2) the student, independently, would be able to read and interpret text materials in the area of developmental psychology that were compatible with an operant/respondent position (Bijou and Baer, 1961).

The course, in its final form, can best be described by discussing each of the instructional sub-objectives, the relationship of these to one or both of the two general goals, and the instructional procedures used to attain the objectives, along with the evaluation of the degrees of success.

Objective A. The student is able to recognize basic operant/respondent terminology. This objective is particularly germane to the design of the behavior modification project as well as to the comprehension of developmental literature.

Instructional procedure: A five-week period at the beginning of the semester was allotted to the attainment of the first objective. Using Holland and Skinner's programmed text, *The Analysis of Behavior* (1961), the students were required to pass, at 75 percent criterion level, five sequential quizzes over a designated number of sets. A minimum number of sets were assigned weekly, but a student could read ahead and finish the text in less than the allotted five weeks. The two-hour lab periods were used for individual testing, as well as reading and reviewing the text.

Proctor's role: Each proctor was assigned to a lab section. The proctor's duties were to construct quizzes over the assigned sets and conduct individual testing of each of the students in his section. Testing took place verbally in a one-to-one situation between student and proctor. If a student failed to reach criterion, he was to return to the lab room, review the material and be re-examined on a comparable quiz.

Instructor's role: The instructor reviewed the proctors' quizzes and made any changes he felt necessary. The instructor helped settle any questions that might arise between proctors and students in the testing sessions. The instructor also assisted the students as they were reading in the text.

Concurrent with the weekly reading-testing exercises occurring in the lab sections, the students in the colloquium were viewing Reese's film, *Behavior Theory in Practice* (1965). The purpose of the film was two-fold: first, to assist the students in recognizing the terminology of the model; second, to give the students an opportunity to see and hear behavior terminology in a different context. The four reels of the film were shown, one at a time, in four successive sessions. After a reel was shown, the instructor and proctors discussed important points with the students. The reel was then shown a second time during that same session for those students who wished to remain.

Evaluation: Evaluation was a two-part process. A student must have successfully passed quizzes, at 75 percent criterion, over all sets of the text. Also, he must pass at criterion level a comprehensive examination consisting of multiple choice questions over the application and interpretation of operant/respondent concepts and principles. The proctor did not take part in the construction of the comprehensive exam.

The statistical analysis of results showed a significant increase in mean scores ($p < .05$), when compared with students who had not had the assistance of proctors and the experience of sequential testing during previous semesters. In addition the distribution of scores of students under this program was negatively skewed when compared with the distribution of scores of previous classes.

Objective B. The student will take an active part in a planned panel discussion presented in the colloquium period. He will review research dealing with behavior modification, interpret the research and present a comprehensive discussion in collaboration with four class members. This was the first formal project used to shape the behavior of the students to the end that they could produce verbal explanations and interpretation of behavior consistent with the model.

Instructional procedures: From a list of about 35 published research reports and position papers on behavior modification and related areas, students in groups of five were required to select an article for verbal presentation before the other students currently enrolled in educational psychology. They were encouraged to read beyond the article itself in order to substantiate the position they would take. To assist them in interpreting research data, they were required to read Elzey's *A First Reader in Statistics* (1967). They were also assigned selected chapters from *The Technology of Teaching* (Skinner, 1968). Their first performance was a discussion of the article lasting 20 to 30 minutes. The panel members were then required to entertain any questions or challenges from the other students.

Proctor's role: The proctor acted as a consultant to the panel members, suggesting research and format for presentation. At the proctor's discretion the panel members were given permission to present the article during the colloquium period.

Instructor's role: The instructor acted as a consultant to the proctors. He furnished the proctors with information concerning research data, typical pro and con arguments that might be expected during the presentation and particular points of emphasis that were relevant to the article.

Evaluation: The instructors evaluated the individual panel members in respect to the clarity of presentation, the amount of evidence presented in support of a position, and the manner in which the questions and challenges were handled. Proctors were also rather subjectively evaluated in respect to the performance of the panel. Needless to say, proctors developed a great deal of pride in producing panel discussions of quality.

Objective C. On the basis of *The Analysis of Behavior* and *Behavior Theory in Practice*, the next step seemed to **require the written and spoken recognition of the variables that control behavior under free operant conditions.**

We considered it imperative that the students make interpretations of behavior that were consistent with the model. Establishment of this behavior can be particularly frustrating, since acquisition of an interpretive point of view is not all that is required. Inherent in our language is a non-parsimonious, inferential, typically circular system of behavior explanation and interpretation. This conventional explanatory behavior is at high strength and incompatible with an operant/respondent interpretation.

Instructional procedures: To the end that written and spoken operant/respondent interpretations be strengthened, a series of behavior modification demonstrations were conducted. A remotely controlled apparatus which greatly restricted the classes of responses that could be emitted, along with a restricted array of antecedent and behavior-consequent stimuli, allowed for the demonstration of a number of basic operant/respondent concepts, using young human subjects. Students were then required to state the specific antecedent stimuli (e.g., a light) that came to control the emission of the behavior (lever press) and the consequent stimulus (poker-chip) that modified the response rate.

Proctor's role: The proctor obtained children from the adjoining college laboratory school, structured the situation for the child if necessary, operated the apparatus, led the discussion on behavior analysis and presented questions for written student analysis.

Instructor's role: The instructor designed demonstrations, supervised demonstrations, operated the apparatus in the more complex demonstrations, supervised discussions, and approved or modified written test questions.

Evaluation: A rather loose criterion was established for both vocal and written responses to questions based on the demonstration. More rigorous criteria could be developed as the demonstrations became more nearly standardized.

Objective D. The student is able to record pupil behavior in a classroom in a manner that contributes to a functional analysis. Deliberate modification of behavior relies heavily on the ability of the behavior manager to quantify behavior. This recording establishes base rates as well as acceleration or deceleration of response rates due to differential consequation.

Instructional procedures: During lab periods, students moved to viewing rooms at the adjacent laboratory school, where they practiced recording behavior of elementary school children. The recording technique utilized was a simple dichotomous classification scheme developed by Smith (1967).

Proctor's role: The proctor was entirely responsible for conducting the training sessions. All members of a section were assigned to watch a given pupil and record his behavior in the fashion dictated by the classification scheme for a five- to ten-minute interval. At the conclusion of the interval, students compared their results and the proctor answered any questions that might have arisen during the recording interval.

Instructor's role: None.

Evaluation: For this objective, practice in recording continued until all students could record to the satisfaction of the proctor.

Objective E. The fact that a student met criteria established for recognition of correct terminology and could read the literature with comprehension in no way guaranteed that he would produce written material consistent with the operant/respondent model. As a result, it was necessary to develop a unit of the course designed to strengthen this behavior.

Instructional procedures: In order to obtain successive approximations of established criteria for written productions, the students were required to design a behavior modification project which ultimately would serve as the basis of project development. Table 1 presents Reese's model (1966), which the students used as an outline for the project design. Under each item of the model the student was to describe in writing the procedures, equipment and kinds of subjects that he would employ in the demonstration. The first requirement, of course, was a written specification of the terminal behavior to be acquired by the subject. The student then described how a baseline rate was to be determined, and so on. The design stage of this unit was complete when the proctor and instructor were satisfied that the written project was suitable in terms of time for development, complexity of the procedures, and the limitations imposed by demonstrating the modified behavior under laboratory conditions.

Proctor's role: The proctor reviewed various items in design, approved items or suggested changes in procedure, measurement, or subjects in preparation for review by the instructor.

Instructor's role: The instructor reviewed the items in the design of the paper, suggested changes and granted approval to write the next item. Final approval

Table 1

A Behavioral Model for Learning

1. Specify the Final Performance (Terminal Behavior)
   a. Identify the behavior
   b. Determine how it is to be measured

2. Determine the Operant Level of Current Baseline

3. Structure a Favorable Situation
   a. Provide discriminative stimuli for appropriate behavior
   b. Remove discriminative stimuli or opportunity for incompatible behavior.

4. Establish Motivation
   a. Locate reinforcers
   b. Deprive (if necessary)
   c. Locate and withhold reinforcers for incompatible behavior

5. Adaptation
   a. Extinguish emotional respondents
   b. Provide or establish discriminative stimuli
   c. Establish reinforcer

6. Shape the Desired Behavior
   a. Reinforce successive approximations of the final performance
   b. Raise the criterion for reinforcement gradually
   c. Present reinforcement immediately, contingent upon the behavior

7. Utilize Stimulus Control: Fading

8. Reinforce Intermittently

9. Keep Continuous Objective Records

of the design resulted in the requirement that the student begin the development procedures.

Evaluation: The evaluation of each written state of the design was based on the judgment and experience of the instructor. The ultimate criterion was the acquisition of the designed behavior by the subject under stated stimulus conditions.

Objective F. The purpose of this objective was the refinement of the behavior modification design to the end that terminal behavior was obtained.

Instructional procedures: After a program was designed in the manner outlined in Objective E, it was used with a series of subjects. Changes were made as a result of each trial, as successive approximations to an effective design.

Proctor's role: The proctor acted as a monitor for all trials of the projects. He also made suggestions regarding contingent stimuli, the method of delivery, the manner in which cues could be faded and the development of discriminative stimuli. The proctor and student judged the adequacy of the program for submission to the instructor.

Instructor's role: During this course division, the instructor consulted with the proctors. The proctors often asked for suggestions in procedural change and as frequently tested their own suggestions that had been made to students. There was little direct contact between instructor and student at this time.

Objective G. At this stage the student must implement his behavior modification design in the presence of the instructor, using a naive subject. A design was judged successful if implementation reached a criterion level of 100 percent.

Proctor's role: The proctor arranged for subjects to be present and scheduled the implementation session.

Instructor's role: The instructor observed the implementation procedures. He gave a "pass-no pass" rating of these procedures. On the few occasions when criterion was not reached, the student was re-cycled into the design or development stage. All programs eventually reached criterion, unless, as on a few occasions, a shortage of time required termination of the project.

Objective H. The student was required to submit a written report of his behavior modification project. The report was to be written in such a manner that an educational psychology student who had no knowledge of the project could implement the design by reading it.

Proctor's role: The proctor monitored the report writing by making suggestions for change and by submitting them to other proctors for evaluation of content and clarity of form. Previously submitted reports were used as models, both positive and negative. The students were encouraged to use the lab periods for writing in order to obtain more immediate feedback on their efforts. The proctor judged the papers to be adequate for submission to the instructor.

Instructor's role: The instructor conferred with both proctors and students regarding the progress of report writing. While the proctors and instructors helped in refining the reports, it was the student's decision to submit the paper for grading. The instructor graded all papers.

Objective I. The ostensible objective here was interpretation of human growth and development using the operant/respondent model as described by Bijou and Baer (1961). Practically, the objective proved to be evaluational, i.e., "Could students transfer skills acquired from the behavior modification units of the course in such a manner that efficient learning occurred in the study of development?"

Proctor's role: None.

Instructor's role: The students were assigned the task of reading the two volumes cited above, in a more or less independent manner. Discussion of the issues tended to be limited to the instructor referring to operant or respondent concepts that students had used in a multitude of ways. The point was made that any difficulties encountered must be those of application. The instructors also constructed and administered a multiple choice examination.

Evaluation: No comparative data were available, hence no objective evaluation of transfer was made. Subjectively, we were of the opinion that the human development unit of the course would require procedures similar to those used in the other units.

The Laboratory

The laboratory was the result of a fortuitous set of construction circumstances. The rooms used and their arrangement were not designed by the authors. Originally the authors had the use of one classroom with an adjoining office. We eventually acquired the privilege of using two additional rooms, separated by a wall of one-way vision windows, which lay directly across the hall from our classroom. In close proximity to this complex were several classrooms, some of which were always available for the use of small groups of students working on the development of programs. The entrance to the laboratory school was about 50 feet from the entrance to the instructors' office, across a small courtyard.

A jerry-rigged amplifier-speaker-microphone allowed students in the observation room to hear what occurred in the demonstration room. On certain occasions a demonstration could be videotaped. One such tape was used frequently to help explain our program, as well as to demonstrate the use of contingency management in the control of complex human behavior.

The laboratory acquired some other pieces of equipment. Typically, this equipment was constructed over a period of time by the students themselves. Most of this equipment took the form of simple manipulanda, small programmed texts and other such materials. One apparatus that was developed, however, was used extensively in every laboratory section. This consisted of a wooden box with five spring-loaded levers and seven small light bulbs projecting from the front. A solenoid attached to an internal lever system could be activated, delivering a poker-chip into a glass jar also attached to the front of the box. A key-board was wired to the box, which allowed remote control of the lights and poker-chip delivery system. With this simple device we could demonstrate virtually all of the operant concepts dealt with in the Holland and Skinner text (1961) using children as subjects.

We were able to purchase some equipment through a research grant (1967). This consisted of a manual-reset cumulative recorder and a six-pen event recorder. A "home-made" 24 VDC power source was constructed to operate the recorders. The recorders were never connected to the manipulanda but were operated by the students using telegraph keys. This was not only convenient but also served to help students attend to the behavior and stimuli being studied.

An inexpensive short-wave (walkie-talkie) set was found useful on occasion. One transceiver of the set was modified, a stenographer's head-phone interrupting the circuit to the speaker. In this way a student or instructor-monitor in the observation room could signal a student in the demonstration room without the subject's knowledge. This signal system was used for such purposes as establishing variable-interval or ratio-reinforcement schedules.

Conclusions

One of the major defects in reporting the course outcomes is the paucity of objective data when so much was available. At the time, the authors were primarily concerned with developing a course that would result in students with behavior management skills, using procedures that were enjoyable and objectively effective. We believed that standardization and data collection methods would follow in good time.

One additional aspect of the use of student proctors in such a course, which has not been mentioned by Keller or others, was their beneficial and voluntary "public relations" function. The students who were required to take this course considered it to be more rigorous than others offered in the College of Education. The subject matter was strange to them and its relevance to education was not always obvious in the early stages of the course. Yet the "teachers" with whom the students had most frequent contact were young men and women they saw and talked with in the student union, in the dormitories and between classes. These "teachers" had not only completed the course, but had done so with considerable success not more than one semester earlier. It was obvious to the students that the proctors enjoyed their work and had a friendly relationship with the professors. They could and did allay the fears of the students regarding the demands of the course.

Our subjective evaluation of the proctors's effects on the course would result in placing this function near the top of the list of benefits derived from their efforts. However, we are convinced that this course had its own built-in reward system. Having had some experience in teaching a traditional course, we were relatively impressed (reinforced) by the frequency of shouts, screams of glee and back-slapping that occurred when a behavior management project was successful. We were impressed by the quality and complexity of the projects undertaken by the students. We spent hours each week simply talking with students and proctors who wanted to discuss their successes and the ideas they had developed for new areas of application.

The students' persistence in pursuing their project goals was reflected in the length of the instructors' working day, which never began later than eight o'clock. The instructors typically had their lunch in an office jammed with happily harassed proctors and students making last-minute preparations for the project demonstration that would "shake the educational world." It was necessary for us to develop a good relationship with janitors, since we were usually in their way during late afternoon cleaning time. Again we made no rigorous analysis of the contingencies that resulted in this happy state of affairs. No doubt they were multitudinous, but we would be interested in hypothesizing that the ability to be systematically successful in managing behavior was important.

Possibly a note should be added about what was *not* taught in this course. Much of the subject matter of textbooks widely used in undergraduate educational psychology courses was not dealt with or even mentioned in our course. Chapters and units of these textbooks usually include a survey of various learning theories; a unit on tests and measurements; some descriptive statistics; the case study; suggestions for the "practical" solution of common behavior problems; and a presentation of the issues of whole versus part learning, verbal learning and serial learning, among others. Our experience suggests that this content results in relatively high interest ranking by education majors when compared with other education courses. Nevertheless, the *skills* that are acquired by teachers as a result of exposure to this subject matter are not remarkable when teachers are observed working in classrooms.

The value of including some of the above-named units in educational psychology will be argued. However, for teachers to acquire effective skills in evaluation, for example, more will need to be done than assigning the reading of a chapter in a textbook and presenting the students with two lectures and an examination. □

References

Bijou, S. & Baer, D. *Child Development, Vols. I & II.* New York: Appleton-Century-Crofts, 1961.

Bulletin. Pocatello, Idaho: Idaho State University, 1965, p. 154.

Elzey, F. *A First Reader in Statistics.* Belmont, California: Wadsworth, 1967.

Holland, J. & Skinner, B. *The Analysis of Behavior.* New York: McGraw-Hill, 1961.

Keller, F.S. Good-bye, Teacher . . . *Journal of Applied Behavior Analysis,* 1968, *1,* 79-89.

Reese, E.P. *Behavior Theory in Practice* (film). Filmed by Charter Oak Studios, New York. Produced by Appleton-Century-Crofts, New York, 1965.

Reese, E.P. *The Analysis of Human Operant Behavior.* Dubuque, Iowa: Wm. C. Brown, 1966, p. 49.

Research Programs Committee Grant, Idaho State University, 1967, A.E. Taylor, Chairman.

Smith, R. *A Primary Investigation of a Method of Categorizing Classroom Behavior.* Unpublished masters thesis, Idaho State University, 1967.

Skinner, B.F. *The Technology of Teaching.* New York: Appleton-Century-Crofts, 1968.

Project LIFE: Developing High Interest Programmed Materials for Handicapped Children

The boy is running to the car.

Figure 1. Pictured above are some sample frames of the Project LIFE programmed language series. The frames are colored, placed on film, and used in a standard remote-control projector. Responses are made on the Project LIFE teaching machine, the "Program Master," to which the filmstrip, slide, or movie projector is attached.

Glenn S. Pfau

Programmed instruction (PI) has been viewed by numerous educators as a teaching medium holding tremendous potential. By combining accumulated learning principles into a system, it has been thought that students could be taken from entry level to mastery level of almost any subject in the most efficient manner.

Glenn S. Pfau is the director of Project LIFE, National Education Association, Washington, D.C.

Among others, PI capitalized on the principles of sequential presentation of learning events (frames), relatively small increments of difficulty between frames, overt responses, immediate knowledge of results (reinforcement), self pacing, high probability of correct responses, gradual fading of prompts to establish the desired repertoires, reinforcement, and systematic repetition and review. Nearly all of the factors of learning were accounted for *except student motivation.* Students were too often viewed as passive receivers of information, who could act as sponges in soaking up information that was presented to them in almost any manner.

As a result of this malaligned focus, the full potential of programmed learning has never been realized. Though efficiency has seldom been questioned, college students have rated this learning medium from dull and listless to tedious and uninteresting. The vast majority of the programs developed to date follow the Skinnerian approach of "fill-in the blank."

More and more programmers have begun, in the 1970's, to concern themselves with critical PI contingencies. These include a careful analysis of the competencies and handicaps of the specific target population, their interests, achievement level, vocabulary and language levels, and their degree of conceptualization. The material must be presented in a meaningful manner, and the learner should see that the knowledge or skills to be assimilated have functional value to him. Most of all, the materials must have such an intrinsic interest level that the student will find his contact with them to be a pleasurable experience.

The Child-Centered Program

In general, it is felt by the author that the PI considerations stated herein have application to all target populations. However, most of the discussion will be in direct reference to handicapped children, and specifically those children with a language deficit resulting from severe, congenital hearing impairment.

Programmed materials can be developed in an interesting and stimulating manner if programmers take into consideration the child's immediate environment, his interests, and his egotistic nature. The child is interested in knowing the names of frequently encountered objects, action words, and terms which will help him to better express his relationship with his home, family, peers, teachers and others.

Every child is interested in those with whom he comes in continual or frequent contact—he wants to know about their possessions, needs, interests and activities. The young deaf child is particularly concerned with acquiring a functional language system in order to communicate. Programmed instruction can satisfy this need by carefully selecting the vocabulary and language concepts that are most needed by this child. The manner in which the material is programmed is as important as the criteria for content selection. The material must be so designed that, in the initial stages, the child will satisfy his desire to *learn to read*; of course, the primary and more distant goal is for the child to *read to learn*.

For PI materials to be intrinsically motivating, they should allow for self-pacing, self-checking and

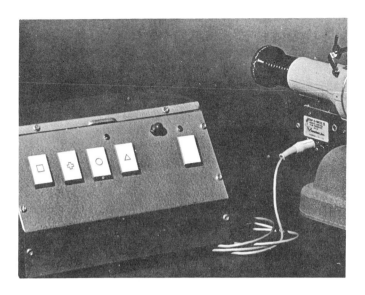

Figure 2. This Project LIFE teaching machine ("Program Master") is used in conjunction with a standard remote-control filmstrip projector (such as that shown at right). The child obtains a green confirmation light upon a correct response, which makes the advance button operative (far right). It can also be used with 35mm slide or movie projectors.

self-correction. In most traditional classroom situations, a child feels shame and embarrassment when he makes a mistake in front of his peers. Usually, if a child cannot correct his mistake immediately, one of his classmates will correct it for him. The importance of this type of independence is vividly pointed out in the book, *How Children Learn*:

> The more a child uses his sense of consistency, of things fitting together and making sense, to find and correct his own mistakes, the more he will feel that his way of using his mind works, and the better he will get at it. He will feel more and more that he *can* figure out for himself, at least much of the time, which answers makes sense and which do not. But if, as usually happens, we point out all mistakes as soon as he makes them, and, even worse, correct them for him, his self-checking and self-correcting skill will not develop, but will die out. He will cease to feel that he has it, or ever had it, or ever could have it.[1]

The above quote has direct relevance to the development of PI materials. The response frames within the program should not call undue attention to the child's errors, nor should the program immediately provide him with the correct answer, but it should allow for the child to self-correct his own mistake by making another response. Such a procedure will develop the child's self-correcting skill—a skill that will be a valuable asset to the individual throughout life.

The above procedure is generally only possible with multiple choice, rather than constructed response, programming. In constructed response programs, the subject is provided the correct answer without responding (prompting frames), he rewrites a portion of the stimulus (copy frames), or he is shown on the subsequent frame what his answer should have been (standard confirmation frame). In all cases, the child's self-correcting skills are not being developed. Multiple choice programming not only develops self-correcting skills but it is uniquely suited for young deaf children who must develop receptive language before expressive language.

It has been estimated that more than 500 teaching machines have been developed since the 1920's; of these, some 60 machines have been used in the past decade to teach some skill to the deaf.[2] In general, it has been found that teaching machines have a high motivational value for the deaf child.[3] A machine *per se* is not intrinsically motivating. The "pin ball effect" will soon wear off, and the child will lose interest in the machine, unless he sees the materials themselves as meaningful, challenging and interesting.

One of the largest and most comprehensive research projects involving PI and the deaf child was conducted by Karlsen.[4] His investigation was initiated to develop a visual presentation via PI for teaching beginning reading. The following statements are extracted from his experiment:

1. A machine can be constructed with which deaf five-year-olds can be taught to read.
2. The development of reading skills and the necessary language concepts to accompany these skills will require an enormous amount of programming.
3. An automated system of non-oral reading instruction can be developed successfully.
4. The teaching machine is uniquely well equipped to effectively present the printed word. It has a place in every classroom for deaf children.

The deaf child must be given thousands of meaningful receptive language contacts (as do non-deaf children) before they can be expected to begin expressing language. It is believed that educators of the deaf have often made the mistake of expecting systematic expressive language long before the children have even receptively internalized their language system. The teaching machine is certainly one method of providing the needed meaningful repetitions. B. F. Skinner concurs when he states:

> The number of reinforcements required to build discriminative behavior in the population as a whole is far beyond the capacity of teachers. Too many teachers would be needed, and many contingencies are too subtle to be mediated by even the most skillful teacher. *Yet relatively simple machines will suffice...* In light of what we know about differential contingencies of reinforcement, the world of the young child is shamefully impoverished. And only machines will remedy this, for the frequency and subtlety of reinforcement cannot otherwise be arranged.[5]

Again, a teaching machine is as good as its software, and the software is only good if the primary motivation is intrinsic (i.e., within the materials), rather than extrinsic (i.e., confirmation lights, tokens, candy, cereal, and the like). The success which is experienced while completing a program is not only a primary reinforcer, but it should also offer a pleasurable and challenging avenue for learning. The following paragraphs will discuss a project that has as its mission the development of intrinsically motivating software.

A Child-Centered Project

Possibly the largest and most comprehensive PI endeavor for the handicapped is Project LIFE— Language Improvement to Facilitate Education of hearing impaired children. The Project was launched in 1963 under the sponsorship of Media Services and Captioned Films, Bureau of Education for the Handicapped, U.S. Office of Education. It is headquartered and administered by the National Education Association, Washington, D.C. For more detailed information concerning the history, scope and various aspects of the Project, the reader is referred to earlier publications.[6] [7] [8] [9]

The success of PI prompted its selection as the nucleus around which to build the Project's instructional material. A linear-type approach for use on the machine was chosen in preference to a programmed book. The machine provides immediate feedback to the learner by means of a green confirmation light.

In view of the reported deficiencies found in the perceptual skills of deaf children, it was decided to precede actual language instruction with programmed lessons in the percepto-cognitive skills. These are being presented through approximately 36 filmstrips of some 45 frames each. They deal with perceptual properties, position in space, additions-omissions and spatial relationships. More specifically, from the child's point of view they involve color, position, shape, relative size, and the like, working into pictures, letters, word configurations and words. Early research findings are indicating that these materials have applicability to language handicapped children, in addition to those with hearing impairment.

To further enhance the child's progress, and to respond to requests by the profession, the Project is developing a series of programmed lessons in thinking activities. Some of the areas for which programs are being sought include those on detecting absurdities and differences, arranging items in logical sequence, recognizing appropriateness or suitability, recognizing relationships, using old information to solve new situations, conceptualizing, and storing information and recalling it.

The Project's largest task is that of developing programmed language lessons. The primary goal for each child is a functional, receptive language system. The beginning programs are built around basic vocabulary and sentence structures that the child will need. The majority of all materials are developed into filmstrips, after having been developmentally tested in 35mm slides. The language filmstrips are organized into hierarchical units, progressing from the very simple to the increasingly complex. The first units are on the themes of self, foods, holidays, community helpers, school, home, clothing and nature.

All programs are constructed on the basis of behavioral objectives. The programmers participate in the development of the objectives for the various units before the units are outlined. Each programmer then formulates, from this background, the necessary behavioral objectives (stated at the beginning of each section within each unit, and selects the vocabulary and the referents to which meaning is to be attached. Only one new word or language principle is introduced at a time, and it is then presented in small, sequential steps. The child must respond to every frame of the student-oriented filmstrip. Special care is exercised to insure that the child arrives at a correct response for the right reason, and not on the basis of some extraneous factor. Though a complete explanation is outside the scope of this article, all materials are critically tested in the developmental stages, and then further validated on a larger population of children.

Project LIFE has sponsored the development of four versions of a teaching machine by specifying the detailed features it must possess. The most recent machine is used in conjunction with a standard remote control projector (filmstrip, slide, or movie). The machine, the "Program Master," serves as a master response-control unit (see Figure 2). It is connected to the remote control outlet of the projector via a specially designed adapter cord. The standard projector becomes a teaching machine, acting as slave to impulses received from the control.

Each program is designed so that the correct-response sequence corresponds to one of eight different response patterns. The predetermined response pattern is placed on a small rectangular plug which is inserted into the back of the machine. The varying patterns give sufficient flexibility to prevent a student from memorizing any given sequence. The child responds by depressing one of four multiple choice buttons. If he responds correctly, he receives a green confirmation light. If he is incorrect, an error is recorded on a counter located on the back of the machine. A separate advance button is operative only when the confirmation light is on.

Several alternate response-control units are under development. Most of these employ a computer card (rather than a counter) on which all of the child's correct, incorrect and skipped responses are punched. This provides for an item by item analysis, and therefore it is preferable for research. It is estimated that all teaching machines will sell at a price under $165.

Several types of supplementary materials are simultaneously being developed. These include specially illustrated children's story booklets, a dictionary series and a series of workbooks. Also, since many language concepts involve motion, a series of programmed movies are being developed. In most cases, the movies are employed with the Kodak MSF-8 Ektagraphic Super 8mm projector. They can be connected to the Projector's teaching machine, which allows for responses on the stop frames of the movies. As far as the student is concerned, the procedure is the same as for the filmstrip or slide presentation.

The Project has begun its initial distribution of teaching machines and materials. It is anticipated that 200 machines and accompanying sets of PI materials will be provided by Media Services and Captioned Films to approximately 100 different schools or institutions concerned with the education of language impaired children. The materials and machines will

"Which button do I press for an instant replay on that last question?"

also soon be available for purchase through a non-profit distribution agency.

Presently, materials are being developed for children at the preschool and primary levels. It is anticipated that the level of material difficulty will later include the intermediate and upper grades.

Project LIFE has 22 full-time personnel located at the NEA. These include specialists in language, deafness, programming, thinking skills, motion and still photography, perception, art and production. The Project also has all of the necessary equipment to perform in-house production. The larger pieces of equipment include a photo-direct camera, offset printing press and a photographic animation stand (for both movies and still pictures).

Developing Child-Centered Materials

In Project LIFE's material development, the learner is the hub of all considerations. This is true in each phase of software construction—planning the Unit and Section concepts, programming, art, production, testing and revision. A careful assessment is made of the child's needs. Only those vocabulary and language concepts are programmed that have definite functional value to the child. The programmers construct short sets of frames or sequences of frames in which phrases and sentences are introduced as soon as the child can handle them. The natural language gives the student the "why" of a given situation, as well as a meaningful contact with appropriate language. This media interaction provides intrinsic motivation. The learner attempts to anticipate the outcome of a given sequence, and verifies his expectancy in subsequent frames.

It was originally proposed that the Project should use black and white line drawings for all illustrations. All pictures were relatively simple and realistic. After a considerable amount of testing, it was found that children relate better to stylized or cartoon art. Also, it has been found that colored illustrations are more appealing and maintain motivation longer than do black and white drawings. Presently, vivid colors are used throughout all of the Project film materials.

From a production standpoint, the frames are constructed in a manner that is intended to cause minimal confusion to the children. The pictures are of a large enough size so that all critical details are easily seen. Also, the print size is maintained above a certain minimal level (as are the symbols). Where possible, the pictures and print are arranged in a manner which forces the child to view from left to right and from top to bottom. In addition, the pictures are colored, and arranged, to the extent possible, so that the child's eyes are directed to the salient features of the illustrations.

As previously indicated, the majority of the Project LIFE filmstrips attempt to develop the child's percepto-cognitive, thinking and language skills. Also being simultaneously developed are "Fun Supplement" filmstrips. These are intended to accomplish the following:

1. Reward the child for the satisfactory completion of a Unit (approximately six filmstrips);
2. Reinforce the language taught in a given Unit, and to extend the meanings to new and different situations;
3. Provide the child with a story that he can read and enjoy independently;
4. Stimulate the child's imagination; and
5. Provide the classroom teacher with another means of rewarding a child for satisfactory completion of other classroom work.

Possibly, the rationale for the Fun Supplements is best presented in a quote from the book, *The Structure of Intellect*. The author, M. M. Meeker, states:

> If almost all information taken in has to be comprehended or cognized before it can be manipulated, then children would need to experience many opportunities for tasks which require only that they do simple comprehending, that they be stimulated or intrigued... If one of our goals is to teach students how to learn, then we need to make some learning enjoyable, 'free of charge,' and unpressured. We

cannot expect young children to generalize to liking-to-learn unless learning has been made pleasurable for them at some time. Preferably, this should occur in the early grades (if a choice must be made) so that if affect tinges conditioning, then learning capitalizes on a good beginning.[10]

In summary, Project LIFE is attempting to develop materials that the child will find meaningful, interesting, challenging, functional and—most of all— enjoyable. It has been said that "the handicapped child is too often the passive victim of the overactive teacher." The Project PI materials might well provide the teacher with another avenue for directly involving the child in the learning process. Hopefully, the materials will assist the child in discovering that he can learn independently *and that learning can be fun.*

□

References

1. Holt, J. *How Children Learn*. New York: Pitman Publishing Corp., 1968.

2. Pfau, G. S. Teaching Machines and the Deaf Child. *Volta Review,* 1970 (In Press).

3. Pfau, G. S. Programmed Instruction: An Exploration into its Effectiveness with the Handicapped Child. *Audiovisual Instruction, 14,* November, 1969, 24-27.

4. Karlsen, B. *Teaching Beginning Reading to Hearing Impaired Children, Using a Visual Method and Teaching Machines.* University of Minnesota, USOE, Project No. 1204, 1966.

5. Skinner, B. F. Why We Need Teaching Machines. *Harvard Educational Review,* Fall, 1961.

6. Wooden, H. Z. & Willard, L. W. Project LIFE: Language Improvement to Facilitate Education of Hearing Impaired Children. *American Annals of the Deaf, 110,* November, 1965, 541-552.

7. Wooden, H. Z. An Audiovisual Approach to Language Instruction of Children with Severe Hearing Impairments. *Audiovisual Instruction, 11,* November, 1966.

8. Pfau, G. S. Project LIFE—Language Improvement to Facilitate Education of Hearing Impaired Children. *Hearing and Speech News, 36,* November-December, 1968.

9. Pfau, G. S. Project LIFE PI Analysis. *American Annals of the Deaf, 114,* November, 1969, 829-837.

10. Meeker, M. M. *The Structure of Intellect*. Columbus, Ohio: Charles Merrill Publishing Company, 1969.

Contingency Management and the Design of Learning Environments

C. Glenn Valentine

The title of this article implies that the reader will get an explanation of the relationship between contingency management and educational technology. In this presentation, I will emphasize the use of contingency management in classroom and learning environment designs. Contingency management is one of the techniques available to the educational technologist; therefore, it should be available to teachers and trainers. This article hopefully will provide those readers who have problems with motivation and classroom control with some insights into this effective technique.

I would like to present some views and suggestions on using the contingency management technique in classrooms and other present-day learning environments, such as learning laboratories, individualized learning centers and computer controlled instruction centers. This collection of my views and suggestions will be presented in three parts:

1. A background section on definition and theory.
2. How and where contingency management fits into the process of programming instruction.
3. Some specific examples of how to use contingency management in the classroom.

Definition and Theory

Contingency management has been used in recent years for many purposes, ranging from classroom control to motivating non-responders. It has also been labelled behavioral management, behavioral engineering and behavior modification. All of these terms evolve from one principle: that if a desirable behavior (or, for that matter, any behavior) is followed by a consequence which is pleasant or rewarding, then that behavior is more likely to occur in the future.

A contingency is a relationship between a response and a reinforcer. The term, "contingency management," simply may mean two things: one, to specify ahead of time what "nice" things will happen as a result of learning a particular skill or knowledge or a set of skills or knowledge; two, to make sure that, when learning occurs, "nice" things do happen.

Many of the methods used in contingency management are derived from the process known as operant conditioning. Operant conditioning in its purest sense

C. **Glenn Valentine** is manager, Technical Product Development, education division of Xerox Corporation.

occurs when the organism that is responding is in a relatively free response situation. The organism or learner generally has some deprivation—such as lack of food. Under proper stimulus conditions, any response which is in the direction of the desired terminal response is followed by reinforcement, and the deprivation is reduced. This increases the probability that the response will be repeated in the future under similar stimulus conditions. Then, through successive approximations, rewards are given each time responses are made which more closely approach the desired terminal behavior. Thus, a learner is shaped to make the desired terminal response through a series of rewards following successively closer approximations of the behavior.

When this process is applied to human learning, the situation is changed. It would be an unusual situation where the human learner would be deprived to a point where food could be used as a reinforcer. Avoiding this extreme, we still use food, but it is usually a commodity such as candy. Due to the value of money to most individuals, coins or other reward tokens also may be used as reinforcers or motivators.

One type of reinforcer that rarely has been used is learning itself. One of our strongest needs is curiosity—man's desire to learn and manipulate his environment. If this particular need can be met as a result of learning desired terminal behaviors, then two objectives are achieved. First, since to satisfy the learner's curiosity *is* rewarding, allowing him to learn some skill or knowledge will be effective as a reinforcer—that is, if the skill or knowledge is also interesting. Second, since the reward itself is learning or satisfying curiosity—i.e., supplying the answer to the learner's questions—that learning will add to his total skills or knowledge.

Instead of using superficial rewards, such as candy or money, a contingency management system can utilize the learning process itself as a reward for other desirable learning. In order for this to be useful, an additional analysis must be made of the learner. Not only must we determine his existing abilities, but it is also necessary to find out his "high probability behavior." That is, if the learner were given the freedom to learn anything he wanted, what would he choose? Consider a contingency management system where a learner is placed in an instructional environment and given the freedom to make any response he wishes: that is, he may utilize any of the instructional materials that are available. Each time the learner makes a response in the direction of a (previously determined) desirable terminal behavior, a reward is given. Suppose that the reward consisted of new information or material related to those things which the learner had previously indicated the desire to know or learn. Then, in theory, the learner would be motivated to learn more of the desired behaviors in order to obtain a reinforcer.

One technique that has evolved out of contingency management systems is the use of a performance contract. This contract is between the teacher or manager of the system itself and the learner. It uses the principles of contingency management in addition to the verbal behavior of the learner. By providing the learner with knowledge of the objectives that he is to meet and a knowledge of the rewards that are available to him, an agreement is made between the teacher or manager of the system and the learner, so that when the learner has acquired the terminal behavior, the reward is given. This contract or agreement that the learner will acquire the goal and then be given the reward provides motivation, since the learner knows what he must do in order to acquire the satisfier. In most behavior modification or contingency management systems now in use, these rewards are artificial or material in nature. They consist of money, food and time rewards, such as time allowed in a particular reinforcing environment, movies and other things of this nature. Again, even in performance contracts, the use of learning itself or the satisfaction of curiosity as a reward is available but rarely used.

Contingency Management and the Process of PI

The effectiveness of contingency management will certainly depend on the process used to design a learning environment or total learning system. The best use of contingencies would be ineffective if the wrong objectives were being used. If the terminal behaviors that were acquired were incorrect or were not transferable to the real world environment, then the system would fail, not because contingency management was ineffective, but because the system was inadequate, i.e., had the wrong objectives. In order to insure adequacy of the system itself, a total process of learning system design must be used. Programmed instruction is such a process. Let me describe the five steps that make up the process of programming instruction and then show where contingency management fits into this total process.

First of all, to design any learning system, it is necessary to know where one is going, that is, what are the terminal behaviors, or what are the criteria for successful performance. This means an analysis or study of the real world to determine just what behaviors need to be taught, the conditions of acquisition, and the measurement techniques to be used to determine when these behaviors are acquired accurately and completely. Following the analysis of the real world environment, the second step is to develop a set of criteria in terms that can be used in the classroom or learning environment. After developing the training objectives, one must move to the third step, which is to analyze the population to be trained. This means determining the entry skills and knowledge the learners will bring to the learning environment, including those terminal objectives they can already meet. Given knowledge of entry behaviors and the behaviors that they must have at the completion of the training or education, we can then go into step four, which is to design the learning environment. It is in this environment that contingency management is used.

Contingency management is used in the design of the activities and situations that convert, change or modify the behavior of the learner so that he can perform successfully in the real world. The process of programming instruction does not end with the design of the learning environment. The fifth step in the process involves a validation procedure or an evaluation of the effectiveness of the system that has been produced. This is accomplished by analyzing the behavior of the learners when they enter the real world environment in an attempt to use their learned skills and knowledge. This is not an article·on the process of programming instruction; therefore, I will not expand on the five steps involved in designing the total system. But keep in mind that it is vital that the process be used. Otherwise, the effectiveness of using contingency management or any other instructional technique may be greatly reduced.

Examples of Contingency Management Systems

These examples cover two of the ways in which the principles of contingency management may be used to improve the effectiveness of a learning system in meeting its objectives. The primary gain in these examples occurs due to the effect on learner motivation.

Example 1

Learning Environment: The environment is an elementary school classroom with individualized instructional materials. The teachers are trained as monitors to diagnose needs, prescribe treatment and evaluate results of learners' progress through those materials.

Population: The population consists of minority group learners with a wide range of input knowledge and skills.

Possible Contingency Techniques:

1. The simplest contingency system is to give rewards, such as candy, for completion of the programmed learning units.

2. A more elegant system of contingency management would be to set up a point or scoring system whereby learners earn points for acquiring knowledge and skill as demonstrated by completing programmed units and passing performance tests. By using charts to show individual and team scores, the reinforcers may be provided by the monitors, giving awards such as money, plaques, banners, trips, dinners, etc., for the high scoring teams and individuals.

3. A contract system of contingency management may be designed in which each learner signs a document agreeing to acquire certain skills and knowledge. The manager (teacher, monitor, etc.) signs the contract, agreeing to provide the reinforcer when the learner satisfies the contract. The reinforcer need only be something desirable to the learner, such as candy, awards, games, trips, access to desirable environments or possibly a very desirable learning experience.

Specific Design: Using any of the available programmed instruction materials, set up the classroom so that each learner has a relatively isolated desk or table space and is given complete instructions on how to use the PI materials. In a properly designed PI system, learners will be tested and diagnosed to determine entry skills and knowledge and a prescription for the needed units of PI.

Using a contingency system similar to the ones described above, identify and select your reinforcers.

The value of the reinforcers will vary among individual children, so the more varied your selection, the more effective will be your system. Each learner must then be managed individually. It is important that the manager knows which children work better with contracts and which ones require random and spontaneous reinforcers. Never overlook the power of attention and love as a reinforcer, especially with children.

Keep accurate records of each learner's progress as well as the particular reinforcer and contingency system used. In this way you can improve individual performance by increasing the use of effective reinforcers and eliminating the ineffective ones.

If you use learning experiences as reinforcers, set up these units of learning in distinctive environments and make sure each experience is a complete program. The effectiveness of this method is enhanced if there is a permanent product output from the learning experience; for example, the child may build a vase, complete a picture, solve a problem or complete a story.

In implementing this system, a substantial amount of record keeping and monitoring is required. Much of this work may be handled by teacher aides such as advanced students and para-professionals. The analysis of learner performance and the application of contingency methods should be handled by a teacher or other qualified staff person, but a teacher can manage a rather large number of learners with sufficient clerical and monitoring support.

Example 2

Learning Environment: The environment is an industrial training center working with about 200 trainees at one time. Instruction ranges from clerical to advanced technical skills, and classes contain from six to 15 learners, depending on the scope and complexity of the training. Some classes are group-paced with a lecture-demonstration method of teaching, while many others are individualized and use programmed instruction materials.

Population: The population consists of varying learner types ranging from new hires, both men and women, up to veteran employees of 20 years or more. New hires are predominantly urban members of minority groups. The new employees are distrustful of the system and have low motivation to attack learning materials, while the veteran employees are reluctant to display skill level and learning ability.

Possible Contingency Techniques:
1. As in the case of the elementary school example, the simplest system would be one where reinforcers such as tokens, extra pay, time off or even prizes (try baseball or football tickets) are given upon completion of the training with satisfactory performance on criterion tests. For group sessions the reinforcers may be used to increase participation, attention level and span, and overt responding such as note taking and asking questions.
2. This environment is excellent for systems using points or other scoring techniques for reinforcers. These points or scores may then be

"cashed" in for time off, extra pay, credit toward promotion or special events such as banquets, theater shows or sports events.
3. The contract system described for the elementary school environment is effective for this adult environment, but care must be taken to keep the contracts simple, direct and relevant. If not properly conducted, the use of a contract with adults can produce a comic aura which decreases the value of the reinforcers and limits the effectiveness of contingency management.
4. The use of learning experiences as reinforcers in this environment is particularly intriguing. In almost all cases, a worker, new hire or veteran will be attracted to the more exotic and higher paying positions in a business. Learning units that cover these areas are usually excellent reinforcers; in addition, they broaden the employees' skills and knowledge of the business. A by-product of this technique is that in evaluating performance in the "reinforcer" learning units, many future "high performance" employees are identified. In many cases, the total time required to complete the desired training plus the time spent in the "reinforcing learning" is less than that now being spent to teach the desired material alone.

These four possible contingency techniques are useful in both group and individualized systems but are usually more easily managed for individualized materials.

Specific Design: Using existing instructional materials and at least one subject matter expert from each job or unique work group, separate and level every possible unit of instruction. Make each unit as short as possible, but not less than one hour in length. Obviously, you should have lists of objectives for each of these units. If not, proceed to specify objectives; but remember that you don't always know if your units are relevant to real world needs. Select one of the possible contingency techniques and identify the reinforcers that will be used. If you are using the learning units themselves, it may be necessary to design some new units, since the existing courses may have too few of these desirable learning experiences.

The managing of this system will require considerable record keeping and clerical support. In most cases, every two instructors (managers) will need a clerk for filing, typing and sometimes test administration and scoring. Clerical support can result in less expense, since the two instructors can usually manage as many learners as three instructors are now managing; and, in most centers, clerks are lower paid than instructors. Again, let me emphasize that the effectiveness of contingency management is directly related to the value of the individual reinforcers used; therefore, careful and consistent treatment of each learner is vital. Find the things on your reinforcer list that are most rewarding for each individual; then manage your system so that when the learner performs or meets a desired behavioral objective, one of the reinforcers is presented.

□

Programmed Instruction, Circa 1666

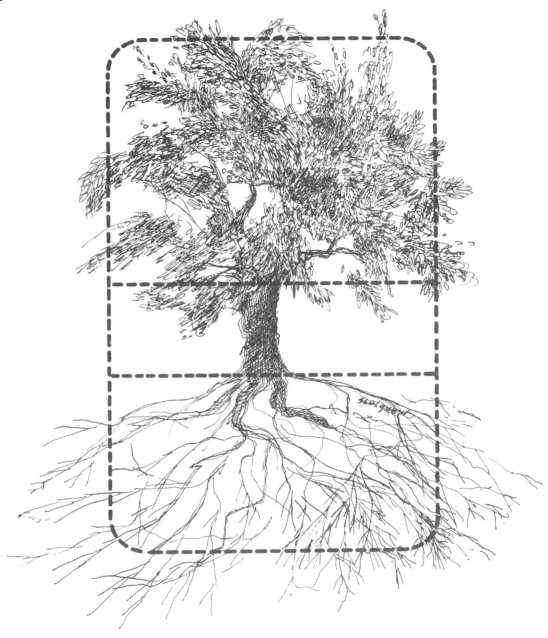

Jim Cockrum

FROM: The Royal Educator

TO: HRH Charles The Second

SUBJECT: The Programmed Instruction of The
Royal Gardeners

Jim Cockrum is a journalist by training. He has written instructional materials, including a programmed text.

Your Majesty, by Your Most Gracious leave, this is to inform you of progress made in a specific PI project being accomplished at the Royal Gardens at Kew.

Having first determined that a need existed, we studied those behavioral responses representing the reaction of a career-successful Royal Gardener when struck by an apple from the royal gardens. The critical incident process revealed these steps to be part of the behaviour process which followed the stimulus specified:

1. He (The Royal Gardener) immediately turned in the direction whence came the apple, stooped down, and picked it up.

2. Upon examination, he determined whether the apple was (a) green or ripe, and (b) a Winesap or a Delicious.

   SUB-ROUTINE A—If the apple were green, he hurled it immediately in the direction whence it came.

   SUB-ROUTINE B—If the apple were ripe, he further determined whether it was Winesap or Delicious.

   SUB-ROUTINE C—Some of the Royal Gardeners would then hurl a Winesap in the direction of origin, but would retain a Delicious apple for eating. Other Royal Gardeners did the converse.

3. After hurling, or retaining, the apple, the career-successful Royal Gardeners invariably rushed off in the probable direction of flight taken by the suspected poacher.

From this analysis, we determined to set several objectives for our programmed instruction project, all of them explicitly behavioural:

1. Upon being struck by an apple, the Royal Gardener trainee shall immediately determine within five degrees its path, relative to his sternum. He shall also determine the angle of trajectory within 40 degrees, which will be useful in estimating the distance whence it came.
2. Upon picking up the apple, the Royal Gardener shall determine whether it is (a) green or ripe, and (b) Delicious or Winesap.
3. He shall decide whether or not to throw the apple, based solely upon his own desires; we did not feel free to encroach on personal preferences in the matter of Winesap versus Delicious.
4. By heft alone, the Royal Gardener trainee shall be able to determine within 2 grams the weight of the apple that was hurled. As you can surmise, this is useful in estimating how far the apple was initially hurled. Some of the apples in your Royal Garden are too light or too heavy for a long, satisfactory hurl. You may wish further training for the Royal Geneticists.
5. The Royal Gardener trainee shall then complete the sequence by determining in which direction to pursue the poachers.

As you can see, our problem was largely one of discrimination training.

For purposes of teaching nomenclature, we constructed a full-scale anatomical dummy. It was marked in degrees, starting at the sternum and proceeding around the right rib cage, across the backbone, and thence to the sternum again, for a complete 360-degree Greenwich orbit. This scale added precision to the training in relative bearing judgment.

Next, we delineated the anatomical model into three vertical segments. The lowest was designated sub-coccygeal, and appropriately labelled in Spencerian script. Just above that region was the supra-coccygeal to sub-clavicular region. Uppermost was the supra-clavicular region, including the cranium.

As you can surmise, an apple striking the sub-coccygeal region must have been hurled from quite a short distance and quite hard, to achieve a horizontal trajectory. An apple striking supra-clavicular would come from a somewhat greater distance. And an apple hurled from the greatest distance would strike in the supra-coccygeal to sub-clavicular area, having roughly a 45-degree trajectory.

It did not seem necessary to teach the Royal Gardener trainees to distinguish green from ripe apples, although we did write 26 frames on the relative health-comfort aspects of eating green as opposed to ripe apples.

To provide a real-life context, we utilized actual Winesap and Delicious apples of many different weights for the discrimination training on those factors.

Appendix A contains a complete report of the response-stimulus mode and the training frames we used.

I am pleased to report that of the ten Royal Gardener trainees who underwent instruction, we had a 90/90 success ratio. Ninety percent of them were 90 percent successful in achieving the behavioural objectives which had been established by the critical incident process.

We were disappointed only by the actions of the tenth young man, a Mr. Newton, and he may have become unhinged when struck by a large and green Winesap apple in the supra-clavicular region. His response to that blow was to whip out a notebook from his pocket and begin to scribble furiously. Muttering to himself about something called gravity," he departed in the direction of the Royal Society. He has since been dismissed, or will be should he return.

Submitted by my hand, most respectfully and obediently, your servant, THE ROYAL EDUCATOR.

□

The Learning Village:

A Behavioral Approach to Early Education

Roger E. Ulrich, Stephen E. Louisell and
Marshall Wolfe

During this century, scientific understanding of the nature of the learning process has tremendously increased. Following the early work of Pavlov, Thorndike, Watson and Skinner, laboratory studies of the interaction between environmental stimuli and observable responses have proliferated. The corpus of data and principles of behavior resulting from this research provide a rich source of methodology for the person interested in changing any type of behavior. When applied in non-laboratory settings, the methodology is known by various names: operant conditioning, behavior modification and contingency management perhaps being most popular.

From the point of view of the public, the main virtue of the methodology has been its striking effectiveness. It has been used to reverse psychotic symptoms (Ayllon & Michael, 1959), to teach autistic children to talk (Risley & Wolf, 1966), to increase time college students spend studying (Fox, 1962; Goldiamond, 1966), to help people lose weight (Goldiamond, 1966), to decrease aggressive behavior (Brown & Elliott, 1965), and to accomplish many other good works (see Ulrich, Stachnik & Mabry, 1966, 1970; Ullmann & Krasner, 1965). In preschool and grade school settings, the techniques have been applied, most commonly, to

Roger E. Ulrich is research professor of psychology and director of the Behavior Research and Development Center at Western Michigan University. In addition, he is president of the Behavior Development Corporation, of which the Learning Village is a facility.

Stephen E. Louisell is educational coordinator of the Learning Village and instructor of psychology at Kalamazoo Valley Community College.

Marshall Wolfe is associate director of the Behavior Research and Development Center at Western Michigan University, and also directs the Learning Village.

remediate behavior problems and deficits (Homme, deBaca, Devine, Steinhorst & Rickert, 1963; Zimmerman & Zimmerman, 1962; Packard, 1970; Hall, Lund & Jackson, 1968; Thomas, Becker & Armstrong, 1968; Hart & Risley, 1968; Madsen, Becker & Thomas, 1968; Buell, Stoddard, Harris & Baer, 1968; Schwarz & Hawkins, 1970; Ulrich, Wolfe & Bluhm, 1968; Surratt, Ulrich & Hawkins, 1969; Schmidt & Ulrich, 1969).

Since one of the principal concerns of behavior modification is with the acquisition of new behaviors, the method is especially appropriate to educational settings. A comprehensive application of the principles of learning to the education of children is currently being made in a private, experimental school system known as the Learning Village. The purpose of the Learning Village is to accelerate and enhance the development of children by applying scientifically sound educational procedures as soon after birth as possible and by continuing their application for as long as the person remains involved in the educational system.

The Learning Village is designed to deliberately create in children the behaviors that most parents hope their children will eventually acquire through ordinary experiences at home and in school. An important group of these behaviors comprises the academic behaviors so necessary to the individual's survival in modern Western society. These include effective use of language and abstract concepts, the ability to extract information from the environment, and the acquisition of information—all of which might be combined under the label of "intelligence." Another group of behaviors is the personal behaviors, such as the ability to keep oneself healthy and productive, and to understand the causes of one's own behavior. Perhaps the most important group of behaviors is that which includes the social and emotional responses important to the individual's, and indeed to society's, survival. Among these are the ability to work cooperatively with others, the ability to demonstrate affection toward others, a concern with the welfare of others, and the skills required to identify and make necessary changes in social systems. When a comprehensive program designed to create desired behaviors is applied very early in children's lives, the children hopefully will develop without many of the behavioral problems and deficits all too familiar to educators. More positively stated, the program of the Learning Village is designed to insure the development of children who read and write well, who think well, who can make the most of their environment, and who love themselves and their fellow men.

The Beginning

The Learning Village grew out of efforts by the Department of Psychology at Western Michigan University to make university training and experience more relevant to cultural concerns (Ulrich & Kent, 1970). Since the education of children is one such concern, an effort was made to institute programs which would permit the involvement of university faculty and students in extra-university educational settings. One program was developed by the Behavior Research and Development Center at Western Michigan University in

69

the Indian Lake Public School, Vicksburg, Michigan, under the jurisdiction of the Kalamazoo Valley Intermediate School District. Initially the program dealt with behavior problems of individual children (Ulrich, Wolfe & Bluhm, 1968). The effort was later expanded to include training programs in behavior modification for teachers in the Kalamazoo public schools (Wood, 1968) and for parents. In addition, work in the public schools gave university students an opportunity to participate in behavior modification in classroom settings. Concurrent with the efforts made in local public schools, a nursery school program was begun, first in a private home and later at Western Michigan University (Wood, Ulrich & Fullmer, 1969). These forays into behaviorally-oriented education were subsequently expanded and consolidated into the private system known as the Learning Village. The private status of the Learning Village allows, within the limits of present knowledge and human frailty, for a rigorous application of behavioral methodology to all aspects of education (Ulrich, Wolfe & Surratt, 1969; Ulrich, Wolfe & Cole, 1970). In addition, private status allows the application of behavioral methodology to the education of people from a wide range of ages. The Learning Village enrolls children as young as two months of age and hopes eventually to develop strategies of comprehensive education which might be applied to the continuing education of adults within an experimental community setting.

Soon after entering the field of nursery school and elementary education, the organizers of the Learning Village encountered the formidable array of traditional ideas, rigid regulations and extensive licensing procedures enforced by local, state and federal agencies which license programs that involve children (Wolfe, Ulrich & Ulrich, 1970; Mabry, Stachnik & Ulrich, 1970). Although the regulations and procedures are intended to better conditions in society, they undoubtedly discourage many persons in their efforts toward the same goal. Complete familiarity with the regulations in the community might prevent some problems. However, unexpected delays and expenses seem, at present, to be inherent in interactions between established institutions and any group that hopes to use new methods to solve old problems.

The Matter of Priorities

No new programs can begin or exist, however, without some support from established institutions, both public and private, and from individuals. The Learning Village receives financial assistance from federal, state and local agencies, as well as from individuals. Some parents pay tuition. The tuition of many infants and nursery school children is paid by the Michigan Department of Social Services. Initial capital was provided by bank loans to founders of the Behavioral Development Corporation and by private funds. Although the support received to date has been greatly appreciated, and the support appears to be increasing, the Learning Village has experienced the shortage of funds inevitably encountered by any day-care center or private school facility that attempts to go beyond minimal care. Programs that are innovative, both in terms of the methods used and the population reached,

are especially difficult to finance. The difficulties have been compounded by the stress the Learning Village places on the prevention, rather than the remediation, of educational mental health and other social problems. Adults soon forget the inadequacies of their early experiences. The problems presented to society by the uneducated teenager or adult generate more concern than the establishment of a system designed to prevent such problems. For example, funds seem easier to obtain when one can alarm the public with exhibits of school failures, extreme mental illness or retardation, drug abuse or crime. Efforts to develop a strategy of education which would make remedial expenditures unnecessary are somehow less inspiring. As anyone involved in education knows, funds are scarce. The education of our children should be one of our top national priorities. At present it is not.

All Day and Year 'round

Children attend the Learning Village all day and on a year 'round basis. A substantial portion of the children's time in school is spent learning academic material. Thus the amount of time spent by the children in school and in structural learning situations is unusual in comparison with traditional educational practices. However, this type of program is gaining support. For example, the Westinghouse Learning Corporation (1969), in its report entitled, *The Impact of Head Start*, makes several pertinent recommendations. It recommends that preschool programs be structured with heavy emphasis on teaching necessary skills; that preschool programs be operated on an all day and year 'round basis; and that special preschool programs be extended downward into infancy and upward into the primary grades. Hopefully an increase in comprehensive, structured early education will follow such "official" endorsement.

Enrollment in the Learning Village does not require that a child be gifted either academically or economically. The Learning Village is also committed to the belief that experience with people of various cultural backgrounds is essential to the true education of any child. The children and staff of the Learning Village, therefore, come from a wide range of economic and cultural backgrounds. In addition, many students, when they enroll in the Learning Village, might be described as academically disadvantaged. They lack the language and conceptual skills usually considered essential to success in school. Although many of the academically disadvantaged come from the less affluent families, academic deficits occur in children from all socio-economic backgrounds.

The Educational Program

The educational program at the Learning Village begins in the infant nursery, which enrolls children aged from two to 30 months. The infant program is designed to teach motor skills, such as sitting, walking and use of the hands; perceptual skills, such as appropriate responses to stimuli differing in quality or intensity; conceptual skills, such as identification of objects and understanding simple concepts; and language skills, such as speech, vocabulary and sentence structure. An effort is made to lengthen the child's attention span, develop imitative behavior, and develop memory. Emphasis is also placed on personal and social skills, such as eating, use of the toilet, cooperative play and affectionate responses to other children and to adults. Creative responses to the environment are also identified and encouraged. Some of these skills and concepts are taught semi-formally in the infant nursery. During such "study" periods each teacher supervises approximately four children. Within this context, the teacher instructs each child individually for periods of approximately 10 minutes. The overall staff-to-student ratio in the infant nursery is 1:3. Since the staff's time is devoted almost entirely to caring for and teaching children, the children in the infant nursery probably receive far more attention from adults than they would in their own homes. In addition, the children are encouraged to interact constructively with the other children in the infant nursery as well as with older children (Ulrich, Wallace & Dulaney, unpublished manuscript). The result is a social environment far richer than that encountered by the infant confined to the typical home environment.

A special effort was necessary to become licensed by the State of Michigan to include infants in the program of the Learning Village. Many psychologists and social workers believe that group day care for children of these ages is damaging, no matter how rich and intensive the care. This unfortunate belief is often based on studies of the development of children in institutional environments that would be considered inadequate by any standards (e.g., Bowlby, 1953; Spitz & Cobliner, 1965). The fact that the environments included group care was secondary to the fact that the children were neglected in countless ways. In the absence of further information, the results of such studies should not be extrapolated to condemn situations which might provide truly constructive experience for infants. Other objections to scientifically based programs for the early education of children may have impeded licensing. These objections relate to philosophical issues such as man's nature and freedom. The issues are beyond the scope of this paper. However, they are frequently encountered by people engaged in modifying human behavior and have been treated elsewhere (Skinner, 1953; Ulrich, 1967; Ulrich, Stachnik & Mabry, 1966, 1970).

Probably because of the difficulty in obtaining a license, infant day care programs, and hence, data on their effectiveness, are rare. However, one infant program which has been in operation for four years at Syracuse University recently reported a study of the attachment behavior of the children enrolled in the program and of their mothers (Caldwell, Wright, Honig & Tannenbaum, 1970). No significant differences were found between the attachment between mothers and the children enrolled in the program and the attachment between mothers and children in typical home environments. However, a relationship was found between the developmental level of children and their attachment behavior. Children at more advanced developmental levels seemed to exhibit a stronger attachment toward their mothers. The stronger attachment was evident both in children enrolled in group day care and in

children who spent their days at home. Since the developmental level of the infants at the Learning Village is greatly enhanced by the program, one might expect an accompanying enhancement of the infants' responsiveness both to their mothers, and to other individuals in their environment.

A rich, well-designed, well-staffed group day-care program for infants is certainly preferable to a deficient home environment. It is also preferable to day care by a single, "babysitting" agent who may not be qualified to give the infant the experiences he needs. Hopefully, as the pressure from mothers for these services increases and as the effects of properly designed and implemented day care for infants become known, the number of centers will increase until the educational and social experiences of children during these crucial months of their development need no longer be left to chance.

At the age of approximately two and one-half years, Learning Village children enter the nursery program (2-½ to 5 years). The personal and social goals of the nursery program are continuations of those of the infant nursery. The nursery program includes four 20-minute study periods each morning. Study periods are devoted to language skills, reading, arithmetic, science, social studies, and the scientific exploration, manipulation and analysis of the environment. "Distar" programs (Englemann & Bruner, 1969; Englemann, Osborne & Englemann, 1969; Englemann & Carnine, 1969) are used in the nursery reading, language and arithmetic instruction. During the study periods, the children are divided, according to their *current* progress, into classes of approximately five children each. The small, individualized groups allow the teacher to give attention to each child, and allow the child to progress at his own rate while remaining in the social context of his own age group.

At the age of approximately five years, the children progress to grade school, where study periods become longer, more time is spent in study groups, and the material, of course, becomes more advanced. Studies (Westinghouse Learning Corporation, 1969) have shown that the continuation of successful educational techniques into grade school is essential to the consolidation of gains made in preschool programs. The staff of the Learning Village anticipates that, as its educational techniques are both implemented earlier in the child's life and continued later in the child's education, results as yet unparalleled in education may be achieved.

The program of the Learning Village is deliberately designed to teach the children certain skills. The emphasis on these skills and the clear structuring of the study periods would be regarded with alarm by some educators (e.g., Neill, 1960). The conviction exists in "humanistic" educational circles that it is somehow damaging to children to *deliberately* teach them the skills which can currently be of use and which certainly will be needed in the future. Such instruction is often thought to stifle children's creativity. When children learn academic skills happily and effectively, they are characterized as being "tricked" or "bribed" into learning these things. Somehow such learning is thought to interfere with the development of a creative personality.

At the Learning Village, quite the opposite seems to be true. Far from stifling the child's personality, the development of skills, even at very early ages, seems to promote active interaction with the environment, to help the child feel good about himself and his abilities, and in general to make the child a happier, more effective, more creative individual. It is difficult to prove scientifically that such effects occur and why. However, it is equally impossible to prove that certain academic deficits promote creativity and freedom. Many adults in our society cannot functionally read or write or work with numbers. These extreme deficits can hardly make these people more free or contribute to their experience as human beings.

Study periods at the Learning Village are designed to be fun and rewarding, just as play periods are designed to be fun and rewarding. During play periods the children are physically more active than during study periods, when they more or less sit in one place and say specific things at specific times. However, the children do not love to play and hate to study. The aversion which some educators have to traditional academic instruction probably relates more to the unpleasant way in which their own educational instruction was enforced rather than to any intrinsically damaging quality in the process of acquiring skills and knowledge. The program at the Learning Village is arranged so that the process of acquiring skills, in itself, enhances the child's development as a human being.

The Behavioral Methodology

The program of the Learning Village, especially of the infant nursery and nursery, allots an unusually large amount of time to the structured learning of academic skills. However, the acceleration of learning which occurs in the Village exceeds that which would occur if the children were simply "exposed" to academic stimuli for the amount of time stipulated in the program. Nor would attempts to promote the social and personal development of the children be as successful if traditional methods were used. As mentioned earlier, the success of the Learning Village depends on the application to the school setting of the principles of learning discovered in the laboratory. The resulting methodology involves arranging the environment, including the behavior of the staff, in such a way that the occurrence of desired behaviors will increase and the occurrence of undesired behaviors will decrease.

The first step in a program of behavior modification is to specify the behaviors ultimately desired. In the Learning Village these "terminal" behaviors include proficiency in reading; correct and creative use of language; acquisition of knowledge about the environment; the ability to use basic concepts of arithmetic and mathematics; a scientific approach to the environment; cooperative, affectionate social behavior; an understanding of the factors which control behavior; an understanding of the factors which make social systems viable and reinforcing to their members; and a good opinion of oneself and one's abilities.

These ultimate goals are translated into specific behaviors which receive daily attention in the Village. The specific behaviors constitute the small steps, or

approximations, from which the terminal behaviors are built. The specification of behaviors is clearly apparent in the academic program, which is systematically broken down into many small steps. In order for a child to learn to speak, read and write, he must make a long sequence of specific responses. Infants imitate sounds, older children make statements about their environment, still older children learn to recognize written symbols, and finally to read and understand words, sentences and stories. The specific behaviors expected of a child are determined by his current behavioral repertoire. If a child is not mastering the material in his study group, he can be moved to a group where more simple responses are required. A special effort is made to match the required responses with the child's progress to insure that the child's experience will include many opportunities for successful responding.

Specific, desired social behaviors include playing with other children, smiling or laughing, absence of crying or aggressive behavior, sharing toys, and being quiet and following instructions when appropriate. Desired personal behaviors include picking up toys at the end of play periods, cleaning up one's own spills, appropriate use of the bathroom, eating a nutritiously balanced diet, and having adequate table manners. The behaviors involved in self-esteem are more difficult to specify, but must certainly involve a willingness to do and learn new things. When a child has a good opinion of himself, he expects to succeed at untried behaviors. He therefore greets new experiences as opportunities for success and good feeling.

Staff members constantly attempt to think about the children in terms of the behavior they exhibit. A child who is sullen or shy is, after all, a child who frowns a lot and plays by himself. If the teacher can arrange conditions so that the child smiles a lot and plays a reasonable amount with other children, the child would no longer be called sullen or shy. When a child does not make the appropriate academic responses, one does not blame the child, or say he is not "motivated," or say he doesn't "need" to learn. One asks, "Does the child have in his repertoire the behaviors prerequisite to the desired behavior?" or, "Is the teacher providing the stimuli which will cause the child to make the desired responses?"

The most important tool used in the Learning Village to promote desired behaviors is positive reinforcement. Non-technically, a positive reinforcer may be equated with a reward. Technically, a positive reinforcer is any environmental event that increases the probability of reoccurrence of the behavior it follows. In other words, the frequency at which a behavior occurs is determined by the events that have followed the occurrence of the behavior in the past. Positive reinforcers must be identified by observing the behavior of children. Events which might not be considered pleasant, such as scolding from an adult, may actually reinforce some children's behavior (Madsen, Becker, Thomas, Koser & Plager, 1968). Conversely, events assumed to be pleasant, such as praise, are not always effective reinforcers (Becker, Thomas & Carnine, 1969). When a child is not responding as expected, one of the questions to be asked is: are the stimuli used as reinforcers indeed reinforcing?

At the Learning Village, the procedure known as contingency contracting (Homme, 1969) is often used to arrange for the reinforcement of students' behavior. "If you do 'X', I will give you or let you do 'Y'," is the basic form of any contingency contract. In this paradigm, "X" is the response that is to be made in order to receive the reinforcer "Y". A good example of contingency contracting is found in the interaction between teachers and school boards. At the beginning of each school year, local school boards or their agents contract with the teachers in their district for a certain salary (Y). If the teachers accept, they must, in turn, make certain responses (X's) during the next nine or ten months. This process is no different from the contingency contracting that goes on every day between teachers and students at the Learning Village. At the beginning of a lesson, the teacher might say, "Class, if you study hard today for twenty minutes, you may, immediately after the lesson, play with a toy for ten minutes." In this case, studying hard has previously been defined as paying attention to the teacher, responding with a high percentage of accuracy, answering and asking questions, and not disrupting the class. Such explicit reinforcement contingencies are readily accepted by the children and, indeed, have become part of the "culture" of the Learning Village.

Of course, not every desired response made by the children is reinforced. Such a procedure would not only exhaust the teachers, but would soon render almost any reinforcer ineffective. Continuous reinforcement is sometimes used to establish behaviors that have a very low probability of occurrence. For most behaviors, however, intermittent reinforcement makes far more effective use of reinforcers. The rate of responding maintained on most schedules of intermittent reinforcement is higher than the rate of responding maintained on continuous reinforcement. In addition, responses maintained on intermittent reinforcement are less likely to fall out of the child's repertoire should a temporary lapse in reinforcement occur.

At the Learning Village, various types of events are used to reinforce behavior. Social reinforcement, such as praise and attention for appropriate behavior, is used lavishly. Attention is given, for example, to the children who are attending during lessons, who are picking up toys after play periods, or who are eating their lunch. The teachers become very adept at delivering enthusiastic social reinforcers. As mentioned above, social reinforcement is not uniformly effective for all children (Baer, 1962; Harris, Wolf & Baer, 1964). However, it is effective for most children. Heavy use of social reinforcers does much to make school a happy, supportive place to be. Since the behavior desired of the child is broken down into small steps which the child can master, the environment is arranged so that the child emits desired responses at a high rate. Many of these small "successes" are greeted with statements acclaiming the child's intelligence, his capabilities, and his willingness to work hard. The result is an atmosphere in which the child feels he is indeed a capable, intelligent human being.

The opportunity to engage in a "fun" behavior is also used as a reinforcer. Such behavioral reinforcers are derived from the Premack principle, which states that a behavior which has a high probability of occurrence can be used to reinforce a behavior which has a lower probability of occurrence (Premack, 1959). Most children find the opportunity to play with certain toys or to go on field trips reinforcing. Other behavioral reinforcers used in educational settings have included the opportunity to push the teacher around the room in a swivel chair, the opportunity to help the janitor sweep the halls, and the opportunity to read a novel. In another nursery school setting, a period in which the children could run and scream was used to reinforce periods of quiet (Homme, deBaca, Devine, Steinhorst & Rickert, 1963).

In order for a reinforcer to be effective it must follow closely the behavior it is designed to reinforce. Physical and temporal limitations often prevent the immediate delivery of reinforcers such as field trips or access to certain toys. To allow immediate delivery of reinforcement, and to provide flexibility in the reinforcement system, a token economy (Ayllon & Azrin, 1968) has been instituted in the Learning Village. When a teacher wishes to reinforce a behavior, he may give the child a token. A token is any small item, such as a poker chip or a piece of play money, that is easily dispensed. The child later exchanges his tokens for a reinforcer of his choice. A designated amount of tokens may buy a field trip, a novel, a puzzle, or the use of a certain toy. Because the tokens can be used to buy so many different reinforcers, they become in themselves powerful reinforcers. The token system not only allows convenient and immediate delivery of reinforcers, but allows the children, within limits, to select their own reinforcers. Different children prefer different toys and activities, and the preferences of children are often surprising. The token economy relieves the educator of the necessity of predicting and standardizing the reinforcers he uses.

The event which occurs most frequently at the Learning Village is the positive reinforcement of a child's behavior. The children come to school expecting many pleasant experiences, and they do, in fact, have these experiences. The traditional academic system is simply not reinforcing enough to make school attractive to many children. For positive reinforcers, schools have traditionally relied on social reinforcers which the teacher may or may not use effectively, on grades, and on the ability of the learning process to reinforce itself. Many educators feel that these are the only reinforcers which can be decently or wisely used. They feel that if the children are rewarded with toys, tokens, or exuberant praise for their good work, they may become dependent on these reinforcers and insensitive to the reinforcers inherent in the learning process. Indeed many teachers refer incorrectly to such reinforcers as bribes. Those with a better understanding of the term "bribe" know that it refers to a reward given to perform an illegal act. Perhaps underlying this general attitude is a sort of Puritanism which dictates that things should be done because one is told to do them, or because they are "good"—not because they may also be really fun.

Nearly everyone has from time to time been reinforced by solving a difficult puzzle or by acquiring new information. However not all the academic behavior required of children is similarly reinforcing. In learning to read, children must learn many things that are of little immediate use to them and which are, after all, not very interesting. There is no harm in "dressing up" this material to make it as interesting as possible. However, the most effective way to make the material truly interesting and important to the child is to make its acquisition necessary to obtain something which the child wants. Deliberate, frequent reinforcement is especially important when very young children are required to learn very simple things. The fact that a reinforcer follows the acquisition of some information does not necessarily reduce whatever "intrinsic" interest that information may have for the child. Rather, the reinforcer makes the child's learning of the material more pleasant and effective and thereby should enhance whatever "intrinsic" interest there is in the material. As the child grows older, some reinforcers should be faded out. Many fade naturally. Children in the Learning Village who initially would not sit in a chair for five minutes without some kind of extrinsic reinforcer, now will sit and read for 45 minutes or longer simply because they now find reading, itself, to be a reinforcing activity. However, one should never assume that everything that even adults are required to learn or do will be so intrinsically reinforcing that no special efforts should ever be made to enhance a person's experience by adding other reinforcers when necessary and possible.

When one neglects positive reinforcers as a means of controlling behavior, one must rely on punishment or other methods which involve aversive stimuli. Neglect of reinforcers has indeed forced on the schools excessive use of aversive control. Problems arise when children are forced to learn because they are shamed or given bad grades and parental censure when they fail. Under such circumstances, even learning material that would otherwise be interesting and exciting, becomes associated with unpleasant experiences and may in itself become unpleasant. The results of this type of aversive control exhibit themselves in many ways, from more dramatic behaviors such as school vandalism, and aggression (Ulrich & Favell, 1970; Ulrich & Wolfe, 1969), to less dramatic, but equally deleterious behaviors such as tardiness, non-attentiveness in class, clockwatching, and failure to complete assignments. School should be a place where children find they can use their skills and intellects to acquire many things which they desire and enjoy. The best way to make learning pleasant and exciting is to reinforce it with a wide variety of satisfying and exciting experiences.

Treatment of Undesired Behaviors

The positive reinforcement of specific, desired behaviors forms the core of the educational program at the Learning Village. The reinforcement procedures build in the children a repertoire of skills; appropriate academic responses; appropriate verbal behavior; cooperative, nonaggressive play; and good eating, toilet and other personal behaviors. In short, the reinforcement procedures help the children develop as happy, active, effective individuals. The emphasis placed on the development of desirable behaviors in itself precludes

development of many of the undesirable responses encountered in educational settings. A child who is reinforced for appropriate academic responses, for smiling and saying, "I like so and so," for playing cooperatively with other children, and for eating his lunch will not lag academically, cry and complain, hoard toys, or throw his food. The preventive approach to problem behavior is by far the most efficient and the most pleasant and constructive from the child's point of view (Ulrich, Wolfe & Cole, 1970; Ulrich, Wolfe & Bluhm, 1968; Ulrich, Stachnik & Mabry, 1970). Time and effort need not be spent on the difficult and unpleasant business of eliminating undesired behaviors. The child seldom needs to be reprimanded, or punished in any way. The development of happy, competent children precludes the development of unhappy, problem children.

However, problems do arise in the Learning Village. When a problem behavior occurs, an attempt sometimes is made to restructure a specific feature of the environment to prevent its reoccurrence. For example, some children would only eat their desserts and drink their milk, without eating the other food in their lunches. The lunch procedure was therefore changed so that the opportunity to eat the food *always* eaten followed the consumption of the food *sometimes* eaten.

The general procedure used most frequently to eliminate undesired behaviors is a combination of extinction (ignoring) of the undesired behavior and reinforcement of behavior incompatible with the undesired behavior. If a child cries and it is known that he is in no physical danger or discomfort that could readily be corrected, he is ignored. Crying of the learned variety thus occurs less frequently. Crying now, when it does occur, contains more information for parents and teachers. When he smiles and plays, he is reinforced. A child who stays by himself and interacts almost entirely with adults is given adult attention only when he plays with another child (Hart, Reynolds, Baer, Brawley & Harris, 1968). A child who is disruptive in a classroom is ignored, and the children who attend to the teacher are praised and otherwise reinforced. Failures to make correct academic responses are ignored and correct responses are reinforced. This procedure gradually eliminates the undesired behaviors and substitutes desired behaviors.

In the case of some behaviors, such as aggression, gradual elimination of the behaviors is not always acceptable, and an attempt must sometimes be made to immediately eliminate the behavior. When absolutely necessary, non-physical punishment is used to attempt to control these behaviors. The punishment may involve loss of tokens in a token economy, or "time out" from the school environment in the form of sitting in an isolated or semi-isolated area. Such aversive control is at the bottom of the list of procedures used at the Learning Village. It is used only when no other method is appropriate. Physical punishment such as hitting the children is never used. Indeed, the use of positive reinforcement, in combination with extinction of undesired behaviors, makes the use of aversive control seldom necessary. As mentioned previously, aversive control can create its own problems in the form of emotional behavior and other undesired behavioral effects. By far the best method of approaching problem behavior is to prevent its occurrence by the deliberate development of incompatible, desired behaviors.

The Teaching Staff

Classes at the Learning Village are very small, and the overall staff-to-student ratio is maintained at 1:5. This desirable state of affairs is achieved, in part, not by hiring numerous people who have been through traditional certification procedures, but by utilizing to the fullest extent possible the teaching capabilities of everyone involved with the Learning Village. Certified teachers, professional psychologists, college students, high school students, parents (41 percent of the Learning Village students have parents on the staff), grade school students, cooks, nurses, in short everyone who crosses the threshold, can become involved in the educational program of the Village.

Most educational systems are isolated from the environment children encounter outside school. The behaviors expected of the children and the methods used to develop the behaviors while in school have little resemblance to the behaviors and environmental controls which the child will encounter during the greater part of his life. The restriction of teaching to individuals who have been through a rigid certification procedure furthers the isolation of the usual educational setting. The traditional methodology of education has been vague and difficult to communicate. Because the behavior somehow expected of teachers has not been adequately specified in traditional education, the system has fallen back on extensive and rigid requirements in the hope that spending years in college or passing an examination will produce skilled teachers. In contrast, the procedures of behavior modification not only specify the behavior expected of the children, but also specify the behavior desired from teachers. Teachers can be taught quite readily to attend to specific, clearly defined behaviors, and to reinforce, extinguish, or perhaps punish those behaviors as necessary. When nearly everyone can be trained to be an effective teacher, the educational setting need no longer be restricted to certain individuals who have been university trained. Newspaper editors, politicians, garage mechanics, law enforcement agents or anyone can teach their skills to children if they are aware of and can apply the principles which control behavior. As more people become teachers, the barrier between community and school, and indeed between student and teacher, can disappear. The entire community can become truly involved in the education of its children.

The formal staff of the Learning Village at present includes a professional psychologist on the Ph.D. level, psychologists and educators on the master's level, psychologists and educators on the bachelor's level, certified teachers, parents, undergraduate college students, high school students, a cook, a nurse, a custodian and a bus driver.

The core of the teaching staff is made up of college students who major in psychology and education. Before beginning work at the Learning Village, these people usually have acquired a background in behavioral psychology. An inservice training program helps them identify and develop the specific teaching behaviors they will need in their work. For many of the students, the Learning Village serves as a laboratory in which they may apply the information they acquire in the college setting (Stachnik & Ulrich, 1969).

High school students are another source of teaching staff. A program has been instituted which identifies and trains high school students interested in education (Arnett, Clark, Spates & Ulrich, 1969; Ulrich, Arnett & DeLoach, in press). These students come both from backgrounds which virtually assure them of a college education and from those which have not typically produced college graduates. Even among the latter group, half the trainees have gone on to enroll in college, planning to specialize in either education or psychology.

To simply describe the students as adequate teachers is to vastly under-rate them. The teaching techniques used in the Learning Village are relatively easy to communicate, and the students have successfully mastered them. Most students approach their work with a thoughtful, critical, creative attitude. In fact, the teaching behavior of a trained high school student is in some cases indistinguishable from that of a certified teacher. In other instances it is distinguishable in that the high school student is much better. The success of these students provides strong evidence that the ability of people in this age group to produce work truly satisfying to themselves and valuable to society is presently being squandered by an extended and isolated educational system. Efforts must be made to liberate our younger colleagues, both by accelerating their formal education and by integrating their formal education with experiences that will allow them to make full use of their knowledge and capabilities.

Yet another source of teaching staff is parents of children attending the Learning Village. Training programs in behavior modification are available both to parents who do and do not intend to teach in the Learning Village. The Michigan Department of Social Services has recently contracted with the Learning Village to train parents and interested lay persons in child care techniques. Parents, even with little formal education behind them, can be trained to be effective teachers and modifiers of their own children's behavior. The training of parents makes an important contribution to the education of children. Continuity is provided between the conditions in force in the home and the school environments. Tantrum behavior may be successfully extinguished at school only to be unwittingly reinforced at home. The training program makes parents aware of the effects of reinforcement and how they can be applied in both the school and the home settings. The training program also serves as a source of enrichment of the parents' lives. Many times it provides a gateway for reentering the educational system at the high school, or more often at the college level. Finally, the training of parents can make an important contribution to the relationship between the parents and their own children. As parents learn to diminish the undesired behaviors of their children, many sources of friction may be eliminated. As parents become able to identify and respond to the behaviors they desire from their children, a new, more positive type of interaction enters many homes.

Pyramidal Instruction

The use of high school and college students as teachers in the Learning Village is one facet of a program which could eventually have a profound impact on the process of education. Throughout American education, the involvement of students in the educational process is inadequate. A fundamental, rigid distinction is made between teacher and learner. Traditional educational methodology requires that students be, for the most part, passive recipients of the wisdom of their teachers or professors. Students are expected to postpone active, constructive participation in the world around them until they have relinquished any identification as learners.

The success with which behavioral teaching methodology can be communicated and effective teaching behavior developed makes rigid segregation of teacher and learner unnecessary. High school and college students have, in the Learning Village, demonstrated that they can be effective teachers. In the Psychology Department of Western Michigan University, a program has also been developed that utilizes college students to teach other college students (Ulrich & Kent, 1970). For example, after completing the first semester of the introductory psychology course, students become eligible to serve, during the second semester, as teaching assistants for the same course (Malott & Svinicki, 1968). This system extends throughout the undergraduate and graduate curriculum. Advanced graduate students teach less advanced graduate students. Graduate students teach upper level undergraduate courses. Advanced undergraduates teach introductory courses, and so forth. Each time a group of students completes a course, a pool of potential teachers of that course is created. At Western Michigan University, an attempt is made to utilize this source of teaching staff to its fullest extent.

A natural extension of the system downward into the high schools and grade schools can easily be envisioned. College students could teach high school students. Upper class high school students could teach first and second year students. Ultimately grade school children could teach kindergarten and nursery children. In fact, grade school children have proved capable of effective teaching behavior. In one study conducted in a public school setting, older grade school children monitored and reinforced the study behavior of younger children (Surratt, Ulrich & Hawkins, 1969). In the Learning Village, grade school children have successfully taught infants to identify pictures (Ulrich, Wallace & Dulaney, unpublished manuscript). In this second study, a programmed booklet was developed to introduce the grade school children to the principles of learning. Several frames from the booklet are shown in Figure 1. The children had had considerable experience with programmed materials and successfully completed the booklet. Each participating child then took an infant aside, determined the number of pictures the infant was able to identify before the teaching procedure was instituted, reinforced subsequent identifications, and

Teachers have learned to use rewards when they teach. A reward is anything that the student likes; such as praise, a piece of candy, or a five minute play period. So, something that a student likes can be used as a r - - - - - by the teacher. [REWARD]

You are now going to learn another name for a reward. The other name is positive reinforcer. Please print these two words here: - - - - - - - - - - - - - - - - - - [POSITIVE REINFORCER]

In this little book we will use the words posi- - - - reinf - - - - - in the place of the word reward. Remember, a positive reinforcer is about the same as a r - - - - d. [POSITIVE REINFORCER AND REWARD]

A piece of candy, or praise, or a chance to play a game are all examples of types of p - - - - - - - r - - - - - - - - -s. [POSITIVE REINFORCERS]

Positive reinforcers should come after a behavior; it is the job of the teacher to give the student a positive - - - - - - - - - after the student has behaved in a way that the teacher wants him to. [REINFORCER]

Positive reinforcers cause the behavior which they follow to happen more often in the future.

Therefore, positive reinforcers are given by the teacher to cause the behavior of the student to happen - - - - often in the future. [MORE]

Let's say that you want your student to increase the number of times he spells his name correctly. If you give a - - - - - - - - - - - - - - - - - - to the child after his name, it will happen - - - - often in the future. [POSITIVE REINFORCER and MORE]

It is easy to see why a behavior which is followed by a - - - - - - - - - - - - - - - - - - would happen more in the future. Let's say that you were given a nickel after every time you printed your name neatly. Don't you think that your behavior of printing neatly would happen more often in the future? [POSITIVE REINFORCER]

Let us say that you gave a piece of candy to a child after he clapped. Wow! He would be clapping his hands all the time. The behavior of hand clapping would happen - - - - often in the future. [MORE]

Figure 1. Sample frames from a programmed booklet designed to train grade school children to teach children in the infant program.

recorded the subsequent increase in correct identification. Further development of training materials, and further experience with use of grade school children as teachers, should allow much broader use of the teaching ability of these children.

The use of students as teachers not only teaches new material to the learner, but allows the teaching student to make use of the material he has previously learned. Many educators, among them Dewey and Montessori, have stressed the importance of the "need to know" in learning. Furthermore, use of sound behavioral principles in a teaching situation demonstrates most dramatically to the teaching student the effect that his behavior has on the behavior of others. Such a behavioral "laboratory" experience (Stachnik & Ulrich, 1969) is a valuable contribution to education at all levels. At the Learning Village it is used especially to help children attain the understanding of behavior which is a primary objective of the program.

The possibility of training people of all ages to teach younger people could allow a restructuring of education so that it is carried on to a great extent by the students themselves. The adult or postgraduate teacher could serve as a source of design, consultation and training. His experience could pyramid downward to create increasing numbers of potential teachers at each descending level. Conceivably, a teacher-to-student ratio comparable to that presently in force in the Learning Village would be possible. When the behavior of children is so developed that they become an active part of the educational environment, they do not cause the discipline problems which now take up much of the teachers' time. Thus teachers could teach more students and teach them well. The restructuring of education to allow complete participation of students would not only relieve educational systems of some personnel and financial problems, but would provide a rich and constructive educational experience for the students themselves.

APPENDIX
Assessment of the Program

Assessment of the effects of the program at the Learning Village has just begun. Indeed, it will not be adequate until the school has been in operation for some time and the long-term development of the children has been observed. As of this date, the nursery school program has been in operation for only two years, and the infant and elementary programs for a little more than one year. Anecdotal information obtained from teachers, parents and visitors as well as test data suggest that the academic behaviors of the students at the Learning Village have indeed been accelerated. At the same time, the children appear to be happy and well adjusted. The undesired emotional behaviors and impeded development predicted as the result of infant day care and the instruction of young children have not been observed. Parents and teachers have reported no incidents of excessive tantrum behavior or regression to behaviors such as bedwetting or thumbsucking. Instead, they are amazed by the gaiety and sophistication of the students at the Learning Village. One mother, who is also a fourth-grade teacher at a local public school, was delighted when she discovered that her three-year-old was learning the same science material that she was teaching her fourth graders. Another mother, whose two children were essentially "expelled" from a local day-care center because of their excessive tantruming, now reports that the Learning Village experience has completely eliminated her children's maladaptive behavior.

Although the staff of the Learning Village is not convinced that a standardized testing program is the best way to evaluate a student's progress, a testing schedule has been implemented. Because nursery programs that teach academic skills are rare, tests scored on the basis of large-group norms are not available for children who are currently in the nursery program. However, results of the Wide Range Achievement Test (WRAT) (Jastak, Bijou & Jastak, 1965) are available for children who are presently enrolled in the kindergarten program. Some of these children have had two years of behaviorally oriented instruction, whereas others have had only one year. The results for the kindergarten children are shown in Table I. Of the 18 kindergarten children, 2 are reading at the fourth-grade level, and 5 children are reading at the third-grade level. The children who scored lowest in reading placed well into the first grade. With one exception, all of these children's reading scores ranked at least in the 90th percentile of their age group's scores. In arithmetic, the results are a little less spectacular, but are consistently good. More than half the children placed in the 90th percentile or better. Spelling has never been explicitly taught in the nursery or kindergarten program, yet the spelling scores, with two exceptions, range from good to adequate. With due respect to the abilities of the children, however, some additional comments are necessary to explain their spelling scores. The children are taught to read *and* spell, but they are initially taught reading and spelling phonetically. As the child progresses, phonetic symbols are faded out and replaced with standard letters of the alphabet. Based on the fact that the children have not altogether reached that stage as yet, they will frequently spell phonetically. Phonetically spelled words, although correct to the children, were not correct by WRAT standards.

Table I
Performance of Learning Village kindergarten students on the Wide Range Achievement Test

Child	Number of Years in the Program	Age: Years-Months	Reading		Arithmetic		Spelling	
			Grade Level: Grade.Month	Percentile in Age Group	Grade Level: Grade.Month	Percentile in Age Group	Grade Level: Grade.Month	Percentile in Age Group
K1	1	4-11	2.5	99	1.8	98	Kg.9	66
K2	1	5-0	1.4	90	1.4	90	Pk.7	04
K3*	1	5-1	1.4	90	1.2	82	Kg.9	66
K4	1	5-3	2.5	99	2.1	99	1.2	82
K5	1	5-5	1.7	97	1.8	98	1.0	70
K6*	1	5-5	1.4	90	1.0	70	Pk.2	01
K7*	1	5-10	2.5	99	2.2	99	1.5	87
K8*	1	7-1	3.8	95	1.9	39	2.3	53
K9	2	5-7	2.6	99	2.4	99	1.8	95
K10	2	5-10	4.2	99	1.9	96	1.8	95
K11*	2	5-11	1.6	90	1.4	82	1.3	79
K12*	2	6-1	3.0	99	Kg.9	34	1.4	63
K13*	2	6-1	2.3	96	1.0	39	1.0	39
K14	2	6-2	3.1	99	2.1	92	2.3	96
K15	2	6-2	3.9	99	2.4	97	1.8	82
K16	2	6-4	4.2	99	2.8	99	2.3	96
K17	2	6-6	1.7	53	1.0	21	1.1	25
K18*	2	6-7	3.6	99	1.9	63	2.0	68
MEAN		5-9	2.6	89	1.7	77	1.3	64
MEDIAN		5-10	2.5	99	1.8	69	1.3	86

*Received financial assistance

For the convenience of readers concerned especially with teaching economically less advantaged children, the children who are supported through some financial assistance plan are indicated in Table I. All of these children placed in the 90th percentile or better in reading. The arithmetic scores have a wider range, the highest being in the 99th and the lowest in the 34th percentile. In spelling the range of scores is extremely wide.

Some data comparing the program of the Learning Village with a more traditional educational experience is provided by tests given in conjunction with the nursery program which was a forerunner of the Learning Village (Wood, Ulrich & Fullmer, 1969). Prior to and during the 1968-69 school year, Western Michigan University operated a traditionally-oriented Campus Nursery School. Concurrent with the operation of the Campus Nursery School, some of the founders of the Learning Village operated an experimental nursery in the same building. Most of the children enrolled in the Experimental Nursery were taken from the waiting list of the Campus Nursery School. Thus neither the Campus Nursery School nor the Experimental Nursery School populations were typical of most educational settings. Most of the children were well-off economically and many came from homes which stressed academic achievement. In the Experimental Nursery, however, five children were added who required financial assistance. At the Campus Nursery School, little attempt was made to teach academic skills. At the Experimental Nursery School, the program was similar to that of the Learning Village. The teacher-to-student ratio was also higher at the Experimental Nursery School.

After approximately one year of half-day attendance, children from both schools were given the Metropolitan Reading Readiness Test and the Weschsler Pre-School and Primary Scale of Intelligence Test Battery. At this point, nearly all of the children from the Campus Nursery School began to attend public school kindergarten. Some of the children from the Experimental Nursery School also enrolled in public school, and some of them enrolled in the newly founded Learning Village. After the kindergarten year, the reading readiness and IQ tests were again administered to those children who could be located and whose parents gave permission for testing. Subsequently, the Wide Range Achievement Test was administered to both groups.

The scores of the children who were able to take the post-nursery school and post-kindergarten IQ tests are shown in Table II. The IQ scores show no glaring differences, yet some trends are apparent. After a year of nursery school education, the mean IQ score of the children from the Experimental Nursery School was 7.49 points higher than that of the children from the Campus Nursery School. Such a difference in itself is not remarkable. However, the scores of the children who subsequently attended the Learning Village kindergarten show a mean

Table II
Post-nursery school and post-kindergarten scores on the Weschsler Pre-School and Primary Scale of Intelligence of children who attended (a) the Experimental Nursery School and Learning Village Kindergarten, (b) the Experimental Nursery School and Public School Kindergarten, and (c) the Campus Nursery School and Public School Kindergarten

	Experimental → Learning Village				Experimental → Public School				Campus → Public School		
Child**	Post-Nursery School	Post-Kinder-garten	Change	Child	Post-Nursery School	Post-Kinder-garten	Change	Child	Post-Nursery School	Post-Kinder-garten	Change
K9	118	139	+21	EP1	122	120	-2	CP1	102	122	+20
K10	124	131	+7	EP2	124	212	-3	CP2	110	108	-2
K11*	105	122	+17	EP3	116	118	+2	CP3	115	U	-
K12*	102	104	+2	EP4	114	116	+2	CP4	105	119	+14
K13*	96	101	+5	EP5	114	116	+2	CP5	114	115	+1
K14	132	135	+3	EP6	121	122	+1	CP6	109	119	+10
K15	124	133	+9	EP7	114	115	+1	CP7	102	116	+14
K16	127	147	+20	EP8*	78	73	-5	CP8	133	134	+1
K17	99	99	0	EP9	124	U	-	CP9	110	112	+2
K18*	120	130	+10					CP11	116	R	-
								CP12	83	U	-
								CP13	108	116	+8
								CP14	86	91	+5
								CP15	106	107	+1
								CP16	104	109	+5
								CP17	108	R	

*Received financial assistance.
**These children's scores on the Wide Range Achievement Test appear in Table I.
U-Unavailable
R-Testing refused by parent

increase of 9.4 points from the post-nursery to the post-kindergarten tests. These means were based only on the scores of children who took both tests. The direction of all changes was positive. In contrast, the scores of the children from the Experimental Nursery School who attended public kindergarten uniformly show no real change. In fact, the mean change of those children taking both tests was -2. However, one child, EP8, did not attend school that whole year. The scores of most of the children who went from Campus to public school show a fairly consistent but smaller increase than did the Experimental to Learning Village children. Of those taking both tests, average improvement was 6.58. Finally, the mean IQ score for those children tested who were involved in behavioral education for two years was 10.1 points higher than that of the children involved in traditional education for two years.

The effects of a first encounter with structured education may be reflected in the slight edge which the Experimental Nursery School children had over the Campus Nursery School children after the initial year, and in the slight increase in the scores of the Campus School children after a year in kindergarten. The failure of the experimental school children who transferred to public school to match the increase in IQ scores of the Learning Village children may reflect the importance of continuing special programs of early education for more than one year. Finally, the difference between the mean post-kindergarten scores of the Learning Village and the public school children does suggest that gains in IQ scores are possible through extended programs of effective early education.

The distribution of percentile ranks of the children given the reading readiness test is shown in Figures 2 and 3. The reading readiness test is designed for administration between kindergarten and first grade. The percentile ranks are therefore not corrected for age. The reading readiness test is not a test of reading ability. Rather it tests knowledge of word meaning, knowledge of numbers and the alphabet, and listening, matching and copying skills. On the post-nursery test (see Figure 2), the scores of the children who attended the Experimental Nursery are widely distributed, whereas those of the Campus School children tend to cluster near the low end of the distribution. After a year of kindergarten, a change occurred in nearly all the scores (see Figure 3). The mean percentile rank of the children who attended the Experimental Nursery and public kindergarten was 80.1 (top graph); of the children who attended the Experimental Nursery and the Learning Village was 82.2 (middle graph); and of the children who attended the Campus Nursery and public kindergarten, 75.9 (bottom graph). The distributions of the three groups given the post-kindergarten test are also very much alike. Apparently, both the public school kindergarten and the Learning Village gave the children the skills they needed to score well on the reading readiness test. Indeed, the skills emphasized by the reading readiness test are often part of the public school kindergarten curriculum.

The scores obtained on the Wide Range Achievement Test present quite a different picture. The mean percentile rank and grade level scores on this are compared in Table III.

The children who attended the Learning Village kindergarten had a mean reading rank above the 90th percentile and placed, on the average, at the beginning of the third grade. The mean reading scores of the children who attended the public school kindergarten fell at approximately the 45th percentile and in the second month of the first grade. Although the public school curriculum did teach the children the skills needed to perform on the average as well as the Learning Village children on the reading readiness test, it did not teach them to read at nearly the same level. In contrast, the program of the Learning Village taught not only the skills measured by the reading readiness test, but actual reading, arithmetic and spelling skills as well. In arithmetic and spelling the mean percentile ranks of the children who attended the Learning Village are above the 70th percentile. The mean percentile ranks for the children who attended public kindergarten are around or below the 50th percentile. In terms of grade level, the mean scores in arithmetic and spelling of the children who attended the Learning Village fall near the end of

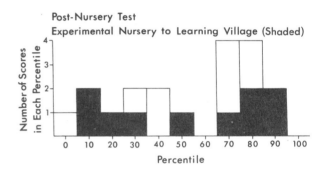

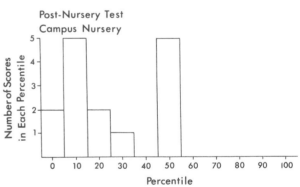

Figure 2. The top graph depicts the distribution of the post-nursery Metropolitan Reading Readiness Test (MRT) scores by percentile for the children who attended the Experimental Nursery. The shaded area represents the scores of the children who attended the Learning Village kindergarten the following year. The bottom graph depicts the distribution of the post-nursery MRT scores by percentile for the children who attended the Campus Nursery. The scores of the children who attended the Experimental Nursery are widely distributed, while those of the Campus Nursery cluster around the lower end of the scale. Ten Experimental Nursery children scored above the 50th percentile while none of the Campus Nursery children scored above the 50th percentile. The MRT is typically administered to children at the end of their kindergarten year. The children in this study were given the MRT a full year before it is normally given.

78

the first grade. The grade level scores of the children who attended public school fall closer to the beginning of the first grade.

Although the Experimental Nursery children had, in the reading readiness skills, a "head start" on the Campus Nursery children, the Campus Nursery children were ultimately able to "catch up." A similar "catching up" in actual reading skills might be proposed for the children attending the public school. The apparently low ceiling of the reading readiness test, plus the superior home and, to some extent, school situations of nearly all the children tested may account for the final similarity of the reading readiness scores. However, some picture of the future reading performance of the Learning Village children might be obtained by examining the current reading performance of the children who have spent one year in the elementary school of the Learning Village.

Perhaps the best picture of reading progress in the elementary school can be obtained by examining the progress of the children on the Science Research Associates (SRA) Reading Laboratory Power Builders. The Power Builders involve reading a story and answering questions designed to develop comprehension and verbal skills. The Power Builders are not tests, but are reading experiences designed to improve the students' skills. In the Language Laboratory, students progress from one grade level

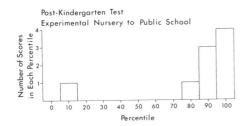

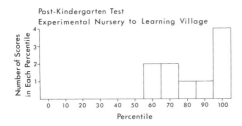

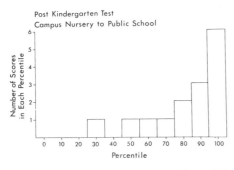

Figure 3. The top graph depicts the distribution of the scores by percentile on the Metropolitan Reading Readiness test for the children who attended the Experimental Nursery and a public school kindergarten. The mean percentile score was 80.1. The middle graph depicts the distribution of the scores by percentile on the Metropolitan Reading Readiness test for the children who attended the Experimental Nursery and the Learning Village kindergarten. The mean percentile score was 82.2. The bottom graph depicts the distribution of the scores by percentile on the Metropolitan Reading Readiness test for the children who attended the Campus Nursery and a public school kindergarten. The mean percentile score is 75.9.

Table III

Mean grade level and percentile scores on Wide Range Achievement Test of children who attended (a) the Experimental Nursery School and Learning Village Kindergarten (b) the Experimental Nursery School and Public Kindergarten, and (c) the Campus Nursery School and Public Kindergarten

School Experience	Reading		Arithmetic		Spelling	
	X̄ Grade Level: Grade.Month	X̄ Percentile in Age Group	X̄ Grade Level: Grade.Month	X̄ Percentile in Age Group	X̄ Grade Level: Grade.Month	X̄ Percentile in Age Group
Experimental Nursery School → Learning Village	3.02	93.64	1.78	72.20	1.68	73.80
Experimental Nursery School → Public School	1.22	44.20	1.25	45.00	.98	30.71
Campus Nursery → Public School	1.25	45.70	1.37	54.40	1.07	42.10

to another according to their performance on individual Power Builders. The grade level at which the child begins is determined by administering the Starter Level Guide, an SRA test coordinated to the Reading Laboratory. Fifteen or 20 Power Builders are included in each grade level, depending on the level. However, if a student meets criteria, he may progress to the next level without completing all of the Power Builders. Criteria are set by the teacher and, in part, by the student. Mrs. Carmen Hren, the elementary school reading teacher, usually requires that the children complete at least six Power Builders at 80 percent accuracy, or three or four Power Builders at 90 or 100 percent accuracy. Incidentally, completion of a Power Builder at 80 percent or better accuracy is reinforced by tokens.

Figure 4 shows the grade level progress of the Learning Village elementary school children on the SRA Power Builders. Temporary "regressions" to previous grade levels are built into the SRA program, which requires some repetition of grade levels. These repetitions appear as level segments in Figure 4, and they do not represent any real set-back in the student's progress. The elementary school children also took the Wide Range Achievement Test near the time of the last entry in the progress charts. The WRAT grade level scores for these children are also shown in Figure 4. For completeness, Table IV gives the full set of WRAT scores of the elementary school children.

As Figure 4 shows, the progress of the children in the SRA Reading Laboratory has been substantial. Within weeks, children progress several grade levels. That this progression is not an artifact peculiar to the SRA program is indicated by the Wide Range Achievement Test grade level scores. In most cases, the children scored at a higher grade level than the grade level of the Power Builders with which they were currently working. Those children who scored below were the oldest, had less experience with the Power Builders and terminated well before the reading test was administered.

Some idea of the lesson-to-lesson performance of the children may be obtained from Figure 5, which shows the scores of two representative children on the individual Power Builders. For each Power Builder, the child records his score on two types of questions (Comprehension and Vocabulary) and records his working time. Child E5's record is typical of the children who progressed rapidly. Accuracy was very high (usually above 80 percent) on both comprehension and vocabulary, even by the SRA standards for the superior learner (Parker, 1969, p. 58). Earlier lessons were completed with apparent speed and ease, several lessons often being completed in a single day. More time was spent on later lessons, but accuracy did not deteriorate. In these later lessons, this eight-year-eleven-month-old child was doing work designed for use in the ninth grade. His WRAT reading score placed him almost at the senior high school level.

Table IV
Performance of Learning Village elementary school children on the Wide Range Achievement Test

Child	Months	Reading Grade Level: Grade.Month	Reading Percentile in Age Group	Arithmetic Grade Level: Grade.Month	Arithmetic Percentile in Age Group	Spelling Grade Level: Grade.Month	Spelling Percentile in Age Group
E1	7-8	8.4	99	3.6	77	5.0	98
E2	8-0	5.1	92	3.9	68	3.5	58
E3	8-4	10.5	99	4.2	75	6.3	99
E4	8-6	5.9	96	4.2	68	4.7	81
E5	8-11	11.7	99	7.2	99	11.5	99
E6	9-0	7.2	98	4.2	53	5.3	79
E7	9-9	6.5	86	4.7	50	3.7	27
E8	11-0	11.7	99	6.1	53	10.9	99
E9	11-5	8.1	86	6.3	55	7.2	73
E10	12-1	7.3	53	7.4	53	5.5	22
MEAN	9-6	8.2	91	5.2	65	6.4	73
MEDIAN	8-8	7.7	97	4.4	61	5.4	80

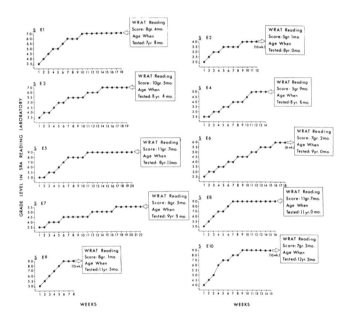

Figure 4. The above graphs indicate the grade level progression by weeks on the Science Research Associates (SRA) Power Builders and the Wide Range Achievement Test (WRAT) scores for the Learning Village Elementary School students. All subjects except E9 and E10 scored higher on the WRAT than their progression level on the SRA Power Builders. This can probably be explained by the fact that the SRA Power Builders place greater emphasis on comprehension skills. The arrows that point toward the last data point indicate that the WRAT was given during that week. For example, the WRAT was administered to Subject E1 during the 19th week of the SRA program. Arrows that point away from the last data point indicate that there was a time lapse between the last week that a student worked on the SRA Power Builders and the date that he took the WRAT. The amount of time between the completion of the last SRA Power Builder and the administration of the WRAT is indicated in parentheses. Temporary "regressions" to previous grade levels are built into the SRA program, which requires some repetition of grade levels. These repetitions appear as level segments (eg. SEI weeks 10-18) on the graphs. They do not necessarily represent any lack of progress.

The lesson-to-lesson progress typical of another child is also shown in Figure 5. Child E7 spent more time on each lesson and did fewer lessons per day. However, his accuracy is excellent. Although this nine-year-old child initially placed below the grade level appropriate to his age, he has now "caught up." In addition, the quality of his work is superior, and the child's reading scores on the Wide Range Achievement Test suggest that his actual reading skills may be above his SRA grade level. A slower worker does not have to be a poor reader.

The reading performance of virtually every one of the children now in the Learning Village elementary school by far exceeds normal achievement in public elementary school. The children who attended the experimental nursery school and the Learning Village have already finished kindergarten with superior reading ability. If they make progress typical of the children now in the Learning Village elementary school, the future contrast with the reading ability of the children who entered public school should be even greater.

One might prefer comparative data showing the effects of the Learning Village program and of traditional education on a more typical population of school children. However, the comparative data do indicate that a Learning Village type program can make a significant difference even in the education of children destined for an above-average academic experience. As mentioned earlier, the general population of the Learning Village is not preselected for academic achievement or "intelligence."

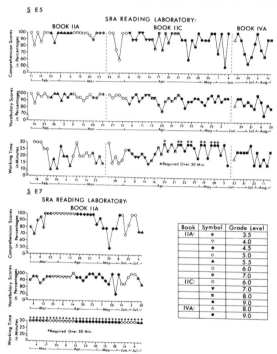

Figure 5. The lesson-to-lesson progressions of two Learning Village Elementary School students are depicted in the above graphs. On each Power Builder, the student graphs his own comprehension and vocabulary scores as well as his working time. Subject E5's graphs closely resemble those of a superior learner (Parker, 1969, p. 58). The graphs of Subject E7 resemble those of a typical slower learner. While Subject E7 always had a working time of over 30 minutes, his accuracy in both the comprehension and vocabulary portions of the Power Builders was quite high. Both subjects are reading above grade level. For each Power Builder, the child records his own score on two types of questions; comprehension (top graphs) and vocabulary (middle graph) as well as on working time (bottom graphs). The chart at the lower right hand side of the figure shows the SRA book from which the child was working and the symbol used in the figures for depicting the grade level.

However, even children who enter the Learning Village with academic deficits are soon indistinguishable in performance from children who enter with good academic backgrounds.

The results of the academic program at the Learning Village are most dramatic in the area of reading. If it is true, as many educators claim, that reading is the key that unlocks the door to knowledge, the students are well on their way to success in education. The experience at the Learning Village has caused the children to learn far more than they would have from the usual elementary school kindergarten or nursery school-plus-kindergarten program. The staff of the Learning Village believes that the results achieved are due primarily to the behavioral methodology used. In the past, attempts to improve the education of children have suffered from a fundamental ignorance of the nature of learning. Technologies of education, to be consistently effective, must be based on a scientific understanding of their subject. Once the results of scientifically based educational methodology become known, a tremendous growth in and refinement of the technology of behavioral education should follow. The ultimate results of long-term, comprehensive behavioral education must be consigned to the void of future happenings. The results could surpass the most fanciful goals of current educators. Indeed, behavioral education may create the very kind of people needed to cope with the extremes of technical advancement and social crisis characteristic of the twentieth century. Whether or not today's children will be given the chance to eventually prove or disprove the above conjecture, of course, as always, depends upon the decisions of those adults who control our present educational systems. ☐

Acknowledgement

Any program such as that described here requires the support of many people and many institutions. In this regard, the authors would like to acknowledge the support of Western Michigan University, the Kalamazoo Community Mental Health Services Board, the Kalamazoo Valley Intermediate School District, the Michigan Department of Social Services, the Michigan Department of Mental Health, the Michigan Department of Education, the National Institute of Mental Health and the Office of Naval Research. In the initial stages, the Learning Village programs were helped especially by Dr. Thomas Stachnik, Dr. Philip Smith, Dr. Vernon Stehman and many other people connected with the Michigan Department of Mental Health. Additional advice came from the Governor's executive staff, namely from Charles Orlebeke, William Whitbeck, Ted Blizzard, David Duncan and Charles Greenleaf. The initial proposal for the Learning Village programs was submitted to the Michigan Department of Mental Health by the senior author, Mr. Paul Surratt and Mr. Marshall Wolfe. Major responsibility for the day-to-day direction and implementation of the Learning Village program is presently assumed by Marilyn Arnett, Helen Brewer, Arlyne Gutmann, Carmen Hren, Madelon Lewis, Alex Luvall, Dorothy Marine, Robert Pierce, James Scherrer, Richard Spates, Carole Ulrich and Robert Wiggins. Teachers and other staff include Marcia Beard, John Bird, Melanie Blanks, Bette Boulding, Debra Briley, Bernice Brown, Janice Brown, Sondra Curry, Lola Dangerfield, Robert Dyche, Anne Farmer, Richard Fearon, Janine Fockler, Margaret Gilligan, Gerald Harper, Ruth Harper, Marie Harris, Red Hartmen, Russell Jones, Tom Louisell, Lois Martin, Delores McGinnis, Mona Mitchell, Fran Pietras, Ruth Shafer, Marilyn Shaw, Brenda Sherburn, Carol Siep, Sharon Sowers, Lois Speck, Joan Spindler, Sue Steiner, Darwin Stier, Paula Van Valkenburg, Opal West, Kathleen Williams, Mary Williams, Cheri Yeager and Mary Ann Zender. Former staff members who rendered indispensable service in establishing the Learning Village program include Sue Anger (our first graduate), Jim Anthony, Al Birdsall, Michael Boyle, Donald Clark, Tony Colasacco, Richard Cole, Jim Cossingham, Sibyl Daniels, Mary Fullmer, Alan Gonick, Tom Kucera, Jan Lindenberg, Helaine Nelson, Chris Nuttall, Paul Surratt and W. Scott Wood. To Judy Favell, Wade Hitzing, John Martin, Max Maultsby, Paul Mountjoy, Roger Pulliam, Donald Roberts, Paul Surratt, Lewis Walker, Velma Watts and Jim Yore on the Behavior Development Corporation Advisory Board and to Ron Hutchinson, Behavioral Development Corporation vice president, we extend a special thanks.

Any attempt to name the people who have been helpful in such a program will probably leave someone unmentioned. To these persons, the authors extend their apologies and appreciation. Special thanks goes to Kay Mueller, who helped prepare and edit the manuscript. Sylvia Dulaney made many useful and essential suggestions. Galen Alessi, Joe Auffrey, Carmen Hren and Lynne Peters were especially helpful in collecting and preparing data.

References

Arnett, M., Clark, D., Spates, R. & Ulrich, R. An In-Service Training Program for High School Students. Paper delivered at American Psychological Association, September, 1969, Washington, D.C.

Ayllon, T. & Azrin, N.H. *The Token Economy: A Motivational System for Therapy and Rehabilitation.* New York: Appleton-Century-Crofts, 1968.

Ayllon, T. & Michael, J. The Psychiatric Nurse as a Behavioral Engineer. *Journal of the Experimental Analysis of Behavior,* 1959, *2,* 323-334.

Baer, D.M. A Technique of Social Reinforcement for the Study of Child Behavior: Behavior Avoiding Reinforcement Withdrawal. *Child Development,* 1962, *33,* 847-858.

Becker, W.C., Thomas, D.R. & Carnine, D. *Reducing Behavior Problems: An Operant Conditioning Guide for Teachers.* Urbana, Ill.: ERIC Clearinghouse on Early Childhood Education, 1969.

Bowlby, J. *Child Care and the Growth of Love.* Baltimore: Penguin Books, 1953.

Brown, P. & Elliott, R. Control of Aggression in a Nursery School Class. *Journal of Experimental Child Psychology,* 1965, *2,* 103-107.

Buell, J., Stoddard, P., Harris, F.R. & Baer, D.M. Collateral Social Development Accompanying Reinforcement of Outdoor Play in a Preschool Child. *Journal of Applied Behavior Analysis,* 1968, *1,* 167-174.

Bushell, D., Jr., Wrobel, P.A. & Michaelis, M.L. Applying "Group" Contingencies to the Classroom Study Behavior of Preschool Children. *Journal of Applied Behavior Analysis,* 1968, *1,* 55-62.

Caldwell, B.M., Wright, C.M., Honig, A.S. & Tannenbaum, J. Infant Day Care and Attachment. *American Journal of Orthopsychiatry,* 1970, *40,* 397-412.

Englemann, S. & Bruner, E.C. *Distar Reading.* Chicago: Science Research Associates, 1969.

Englemann, S. & Carnine, D. *Distar Arithmetic.* Chicago: Science Research Associates, 1969.

Englemann, S., Osborne, J. & Englemann, T. *Distar Language.* Chicago: Science Research Associates, 1969.

Fox, L. Effecting the Use of Efficient Study Habits. *Journal of Mathetics,* 1962, *1,* 75-86 and in R.E. Ulrich, T. Stachnik & J. Mabry (Eds.) *Control of Human Behavior: I. Expanding the Behavioral Laboratory.* Glenview, Ill.: Scott, Foresman, 1966, Pp. 85-93.

Goldiamond, I. Self-control Procedures in Personal Behavior Problems. In R.E. Ulrich, T. Stachnik & J. Mabry (Eds.) *Control of Human Behavior: I. Expanding the Behavioral Laboratory.* Glenview, Ill.: Scott, Foresman, 1966, Pp. 115-127.

Hall, R.V., Lund, D. & Jackson, D. Effects of Teacher Attention on Study Behavior. *Journal of Applied Behavior Analysis,* 1968, *1,* 1-14.

Harris, F.R., Wolf, M.M. & Baer, D.M. Effects of Adult Social Reinforcement on Child Behavior. *Young Children*, 1964, *20*, 8-17 and in R.E. Ulrich, T. Stachnik & J. Mabry (Eds.) *Control of Human Behavior: I. Expanding the Behavioral Laboratory*. Glenview, Ill.: Scott, Foresman, 1966, Pp. 130-137.

Hart, Betty M., Reynolds, Nancy J., Baer, D.M., Brawley, Eleanor R. & Harris, Florence R. Effects of Contingent and Non-contingent Social Reinforcement on the Cooperative Play of a Preschool Child. *Journal of Applied Behavior Analysis*, 1968, *1*, 73-76.

Hart, B.M. & Risley, T.R. Establishing Use of Descriptive Adjectives in the Spontaneous Speech of Disadvantaged Preschool Children. *Journal of Applied Behavior Analysis*, 1968, *1*, 109-120.

Homme, L.E. *How to Use Contingency Contracting in the Classroom*. Research Press, P.O. Box 2459, Station A, Champaign, Ill. 61820, 1969.

Homme, L.E., deBaca, P.C., Devine, J.V., Steinhorst, R. & Rickert, E.J. Use of the Premack Principle in Controlling the Behavior of Nursery School Children. *Journal of the Experimental Analysis of Behavior*, 1963, *6*, 544; and in R.E. Ulrich, T. Stachnik & J. Mabry (Eds.), *Control of Human Behavior: I. Expanding the Behavioral Laboratory*. Glenview, Ill.: Scott, Foresman, 1966. Pp. 93-94.

Jastak, J.F., Bijou, S.W. & Jastak, S.R. Wide Range Achievement Test. Guidance Associates, 1526 Gilpin Ave., Wilmington, *Del., 1965.*

Mabry, J.H., Stachnik, T.J. & Ulrich, R.E. Cultural Impediments to the Implementation of a Behavioral Technology. In R.E. Ulrich, T.J. Stachnik & J.A. Mabry (Eds.) *Control of Human Behavior: II. From Cure to Prevention*. Glenview, Ill.: Scott, Foresman, 1970.

Madsen, C.H., Jr., Becker, W.C. & Thomas, D.R. Rules, Praise and Ignoring: Elements of Elementary Classroom Control. *Journal of Applied Behavior Analysis*, 1968, *1*, 139-150.

Madsen, C.H., Jr., Becker, W.C., Thomas, D.R., Koser, L. & Plager, E. An Analysis of the Reinforcing Function of "Sit Down" Commands. In Parker, R.K. (Ed.) *Readings in Educational Psychology*. Boston: Allyn & Bacon, 1968.

Malott, R. & Svinicki, J. Contingency Management in an Introductory Psychology Course for 1000 Students. Paper presented at the American Psychological Association, San Francisco, 1968.

Neill, A.S. *Summerhill: A Radical Approach to Child Rearing*. New York: Hart, 1960.

Packard, R.G. The Control of "Classroom Attention": A Group Contingency for Complex Behavior. *Journal of Applied Behavior Analysis*, 1970, *3*, 13-28.

Parker, D.H. Teachers Handbook. SRA Reading Laboratory. IIa. Science Research Associates, 1969.

Premack, D. Toward Empirical Behavior Laws: I. Positive Reinforcement. *Psychological Review*, 1959, *66*, 219-233.

Risley, T. & Wolf, M.M. Experimental Manipulation of Autistic Behaviors and Generalization into the Home. Paper read at American Psychological Association, September, 1964, and in R.E. Ulrich, T. Stachnik & J. Mabry (Eds.) *Control of Human Behavior: I. Expanding the Behavioral Laboratory*. Glenview, Ill.: Scott, Foresman, 1966, Pp. 193-198.

Schmidt, G.W. & Ulrich, R.E. Effects of Group Contingent Events Upon Classroom Noise. *Journal of Applied Behavior Analysis*, 1969, *2*, 171-179.

Schwarz, M.L. & Hawkins, R.P. Application of Delayed Conditioning Procedures to the Behavior Problems of an Elementary School Child. In R.E. Ulrich, T. Stachnik & J. Mabry (Eds.) *Control of Human Behavior: II. From Cure to Prevention*. Glenview, Ill: Scott, Foresman, 1970, Pp. 271-283.

Skinner, B.F. *Science and Human Behavior*. New York: Macmillan, 1953.

Spitz, R.A. & Cobliner, W.G. *The First Year of Life*. New York: International Universities Press, 1965.

Stachnik, T.J. & Ulrich, R.E. A Laboratory Section for Educational Psychology. *The Psychological Record*, 1969, *19*, 129-132.

Surratt, P., Ulrich, R.E. & Hawkins, R.P. An Elementary Student as a Behavioral Engineer. *Journal of Applied Behavior Analysis*, 1969, *2*, 85-92.

Thomas, D.R., Becker, W.C. & Armstrong, M. Production and Elimination of Disruptive Classroom Behavior by Systematically Varying Teacher's Behavior. *Journal of Applied Behavior Analysis*, 1968, *1*, 35-46.

Ullmann, L.P. & Krasner, L. (Eds.) *Case Studies in Behavior Modification*. New York: Holt, 1965.

Ulrich, R.E. Behavior Control and Public Concern. *The Psychological Record*, 1967, *17*, 229-234.

Ulrich, R.E., Arnett, M. & DeLoach, T.G. Teaching the Disadvantaged. In J. Bergeson & G. Miller (Eds.) as yet untitled. New York: Macmillan, in press.

Ulrich, R.E. & Favell, J.E. Human Aggression. In C. Neuringer & J.L. Michael (Eds.) *Behavior Modification in Clinical Psychology*. New York: Appleton, 1970, Pp. 105-132.

Ulrich, R.E. & Kent, N.D. Suggested Tactics for the Education of Psychologists. In R.E. Ulrich, T. Stachnik & J. Mabry (Eds.) *Control of Human Behavior: II. From Cure to Prevention*. Glenview, Ill.: Scott, Foresman, 1970.

Ulrich, R.E., Stachnik, T. & Mabry, J. (Eds.) *Control of Human Behavior: I. Expanding the Behavioral Laboratory*. Glenview, Ill.: Scott, Foresman, 1966.

Ulrich, R.E., Stachnik, T. & Mabry, J. (Eds.) *Control of Human Behavior: II. From Cure to Prevention*. Glenview, Ill.: Scott, Foresman, 1970.

Ulrich, R.E., Wallace, F. & Dulaney, S. Pyramidal Instruction: A Proposed Solution to an Educational Problem. Unpublished manuscript.

Ulrich, R.E. & Wolfe, M. Research and Theory on Aggression and Violence. *The Science Teacher*. 1969, *36*, 24-28.

Ulrich, R.E., Wolfe, M. & Bluhm, M. Operant Conditioning in the Public Schools. *Educational Technology Monographs*, 1968, *1* (1).

Ulrich, R.E., Wolfe, M. & Cole, R. Early Education: A Preventive Mental Health Program. *Michigan Mental Health Research Bulletin*, 1970, *4*, (1).

Ulrich, R.E., Wolfe, M. & Surratt, P. New Methods for Treatment Delivery. *Michigan Mental Health Research Bulletin*, 1969, *3*, 41-44.

Westinghouse Learning Corporation. *The Impact of Head Start, An Evaluation of the Effect of Head Start on Children's Cognitive and Affective Development*. Office of Economic Opportunity Publ. No. B894536. Springfield, Va.: U.S. Govt. Clearinghouse, June, 1969.

Wolfe, M., Ulrich, R. & Ulrich, C. Administrative Hurdles Blocking Preventive Mental Health Programs for Children.*Michigan Mental Health Research Bulletin*, 1970, *4*, 44-48.

Wood, W.S. The Lincoln Elementary School Projects: Some Results of an In-Service Training Course in Behavioral Psychology. *Educational Technology Monographs*, 1968, *1*, (2).

Wood, W.S., Ulrich, C. & Fullmer, M. Early Education: An Experimental Nursery School. Paper read at Michigan Academy of Arts, Letters and Sciences, Ann Arbor, 1969.

Zimmerman, E.H. & Zimmerman, J. The Alteration of Behavior in a Special Classroom Situation. *Journal of the Experimental Analysis of Behavior*, 1962, *5*, 59-60 & in R.E. Ulrich, T. Stachnik & J. Mabry (Eds.) *Control of Human Behavior: I. Expanding the Behavioral Laboratory*, Glenview, Ill.: Scott, Foresman, 1966, Pp. 94-96.

A Reinforcement Theory Perspective of Early Child Rearing and Education

Richard P. Toister

The ebb and flow of advice to parents and teachers on how to rear and educate young children, oft-times contradictory from one generation to the next, has been well documented (Wolfenstein, 1953; Brim, 1959; Caldwell, 1964). Why this has been the case is not entirely clear but, for the most part, two complementary factors have been involved. First, there has been a general lack of systematic empirical information on behavior development itself; second, professionals have historically exhibited a propensity to deduce child rearing practices from past and current theoretical ideas about how and why children learn.

The reasons for the lack of systematic information about child development are many and include methodological problems of conducting such research (Gewirtz, 1969). The reasons for the popularity of various theories of child development are not as evident, but the practice of teaching both parents and educators a given theoretical language is widespread.

Yet, as most parents and teachers will testify, the relative lack of systematic data notwithstanding, having a theoretical point of view does not necessarily result in answers to the practical everyday questions of behavior management generated in the home or in the preschool classroom.

At this level both educators and parents require more or less specific principles or guidelines which they can apply to foster cognitive and social development in the young child. In addition, these principles should, ideally, make few unreasonable demands for special equipment or highly technical skills, or require undue staff or assistants. Put simply, a child rearing technology based upon existing systematic analyses of behavior capable of providing specific objective principles to parents and teachers should be of great interest to lay persons and professionals alike. In recent years such a technology of behavior management has been developing at a geometric rate and is generally referred to as reinforcement theory. The present discussion is meant only as an overview of some of the basic principles of

Richard P. Toister is assistant professor of psychology at the Mailman Center for Child Development, University of Miami.

this orientation which are particularly relevant to early childhood education. The interested reader should consult the more extensive reviews and discussions readily available in the literature (Baer & Wolf, 1968; Homme, et al. 1968; Ferster & Perrott, 1968; Staats, 1968; Franks, 1969).

Reinforcement Theory—Basic Principles

A 5-year-old child, hearing the bell of an ice cream truck, runs into his house, requests some money from his mother, runs back into the street and purchases an ice cream pop.

A 2-year-old toddler while being wheeled around the supermarket points to a box of cookies and says, "I want cookie," yet because lunch is imminent the request is denied; the result is a crying tantrum on his part, and because of her wish not to disturb the other shoppers, mother relents and supplies the cookies.

A 3-year-old preschooler is observed to remain on the periphery of social activities and in these situations his teacher, desirous of fostering cooperation and social interaction, continually pleads and prods the child to participate; the prodding does not have the desired effect.

Are there any similarities in the above examples? What is common to all three illustrations is the fact that in each there is an antecedent event (bell of an ice cream truck; cookies on a shelf; children playing a social game); a behavior (running and requesting; crying and screaming; standing apart from the group); and a consequence (ice cream; cookies; teacher attention). Thus, one can explain or describe all three behaviors similarly in a functional way by pointing to the relationship between these three events—the antecedent event or *discriminative stimulus*, the behavior or *response*, and the consequence or *reinforcer*. To demonstrate that these events are in fact functionally related one might withhold the money for the ice cream, not supply the cookies, and only attend to the child if he approached the group. If, as a result, the child ceased running in and requesting money at the sound of the bell; stopped crying and screaming in similar supermarket situations; and began to approach the group in play activities, we would say that those consequences (ice cream, cookies, attention) served as reinforcers because they altered the frequency of certain behaviors they followed. The relationship between all three events—a discriminative stimulus, a response and a reinforcer—describe a contingency of reinforcement whereby a performance may be increased, decreased or unchanged in frequency over time.

Techniques Which Increase the Frequency of a Performance

It would certainly be convenient if young children began preschool already demonstrating consistent peer cooperation, good work habits, attentiveness, appropriate language and perceptual-motor skills, and so on. Usually, however, not only are there gross individual differences in competence between children, but the same child might display differences in competence across these skills. The techniques presented in this

83

Photos courtesy of Fisher-Price Nursery School

section are very relevant to both inter- and intra-behavioral differences and are important in the establishment of behaviors which are deficient, which occur at a low rate or in inappropriate circumstances. Specifically, these procedures are shaping, fading and imitation or modeling.

Again, it should be noted that the techniques presented are but a few relative to a reinforcement theory technology applicable to early education, and the reader should consult those references cited in the text for more complete analyses.

Shaping

Shaping refers to the differential reinforcement of successive approximations toward a final performance. The most notable example of shaping in educational environments is programmed instruction, where shaping is used to introduce complex concepts one step at a time. Thus, for example, the spelling of a difficult word such as DEMOCRACY could be achieved by first requiring the student to give the first letter, next, the first two letters, and so on until reinforcement is given only if the entire word is spelled correctly. Relating this procedure to early education, various tasks can be "programmed" or broken into simple steps and the child led through the sequence until the final goal is achieved. Puzzles, formboards and copying are all tasks which readily lend themselves to a shaping or programming analysis. For example, a child having difficulty completing a five-piece formboard might first be required to place one piece to receive a positive consequence (attention or praise). Next two pieces, three, and so on until attention was given only for the complete performance of placing all the formboard pieces. Not only can perceptual-motor skills be programmed in this manner, but social behavior such as paying attention, cooperation and language skills can also be increased in accuracy and frequency. The teacher employing shaping should be able to describe the final performance objectively; break the performance down into small, discrete but progressive steps; and make reinforcement

contingent on the successive approximations or mastery of each step toward the final behavior.

Fading

Fading involves two processes, prompting and the eventual or gradual reduction or fading of the prompt. By appropriately arranging stimuli or materials, a teacher can successfully change the stimuli controlling a behavior with little or no decrease in the rate or accuracy of the performance. For example, a child who can say the word "blue" when shown a blue card can be taught to say "blue" to the written word by gradually fading the blue color as the word BLUE eventually appears on successive cards. The end result is the verbal response "blue" to the written word with a minimum of errors if the materials were carefully arranged. Copying skills also offer a good instance where fading is a valuable technique. Thus, a child may trace a complete form and gradually the prompt is faded into a dotted outline until the child is correctly drawing the figure on a blank space. Again, the significant feature of fading is that it eliminates or greatly reduces errors in learning and hence enhances motivation to perform. The importance of fading in the development of complex skills in early childhood has been discussed at length by Ferster & Perrott (1968).

Modeling

Children are taught to imitate the behavior of parents, siblings, peers and teachers by repeated instances of such behavior being followed by positive consequences and/or avoiding negative ones. In fact, imitative behavior is so strong by age 3 that many children will imitate tape recorded messages, TV cartoon characters, and so forth. Technically, modeling refers to the matching of behavior between the child and the model. "Simon Says" is a game that exploits imitative behavior in a competitive and reinforcing format. The use of imitation in early child rearing and education is legion, since it is so efficacious in establishing new performances. It is not necessary to discuss "how" a teacher or parent can use modeling to increase the occurrence of behaviors, but it should be noted that the behavior consequated in the reinforcement contingency is the correct match between the child's performance and the model.

Techniques which Reduce the Frequency of a Performance

These procedures include extinction, time out from positive reinforcement and punishment.

Extinction

Extinction refers to the gradual reduction in behavior when reinforcement is no longer forthcoming. For instance, a child whose disruptive classroom behavior has been characteristically followed by teacher attention may stop this behavior if the teacher begins to differentially ignore him when he misbehaves. The exact course of reduction in the rate of behavior is a function of the previous contingencies of reinforcement as well as emotional factors such as frustration. Thus, the child might initially show more frequent and intense disruptive behavior when he is ignored. Parents, mothers in particular, are all too familiar with the increased volume in crying of their infant when they fail to respond to his first protestations, especially at three in the morning. For this reason, consistency and persistence on the part of the parent or teacher are especially important in reducing behavior through extinction procedures.

Time Out

In the time out procedure (TO) a child is prevented from contacting positive reinforcement for a behavior by contingent removal from the reinforcing situation. A TO room or space may be used in which a child is placed for a brief period of time, usually 10 to 15 minutes, immediately upon the occurrence of a behavior. Or, in ongoing training sessions, the teacher may look away from the child for a brief period of time (about 10-15 seconds) when an objectionable or incorrect response is made (Risley & Wolf, 1967). The practical implications of TO for early child rearing and education are many, particularly as a technique to reduce inappropriate social behaviors.

Punishment

In behavioral terms, a punishing consequence is defined by its suppressive effect upon the frequency of the behavior it follows. However, because of this usually immediate suppressive effect, punishment may reinforce the punisher. One outcome may be that punishment will be more likely to occur in similar situations when more positive techniques might accomplish the same results. In other words, the parent or teacher who is reinforced for punishing by the immediate suppression of a behavior is likely to punish for another behavior. There is no easy solution to this problem since many behaviors, such as running into the street or injuring peers, require immediate reduction. Nevertheless, in many instances where an objectionable behavior (shouting out in class) can be suppressed by punishment, a more

desirable behavior (raising one's hand) can be increased in frequency by applying appropriate contingencies of extinction (ignoring the child when he shouts) and positive reinforcement (praising or attending to him only when he raises his hand).

Gardner & Briskin (1969) have reviewed punishment procedures with retarded children, but their conclusions and recommendations for using punishment as a technique to reduce behavior are applicable to normal children as well.

Summary

Several techniques, derived from reinforcement theory, which have been shown to effectively increase or decrease the frequency of behavior were presented and related to early child rearing and education. The former included shaping, fading and modeling. The latter included extinction, time out and punishment. In addition, it should be emphasized that it is *the systematic application of consequences* which is crucial in behavior management with children. Finally, in most instances, it is the contingent use of attention, praise and disapproval alone coupled with the effective programming of tasks which results in significant increases in the development of cognitive and social behaviors in young children. Thus, the careful manipulation of a parent's or teacher's own behavior can be a most powerful technique in early child rearing and education. □

References

Baer, D. & Wolf, M. The Reinforcement Contingency in Preschool and Remedial Education. In Hess & Baer (Eds.) *Early Education.* Chicago: Aldine, 1968, 119-129.

Brim, O.G. *Education for Child Rearing.* New York: Russell Sage Foundation, 1959.

Caldwell, B.M. The Effects of Infant Care. In L. Hoffman & M. Hoffman (Eds.) *Review of Child Development Research: Volume One.* New York: Russell Sage Foundation, 1964, 9-87.

Ferster, C. & Perrott, M.C. *Behavior Principles.* New York: Appleton-Century-Crofts, 1968.

Franks, C. (Ed.) *Behavior Therapy: Appraisal and Status.* New York: McGraw-Hill, 1969.

Gardner, W.I. & Briskin, A.S. Use of Punishment Procedures in Management of Behavior Difficulties of the Severely Retarded. *Journal of Psychiatric Nursing and Mental Health Services,* 1969, 5-16.

Gewirtz, J.L. Levels of Conceptual Analysis in Environment-Infant Interaction Research. *Merrill-Palmer Quarterly,* 1969, *15,* 7-47.

Homme, L., C'de Baca, P., Cottingham, L. & Homme, R. What Behavioral Engineering Is. *Psychological Record,* 1968, *18,* 425-434.

Risley, T. & Wolf, M. Establishing Functional Speech in Echolalic Children. *Behavior Research and Therapy,* 1967, *5,* 73-88.

Staats, A. *Learning, Language and Cognition.* New York: Holt, Rinehart and Winston, 1968.

Wolfenstein, M. Trends in Infant Care. *American Journal of Orthopsychiatry,* 1953, *23,* 120-130.

APPLIED ACCOUNTABILITY

William A. Deterline
Contributing Editor

Objectives

Upon completion of this article, including the search for answers to the questions at the end of the work, you should be able to do the following:

1. Explain what "accountability" means in the broad sense.
2. Describe what impact accountability would have on your training/education setting; or, if you are not involved full time in training or education, describe the impact that accountability would have on a hypothetical training/ education operation.
3. Explain what is meant by the "information presentation" approach to instruction, and describe briefly three objections that the author expresses to that approach. Prepare at least a 100-word rebuttal to one of his objections.
4. Clarify the distinction the author makes between *training* and *education*. From your own experience—either as an instructor or student—describe an example of each, without going back to your elementary or secondary school courses.
5. Describe each of the three accountability "directives." Describe, in terms of a real or hypothetical course, how each of these directives might be implemented.
6. In terms of your own involvement with instructional design, development, implementation, or management, describe the following:
    a. Changes that you could make now, under present conditions, with your present skills, to utilize any aspect of the accountability approach.
    b. Changes that could not be made because of existing constraints; and describe those constraints.
    c. Skills or methodologies that appear to be required, but which you do not understand, or do not think are feasible.
    d. Procedures, techniques, skills that appear to be a necessary part of applied accountability that probably do not exist where you are, and which would have to be obtained or developed.
7. Considering your answer to 6a, above, prepare a plan detailing the steps that you would take, and then, ideally, *go take them.*

Subject Matter Experts, Skilled Performers and Instruction

Consider a group of people all doing basically the same job. The group might be a group of surgeons in a hospital, a group of assembly line workers in a factory, or a group of white collar workers doing related but not completely similar activities. One day it becomes necessary to appoint a supervisor or coordinator for the group: a chief surgeon, a foreman or a chief clerk. Too often, what happens is that the best performer gets the job, and sometimes the hospital loses its best surgeon to administrative detail, which he fouls up; the plant loses an excellent worker and gets an incompetent foreman; and the office loses a highly skilled clerk and gets a lousy supervisor. This is one example of the Peter Principle in action (see article by Lessinger, this issue): people tend to be promoted out of jobs they do well, and eventually they end up in a job they don't do well; there is, therefore, no reason to promote them, and there they sit, having risen to the level of their own incompetence!

That sad example is all too familiar. There is another, related kind of problem that is neither as obvious nor as well-known. There is a myth that says, "Any competent subject matter expert and/or skilled performer of a job or activity is, by the nature of that competence alone, automatically a highly competent teacher of the competence." Often—but not always—those two competencies *do* go together. And because we see that happen frequently, we apparently assume that it is true all the time. But we have all encountered many exceptions: The instructor of whom we have said, "He knows his subject, but he is way over my head," or "It is obvious that he knows his stuff, but he sure can't teach it!" So, sometimes, for one reason or another, a competent subject matter expert is assigned the task of participating in the design, development and implementation of a course of instruction. And sometimes we lose a competent worker or supervisor, and find him operating at a level of relative incompetence in the training field.

There is another myth, perpetuated by much of the training and education community, that says that teaching means a competent subject matter expert *presenting information*, and then, through testing, identifying learning deficiencies—and blaming them on the students.

Some people believe those myths—really *believe* them. Other people act as if they believe them, because it is certainly easier that way. But those myths are not true. Being an effective teacher requires more than subject matter expertise, and consists of more than a technically accurate and clear and interesting presentation of information.

Visit schools, colleges, universities, industrial, military and government training facilities, and you will find many people acting out the myths. What sense does a lecture make? If the students need the information being presented by the lecturer, why make them try to take accurate and complete notes while the lecturer is talking? Why not record and transcribe them, and pass out copies? If the lecture is actually a lecture/discussion, with considerable participation by the students, again, why not eliminate the lecture—the information presenting part of it—and concentrate on interactive discussion? Get the information to the students by more effective and efficient means, and use the discussion periods for diagnostic, remedial, application, implication and practical consideration-types of discussion. The most obvious thing for us to do, when, as subject matter experts we are asked to become involved in course development or teaching, is to do what our teachers did to us. So we do, and it doesn't work very well. But since all failures and ineffective aspects of our instruction are slyly laid on the students, in the form of a grade or rating, we never really have to face the facts of our own incompetence in the field of instruction.

Consider your own job, whatever it might be: would you expect a brand new person—a cook, nuclear physicist, accountant, mechanic, bank president, clerk, or confidence man—to be able to walk in and do your job without any training, or without being taught any tricks of the trade? Would you expect him to sit at the desk next to yours and with little direction do the same thing that you are doing? Not very likely. *Yet we do exactly that* and perpetuate those myths when we say, "Hey, subject matter expert, sit down here and design and develop a course to teach something." Where is he supposed to get the skills, and procedures, and techniques to do it with? That's where the first myth comes in: if he can do a job, we assume that he has all the necessary instructional skills, and that isn't fair to

him or to his students. So he relies on the other myth: he prepares barrages of information to present to the students.

How does he decide *what* information to present? Intuitively, from his own experience, or from reference materials that also present information. And there is a very real limiting factor. In education and training for scores of years we have attempted to present information as skillfully as possible, using a great number of methods, audiovisual devices, games, demonstrations, all designed toward the impossible, ultimate form of the second myth: that there is a *perfect* presentation of information possible, such that every student will learn everything, understand everything, and remember it all. When we concentrate on the presentation of information, we strive for that unattainable *perfect presentation*. No one has ever gotten there; most fall far short.

Accountability

Most of us are held accountable for our work. We are expected to earn our salaries by producing results, by carrying out the tasks assigned to us with at least a minimum acceptable level of competence. Certainly we tend to look for and give excuses when our performance is less than it should be, but that only works a little bit, sometimes. Basically, we are accountable and are held to be accountable. There is, however, a never-never quality about the instructional world that says, "You are the professional, you are the competent person here, and the students are dependent upon you. Yet we won't hold you accountable if they fail to learn from you; we'll blame them. We will hold them accountable for any failures, deficiencies and incompetence in your teaching. And we will use the instructional setting as a screening device: if the students can not learn in spite of what goes on here, we will penalize them. Their records will show that their intelligence and motivation were not enough; and sometimes those records will haunt them, and affect their careers, and their lives. You will not be affected in any way. You are not accountable for the results of your activities.

Now, however, we find education talking about "accountability" in teaching and in the operation of schools. Teachers and schools are to be held accountable for the results of instruction, and rewarded or not rewarded depending on those results. What is a teacher to do? Suppose a teacher had worked very hard, very conscientiously, trying to achieve perfect presentations. That teacher learned the hard way that there are limiting factors—constraints—and that reality and practicality prevented that ideal from being attained. Why should that teacher welcome the notion of accountability?

Some parts of the training world have been able to avoid accountability because of the nature of the subject matter being taught. Some topics are so ill-chosen, so irrelevant, that it doesn't really matter what happens—whether the students learn or not! A training manager who is involved in the training of flight crews for jets told me recently that, in the past, although the cockpit procedures trainer and flight simulator provided very relevant practice, much of what went on in the classroom was largely irrelevant to anything the crews needed to know, or had to be able to do. For example, when an aircraft manufacturer sent the airline all of the specifications and information about the construction and operation of the aircraft and all of its systems, the trainers attempted to teach the crews how the plane was built, and how it worked. Some of that is relevant, of course, and some is critical, but no attempt was made to separate the relevant and critical from the irrelevant. So pilots were trying to learn the dimensions and capacity of tiny flutter values, and components and systems of many kinds that were irrelevant to the requirements of flying the aircraft. And the irrelevant got in the way of the critical things, making the course harder, duller and longer, and, most important of all, less effective. Fortunately, following the classroom sessions, the other methodologies did adequately prepare the crews to do their jobs! For those results the training staff has always been held accountable. They have never been able to do a poor job, and then blame it on the students if any deficiencies slipped through.

Some training courses have avoided accountability because no one has bothered to follow-up to see if the training really accomplishes anything. Sometimes the course examinations are so simple—far less complex than the job performance requirements for which the course was to prepare the student—that most of the students are able to demonstrate high levels of competence on the examinations, and this is a fine feather in the cap of the training staff. Occasionally a surly malcontent on the line or in the field will scream that the newly trained people assigned to him are incompetent, but often his is only a single voice. The "silent majority"—like any silent majority—can be interpreted as expressing—through their silence—approval, and a lack of criticism. Often, however, line supervisors and managers are silent because they have learned not to expect anything better; they have learned that the training courses will turn out some skills, but with many holes, many deficiencies that will have to be repaired on the job, through direct and close supervision, and on-the-spot correction and guidance. Why make a fuss, they reason, next year it might be their turn in the barrel, assigned to the training department!

In training there is usually an external criterion that can be used to evaluate the results of training: job effectiveness. An analysis of the job performance requirements can improve the relevance and effectiveness of instruction, and that same analysis permits a very precise analysis of the effectiveness of instruction. But if the training instructors have also learned about the very limited features of information presentation as a teaching method, then why should *they* welcome or seek accountability if they can avoid it?

So we can conclude that both teachers in educational settings and instructors in training settings might be expected to cry "foul and unfair" when faced with the notion of accountability. And I don't blame them a bit. Unless someone else accepts accountability for teaching those teachers relevant skills beyond those they already possess, and unless the conditions that limit their effectiveness can be changed, then there is no justification for expecting them to do better, or for holding them accountable for doing so. They need more effective techniques, procedures, methods, materials and other components of instruction. And then, when new components are added, no matter how innovative, how effective, there will be a limit to the overall effectiveness of that totality, probably still short of that ideal of all students learning everything. That new limit will have to be determined empirically, and then additional research and development efforts can be aimed at raising that ceiling.

The foregoing is *not* intended to imply that accountability is not feasible, or that it would be premature to explore the concept in action. It *would* be a mistake to attempt to impose accountability within the existing system of information-oriented instruction, where it would be, in effect, nothing more than a punitive structure. Teachers and students fail, not because they don't try hard enough, but because of the limitations imposed on them by the way they are forced to go about it! Students are presently held accountable for failures; accountability does not mean—although it has often been interpreted to mean—simply assigning accountability to teachers and arranging some form of reward system for teachers based on results. Accountability must start at the top, and must be applied to everything that has an instructional or instructional management function. The purpose is not punitive; the purpose is—to use a manufacturing term—quality control. The systems approach—and we are all tired of hearing about the systems approach—is basically a methodology which requires exact specifications of what is to be accomplished by each component, and the use of techniques to see that each specification is achieved; meeting specifications is quality control. Seeing to it that specifications and quality control work—at all levels—is accountability.

I recently heard a prominent educator refer to accountability as a "new theory of education." It is not. There is nothing theoretical about it. While discussing accountability with a group of industrial training specialists, who were involved in sales training that might or might not have been having an effect on sales skills, I suggested that they do some follow-up studies to find out what impact—if any—their instruction made on the real-world activities of the salesmen they trained. One member of the group exclaimed, "Wow, that would really be laying it on the line, wouldn't it!" Yes, it would, and that seems only fair, because the salesmen they train are laying it on the line, presumably assisted by skills learned during training. Again, what I was suggesting was not a fault-finding procedure, but an empirical approach to developing, implementing and managing instruction. We may *think* that we are accomplishing something; if we are wrong, we need to find it out as quickly as possible, so we can do something about it.

Applied Accountability

There are many examples of accountability in training, not because someone thought that accountability sounded like a good idea, but because of the criticality of the job performance requirements. Obviously the punitive interpretation of accountability would make no sense in the airline setting, where flight crews must, as a result of training, meet very precise performance standards: holding the training department accountable for pilot error accidents is not much of a solution. The training department must do everything necessary to provide relevant and effective training, and identify any deficiencies in time to correct them, both in their trainees and in their training methods and materials. They have to know what they are trying to accomplish in precise and measurable terms; they have to have effective methods for determining when they have or have not been successful; they have to be as empirical as possible in their approach in order to identify problems and deficiencies; they have to have effective diagnostic and remedial methods available for trainees who for any reason are in difficulty; and they must collect relevant data, and use the data to revise, improve and maintain the resulting instructional effectiveness.

How does one introduce accountability into instruction where it did not formerly exist? The easiest setting, relatively speaking, is in a training environment, preparing trainees to perform a specific job, all components of which are readily identifiable. The job itself is the criterion. The job can be analyzed as a basis for instructional design. Later the job serves as the source of quality control data for determining how well the instruction works, and where it must be improved. A non-accountable approach to training in that setting— difficult to justify, but all too common—pays very little attention to the job itself *as it really exists.* Instead, rather vague job descriptions and subjective judgments are used as a basis for selecting information that is to be presented, probably in a lecture setting. Gathering information and lecturing about it is the easiest and most convenient method available, so, whether or not it is the most appropriate approach, some training staffs make very little contact with the job itself, with people who can do it, or with those who supervise those who can do it. A non-accountable approach can afford to ignore the job and make intuitive rather than empirical-

ly-based judgments about the design of instruction. Moving one step closer to the job, using subject matter experts as sources of information, or even going so far as having them design or assist in the design of the content, does not solve all of the problems. It obviously does not solve the problems created by the information-presenting approach; nor does it adequately replace the missing empirical and objective analysis of the job performance requirements.

The first step in introducing accountability is setting some basic standards or rules or specifications. The first directive says that no trainee will proceed from training to the job until we have complete and objective evidence that he can do the job according to the established criteria. There are many implications of that prime directive, which applies—incidentally—to education as well, although couched in different terms and involving slight modifications in methodology. One implication is the dependence on *established criteria,* which may never have been established beyond the level of vague and ambiguous job descriptions. Who is to establish the criteria, the descriptions of the job performance requirements in objective, measurable terms? We might do several kinds of task analyses: an observation task analysis, observing people doing the job in order to see what they do and the way in which they do it; a consensus analysis, asking workers, supervisors, equipment designers and anyone else who purports to know how the job should be done; or a content analysis, determining what the manufacturers of equipment put into the directions for operation, and so on. The consensus and content analyses would probably yield very similar kinds of information, but both might disagree markedly with the results of the observation tasks analyses. Suppose we find that the job, as it is being done, does not agree with the experts' descriptions of the way they think that it should be done? Which description is "right?" The establishment of objective criteria in the form of performance specifications is a complex problem in itself. Some training departments operate without such specifications; some apparently never hear of such things. Sometimes the responsibility for establishing such specifications is left to the training staff; sometimes there is a separate department responsible for performance specifications and job simplification. It should be obvious at this point that this is a complex requirement, but the complexity and difficulty are not justification for ignoring the problem, hoping that it will go away or take care of itself!

What form does the prime directive take in education, or in the education portions of training? First of all, consider the distinction that has just been implied, between education and training. Many people have made such a distinction, which in its harshest form becomes: when we know what we are doing, that's training; when we don't, that's education. A less critical—and more sympathetic—distinction is made here: training implies objective criteria in the form of job performance requirements; education is instruction of a more general nature, possibly specifically job-related, but also "general knowledge" and skills relevant to many kinds of jobs, or to activities outside of job settings. Some academic subjects have certain aspects of training, in that objective criteria are available, and the performance components are relatively unchanging no matter what kind of job or real world application is involved (e.g., reading, mathematical skills, language skills, including foreign languages, operation or use of measuring devices, etc.). A course in "principles of electricity" would fall under the heading of *education*, whether taught in a training or education environment, but the specific application of those principles as job performance activities would be the *training* part of the course. In any case, and regardless of the nature of an appropriate distinction, or in the absence of any distinction, one requirement stands out: the prime directive, independent of any job referent, states that no student will be considered to have completed a course of instruction until we have complete and objective evidence that he has achieved the objectives according to the established criteria. The common denominator for training and education is the use of established criteria and evidence of attainment.

Education requires some form of commitment to a set of criteria. Unless we are willing to commit ourselves to a specific set of criteria, no "complete and objective evidence" can be obtained indicating that our students have or have not attained them! If we don't care about all of our students attaining at least some uniform minimum level of competence, then we can do without criteria, and quality control and accountability. We can then continue to present information and grade on a curve and let it go at that. Once we commit ourselves, however, and agree on a set of criteria—even if it is necessary to establish a tentative set of criteria, planning to improve that set as we collect relevant data—we can make accountability a viable concept and methodology. Obviously, I am referring here to the use of instructional objectives.

The second directive says that we have to assemble a set of "learning experiences" and evaluation and management procedures that will allow and assist every student to reach that specified criterion or set of criteria. We can start by assembling components intuitively, using our own best judgment about the requirements of each objective. We might develop or select conventional text materials, programmed materials, audiovisual materials of various kinds, hands-on practice materials and simulators, and we might schedule field trips, use both individualized and group instruction, and a variety of methods. We should use past experience, not just our own, but the vast applied and methodological research, media, training and learning research data, and the practical know-how collected as part of thousands of developmental and implementation projects.

And that is only a start. All we have so far is an experimental version of a course of instruction; we do not know whether it will meet the requirements of the first two objectives. Total accountability means that each component has a specified function; we have to determine how well each component succeeds, and revise and improve where necessary. Accountability also means that we must identify the weaknesses and provide corrective back-up so that no student is lost to us. This is also part of the game specified by the first two directives.

The third directive says that we must rely on data. Too many courses are considered to be "finished, polished, and perfect," because a group of subject matter experts or instructional specialists pronounced them so. In their best judgment, the course *should* teach. An empirical approach requires more than that. The subjective, intuitive and experiential judgments of the experts are interesting, encouraging and nice to have. But the final judges are the students. The data they produce as they proceed through the various components of the course, and the evaluation data, and any available follow-up data tell the story. We are accountable for the data; if the data are not adequate in comparison with the data we had hoped for, we have not met the requirements of the first two directives, so now we must act on the third directive as our only hope for attaining the first two!

The teachers, the instructors, in an accountability setting, have to function effectively as tutors, diagnosticians, remediators, managers, counselors, advisors, conversationalists and stimulating consultants. These skills are not part of most teacher-training or instructor-training curricula. Some will have to be learned by experience on the job, and some people will be able to develop higher levels of proficiency at one skill than another. Eventually we will have to learn how to analyze and teach these skills, and be accountable for doing so, to at least a minimally adequate level. At that time we will be able to establish and implement a reasonable merit reward system. The teacher or instructor who can "service" the most students with the best results deserves to be rewarded.

At present, education and training are *time-oriented*, not *performance-oriented*: a student completes a course at the end of a fixed period of time, not when he reaches a specified level of proficiency; instructional staff members are promoted and given salary increases on the basis of longevity, or for credits accumulated for spending specified numbers of hours, days, or years in training courses, workshops, or graduate courses. All that can be changed, and changed now.

Only a vocal minority sees much need for accountability and its requirements. The instructional world is primarily structured on subject matter content and presentations of information. In effect, that world doesn't seem to care about results, about learning, about student competence. Yet those are all that count. I have collected a number of objections to accountability, from representatives of all parts of the instructional world:

- A teacher asked, "Are we then to stop educating the whole child?"
- Another teacher said, a bit sadly, I thought, "It sounds exciting, but it is obviously impractical, or immoral, or something, or we'd be doing it already."
- A training director growled, "We don't have time for all that."
- Another training director said, "If I tried to sell that idea to our management, they would either think I had lost my mind, or would accuse me of admitting that everything we had done previously was wrong, incompetent, or irrelevant!"
- A dean told me, "Those activities would get in the way of the scholarly activities of our faculty."
- A college professor, avoiding the term "scholarly activities," was more blunt when he said, "We are *not* accountable and never will be. The system specifies that the student is responsible and accountable in higher education. I must talk to them about what I know, help them, try to interest them, and guide and steer their curiosity and interests. And I help them in their career decisions if they commit themselves to my field. But my profession, my professional advancement, and my professional activities come first. That's the name of this game!"
- A harassed instructor cried, "What the hell are you talking about? I have to squeeze an hour or two out of each day for the next week in order to put together a one-day course on something I'm still learning about myself!"

If all of the real world, the practical world, indicated that accountability is not feasible, or that universal constraints make it impossible, then we would have to assign accountability to the pipe-dream category. But the constraints are *not* universal; the system can be changed or the constraints by-passed. Many companies, both large and small, many government agencies, and instructional projects in schools of all kinds have demonstrated that accountability can be implemented on an efficient, cost-effective basis, and made a way of life. As I said above, none of it is easy, but hell, the things that we are doing now aren't easy either, so we might as well do it right!

Summary

Instruction too often relies on subject matter expertise and information-presentation methods to be the primary—or entire—set of resources and tools of design, development and implementation. Sometimes this is the only approach possible, but most of the time alternatives are available. Accountability imposes three directives: specified performance capability will be produced; the instructional components must produce those results; and an empirical development and management process must be employed. Accountability is not a punitive method of assigning blame for failure, or a method of rewarding teachers who work harder. An overhaul of the entire instructional environment—its components and its methods—is a basic requirement. The entire operation must become results-oriented, results measured in terms of students' performance capabilities stemming from the instructional events arranged for them.

Questions

1. The "accountability" concept does not hinge on a punitive and/or reward system for instructors. What then is its basis?
2. Accountability requires several new implementation procedures and criteria. Describe them.
3. Industry does training, and also provides education. The educational community educates, and also does some training. How are "training" and "educating" defined in this article?
4. Describe each of the accountability "directives" and their implications for both training and education, not in the abstract, but in terms of the procedures necessary to act on these directives. □

Who Thought of It First?

A Review of Historical References to Programmed Instruction

Dene R. Lawson

Most educational technologists credit B. F. Skinner, Harvard experimental psychologist, with being "father of the teaching machine," even though Mellan[1] in 1936 had reported over 600 teaching devices which have been registered with the U. S. Patent Office. Skinner's article[2] in 1954 set the stage for a tremendous wave of interest in the development of mechanical teaching devices. Unfortunately, too much emphasis was placed on gadgetry and not enough on the basic learning theory which had originally prompted Skinner to utilize a mechanical device for presenting sequential subject matter to students.

Dene R. Lawson is a doctoral student at Stanford University.

Only recently, the technology of programmed instruction has shown signs of surviving the justifiable criticism of that frantic period of the early 1960's when most programs were being written (and sold) by non-qualified opportunists.

With the return to popularity of auto-instruction, as it is frequently referred to now, comes renewed interest in historical aspects of this approach to learning. Numerous references in historical accounts of early educators indicate that programmed instruction also had a "grand-daddy." Who should get credit for this honor, however, is speculative.

In Skinnerian terms, programmed instruction is a means by which a student 1) may be presented material to be learned in sequential order, whereby 2) he can respond overtly to the material, and 3) receive immediate feedback (awareness of results) with respect to the adequacy of his response. The basic characteristic of programmed instruction (with or without a mechanical device) is the interaction which occurs between the student and the material to be learned. Based on reinforcement theory, programmed instruction provides a means by which the learner becomes aware of the correctness of his response. While somewhat sketchy, this description of programmed or auto-instruction should be sufficient to make relevant the following historical examples of early educators who were on the threshold of programming instruction.

Quintilian (35-100 A.D.) developed a technique for training students in writing the alphabet. He grooved the letters on a board, and the neophyte student traced the letters in guided fashion. With the teacher's minor assistance, this procedure fulfills the criterion of a teaching machine, and thus pushes back the likelihood of the first teaching machine to the time of Christ.

In Book I of his **De Institutione Oratora,** Quintilian recommended the following:

As soon as the child has begun to know the shapes of the various letters, it will be no bad thing to have them cut as accurately as possible upon a board, so that the pen may be guided along the grooves. Thus mistakes such as occur with wax tablets will be rendered impossible; for the pen will be confined between the edges of the letters and will be prevented from going astray.[3]

Quintilian emphasized the fact that different natures demand different treatments, and urged that teachers study the dispositions of their pupils.

Central to almost all current psychological theories of learning is the principle of reinforcement. Behavior which is rewarded or reinforced is more likely to occur again when a situation arises which is similar to the one in which the behavior first occurred. Knowledge of results is one of the most effective reinforcers for human beings, and in auto-instruction an essential feature is the immediacy of the student's feedback. The student "knows" he is right, for example, and gets reinforcement from knowing.

While this complex topic is still not completely settled by present-day educational psychologists, most students of reinforcement theory will appreciate the insightful remarks of Plutarch (46-120 A.D.) who wrote in "The Education of Children" (Volume I of Plutarch's **Moralia):**

. . . Praise and reproof are more helpful for the free-born than any sort of ill-usage, since the praise incites them toward what is honorable, and reproof keeps them from what is disgraceful.[4]

One of the first educators to stipulate the conditions for learning in the language of auto-instruction was Comenius (1592-1670 A.D.). In **The Great Didactic** Comenius included among his postulates for teaching and learning:

Seventh postulate: Nature does not skip but proceeds evenly. . . . Therefore in the future:

1. The totality of studies ought to be classified so that each step prepares for the next one . . .[5]

In his chapter on "Requisites for easy teaching and learning," Comenius specifies:

. . . we will succeed if we follow in the steps of nature. This means that instruction:

3. . . . must proceed from the general to particular, and

4. From the easier to the more difficult.

5. Progress must not be rushed.

6. The minds must not be forced to do anything but that to which they aspire according to their age and motivation.

7. Everything must be related through sense impression, if possible.

8. Everything must be applied immediately . . .[6]

Monroe[7] highlights another of Comenius' statements:

The object of study must be a real, true, useful thing, capable of making an impression upon the senses and the apprehension. This is necessary that it may be brought into communication with the senses; if visible, with the eyes; if audible, with the ears; if odorous, with the nose; if sapid, with the taste; if tangible, with the touch. The beginning of knowledge must be with the senses.

In "Some Thoughts on Education," John Locke (1632-1704 A.D.) is reported by Ulich[8] to have written:

. . . Much less are children capable of reasoning from remote principles. They cannot conceive the force of long deductions; the reasons that move them must be obvious, and level to their thoughts, and such as may, (if I may so say), be felt and touched.

In **Emile, or A Treatise of Education,** Jean Jacques Rousseau (1712-1778 A.D.) wrote:

The sciences are connected together by a series of propositions, all dependent on some general and common principles, which are gradually displayed. The philosophers make use of these; with us they are as yet out of the question. There is another chain of reasoning, of a different construction, by which every particular object is connected to some other, and points out that which succeeds it. This order of succession, which, from our natural curiosity, keeps alive our attention, is generally made use of by grown persons, and is peculiarly adapted to children.[9]

A forerunner of the teaching machine was devised by Johann Bernhard Basedow (1723-1790 A.D.) who used the back side of a blackboard for the missing word in a sentence, much in the same way that some modern linear programs require the student to look elsewhere for visual reinforcement.

A more elaborate teaching machine was used for the training — and amusement — of knights in the Middle Ages. Called a **quintain,**[10] it varied in style but in general was a figure of a swordsman mounted on a pivot. In one hand was a sword or other flailing instrument, and in the other hand, a shield which served as a target. The horseman tilting at the quintain with his lance had to strike the shield squarely in the center. Otherwise, the quintain would pivot quickly, and slap the knight with his sword as he raced by. The negative reinforcement served as a strong inducement to improve the knight's performance.

While the quintain can be called a teaching machine, many early teaching devices cannot. The abacus, for example, does not provide for sequential steps in its use, nor does it allow for immediate feedback. The patented devices reported by Mellan[11] would not qualify in most cases. Some, such as the device for teaching spelling patented by Halcyon Skinner in 1866 (Patent No. 52758), do not provide immediate feedback. To check on the other 300 patents which were issued for educational appliance prior to 1910 requires a substantial investment in time and money.

On February 16, 1809, H. Chard received a United States patent on a device for which he bequeathed the title, "A Mode of Teaching to Read." Shortly after, S. Randall received two patents on a teaching device described as "A Mode of Teaching to Write." T. Weston filed for a patent on June 26, 1812, to protect his invention, "Plummets of Lead in Teaching Writing." A device for teaching geography and astrography was patented in 1842; and in 1846, a mechanism for teaching arithmetic.

One might just as well speculate on the teaching devices that John Henry Pestalozzi (1746-1827 A.D.) could have created, had he been so inclined. His writings[12] disclose an appreciation for the small, sequential steps that characterize individualized instruction:

4. In every department instruction must begin with the simplest elements, and starting from these must be carried on step by step according to the development of the child; that is, it must be brought into psychological sequence.

5. At each point the instructor shall not go forward till that part of the subject has become the proper intellectual possession of the learner.

6. Instruction must follow the path of development, not the path of lecturing, teaching, or telling.

7. To the educator, the individuality of the child must be sacred.

Madame Maria Montessori (1869-1952) borrowed a page from Quintilian's method of teaching children to write letters of the alphabet. Emphasizing sensory perception, she substituted sand paper for grooves in wood. With eyes closed, a young student would trace the letters of the alphabet with the tip of his finger. While not an elaborate device, it provides opportunity for sequential presentation of material, overt response to the material, and immediate feedback with respect to the adequacy of the response — the criteria for describing a teaching machine.

In addition, Montessori borrowed ideas from the French physician, E. Sequin, and the German educator, Friedrich Froebel, by her own admission,[13] to develop other teaching devices, obtaining a patent (No. 1103369) on one of them in 1914. Cylindrical pieces of varying dimensions are placed in appropriate holes by the student. If he makes a mistake, the materials tell him about it automatically. Sloppiness of fit or something which will not fit in a remaining hole gives immediate feedback to the student. Variations in shapes of blocks of wood extend this technique to greater degrees of difficulty, accentuating sensory acuity, particularly **visual,** which Montessori felt was a sadly neglected sense in most learning processes in other schools.

In 1912, Thorndike developed a plan that might have led to auto-instruction as it was later introduced by Skinner and his followers. Said Thorndike[14]:

If, by a miracle of mechanical ingenuity, a book could be so arranged that only to him who had done what was directed on page one would page two become visible, and so on, much that now requires personal instruction could be managed by print.

This was the philosophy of the programmed textbook which hit the educational scene a half century later. Since all three elements of a teaching machine definition (sequential order, overt response, and immediacy of feedback) are included in the programmed textbook, the latter receives the same accord as any mechanical device which also passes the criterion test of definition.

It is not the purpose of this article to mention all the countless contributors to programmed instruction. An excellent resource on the history of the movement is provided by Lumsdaine and Glaser,[15] and it is recommended to those readers who wish to learn about more recent advocates of the technology, such as Sidney L. Pressey and Norman A. Crowder, as well the work of B. F. Skinner. Perhaps the references herein cointained will serve to disclose the reasons why it is difficult to label any early educator as "the forerunner of programmed instruction." ☐

References

1. Ibert Mellan. Teaching and Educational Inventions. **Teaching Machines and Programmed Learning** (A. A. Lumsdaine and Robert Glaser, Editors), National Education Association, 1960; pp. 265-274. (Reprinted from **Journal of Experimental Education,** Vol. 4, March, 1936, with minor changes in format.)

2. B. F. Skinner. The Science of Learning and the Art of Teaching. **Harvard Educational Review,** Vol. 24, No. 2, 1954. (Reprinted in Lumsdaine and Glaser, previous reference, pp. 99-113.)

3. Elmer H. Wilds and Kenneth V. Lottich. **The Foundations of Modern Education.** New York: Holt, Rinehart and Winston, 1966, p. 95.

4. Robert Ulich. **Three Thousand Years of Educational Wisdom.** Cambridge: Harvard University Press, 1965, p. 90.

5. **Ibid.,** pp. 344.

6. **Ibid.,** pp. 344-346.

7. Will S. Monroe. Comenius, The Evangelist of Modern Pedagogy. **December Education,** 1892.

8. Ulich, **op cit.,** p. 364.

9. Ulich, **op. cit.,** p. 410.

10. A facsimile of a miniature painting of a quintain appears in Paul Lacroix's **Military and Religious Life in the Middle Ages.** London: Chapman and Hall, 1874, p. 145. For a complete description of a quintain in one of its many variations, see T. H. White, **The Once and Future King,** London: Collins, St. James Place, 1958, p. 54.

11. Mellan, **loc. cit.**

12. As summarized in R. H. Quick. **Essays on Educational Reformers.** New York: Appleton, 1897, p. 369.

13. Maria Montessori. **The Montessori Method.** New York: Schocken Books, 1964 (first published in 1912, translated from Italian by Ann E. George).

14. Edward L. Thorndike. **Education.** New York: Macmillan Company, 1912, p. 165.

15. A A. Lumsdaine and Robert Glaser (Eds.). **Teaching Machines and Programmed Learning: A Source Book.** Washington, D. C.: Department of Audio-Visual Instruction, National Education Association, 1960.

Costs of Automated Instruction in Higher Education

Harold S. Sloan

Now that automated instruction is moving into the schools and taking over the teaching of regularly scheduled courses, it is time to think about **costs.**

Many private colleges and universities are facing financial difficulties. In 1967, one estimate put the combined 1968 deficit of 20 of the wealthiest colleges in the country at $3 million, and, if the present trends continue, a deficit of $45 million four years hence is anticipated.

President Etherington of Wesleyan University gave credence to this estimate last winter when he told the Economics Club of Greater Hartford that "even in New England, where the thought is unthinkable, these institutions [independent colleges] have been dipping — sometimes gouging — into capital."

Teaching methods in higher education have not changed materially in years — some would say since the Middle Ages — while increased productivity has characterized nearly every other phase of American life. But now we must ask whether automated instruction can not only increase the effectiveness of teaching, but also its **efficiency** as expressed in instructional costs, thus relieving, to some extent, the financial pressure felt by private institutions of higher education. The answer requires a **quantitative** measure.

An instructional cost index

Consider conventional teaching first. In 1965, Dr. Harold Feldman made an exhaustive study of instructional costs at Fairleigh Dickinson University in New Jersey by calculating the ratio of expense to

Harold S. Sloan is president of the Institute for Instructional Improvement, New York.

income of every class or class section throughout the University. Expense was calculated on the basis of the instructor's salary and the percentage of his time devoted to a class; income was considered the amount of tuition derived from the class.

These relationships might be expressed in a generalized formula such as

$$P = \frac{A/2 \times C/B}{abc}$$

when:

P = percent of tuition income devoted to instruction.

A = annual salary of the instructor (2 semesters).

B = instructor's maximum teaching hours per week.

C = instructor hours per week devoted to course under consideration.

a = tuition per credit hour, or point (one hour per week per semester).

b = number of students attending the course under consideration.

c = credit hours or points assigned to the course under consideration.

The instructor's salary, per semester, calculated at half of his annual salary, or A/2; the proportion of the instructor's time devoted to the class in question is the number of weekly hour meetings of the class, divided by the instructor's total weekly hour teaching load, or C/B. The instructional cost, therefore, is the proportion of the instructor's time devoted to the course, times the instructor's semester salary, or A/2 x C/B.

The semester tuition income, yielded by the class, is the tuition per hour credit or "point," times the number of credit hours or "points" assigned the class, times the number of students in the class, or abc.

The per cent of tuition income devoted to instruction, therefore, is A/2 x C/B divided by abc.

Example: An instructor, teaching 15 hours a week at a salary of $12,000 for 2 semesters, teaches a class of 60 students in 3 sections of 20 students each. Each section meets 3 hours a week, and the course earns 3 credit hours. The tuition is $33.00 per credit hour.

A = $12,000 instructor's salary (2 semesters).

B = 15 hours, instructor's teaching load per week.

C = 9 hours, instructor hours per week devoted to course in question; 3 sections, each meeting 3 times a week.

a = $33.00 tuition per credit hour.

b = 60, number of students taking the course.

c = 3, credit hours assigned to the course

$$P = \frac{A/2 \times C/B}{abc} = \frac{12,000/2 \times 9/15}{33 \times 60 \times 3} = \frac{3600}{5940} = .606$$

The proportion of tuition income devoted to instructional expense, then, is .606. It might be called an instructional cost index.

Many indices, of course, will be over 100. Even a high tuition university expects loss areas. A low tuition institution will have more, and a free tuition institution will have nothing else.

Automated instruction

The basic formula applicable to conventional teaching can easily be extended to apply to automated instruction by adding the percentage of **machine** time, absorbed by a given class, to the percentage of the instructor's time assigned to the same class as follows:

$$P = \frac{(A/2 \times C/B) + C'/B' \,(A'/2 \times D)}{abc}$$

when (as before)

P = per cent of tuition income devoted to instruction.

A = annual salary of the instructor (2 semesters).

B = instructor's maximum teaching hours per week.

C = instructor hours per week devoted to course under consideration.

a = tuition per credit hour, or point (one hour per week per semester).

b = number of students attending the course under consideration.

c = credit hours or points assigned to the course under consideration.

and when (as added)

A' = cost of one machine per year.

B' = total possible machine use in hours per week. (This is computed as 45 hours; 3 hours in the morning, 3 hours in the afternoon and 3 hours in the evening for 5 days.)

C' = machine use-hours devoted to the course in question.

D = number of machines.

Just as the proportion of the instructor's weekly teaching load (15 hours) is allocated to a given class, so the proportion of total weekly time that the machines are available for use (estimated at 45 hours) must be allocated to a given class using the machines. This is represented in the equation by C'/B'. And just as the proportion of the instructor's time allocated to a given class absorbs that same proportion of his salary, so the proportion of machine time allocated to a given class absorbs that same proportion of the machine cost. This is represented by A'/2 multiplied by the number of machines represented by D.

Example: This is the same as the former one except that the 3 sections of 20 students each, meeting 3 hours a week, use machines, and the instructor is available 3 hours a week for personal conferences with students who require his help. Thus, while the students are in "class" 9 hours a week, the instructor is available 3 of these 9 hours. The machine cost is estimated at $45.00 a month for each machine, the actual cost of one widely used machine.

A = $12,000 instructor's salary (2 semesters).

B = 15 hours, instructor's teaching load per week.

C = 3, instructor hours per week for course in question.

a = $33.00 tuition per credit hour.

b = 60, number of students taking course.

c = 3, credit hours assigned to course.

A' = $540.00 cost of one machine per year (12 x $45.00)

B' = 45, total possible machine use hours per week.

C' = 9, machine use hours devoted to course in question.

D = 20, number of machines.

$$P = \frac{(12,000/2 \times 3/15) + 9/45 \times (540/2 \times 20)}{abc} = \frac{1,200 + 1,080}{5940} = \frac{2,280}{5940} = .384$$

index of instructional costs.

Through the use of machines, then, the cost level has been decreased from .606 to .384. A comparison of the two examples indicates that, while the tuition income has remained the same, the instructional expense has been reduced by $1,320 (3,600 — 2,280). This is accounted for by a savings in the instructor's time of 6 hours (9 — 3 = 6), amounting in expense to 6/15 of $6,000 or $2,400, from which must be deducted a machine expense of $1,080 ($2,400 — $1,080 = $1,320).

It should be noted that this saving is effected only if the machines are used to the full extent of their capacity (figured at 45 hours a week), and if the saving of the instructor's time is scheduled for other teaching duties.

The formulas may, if desired, be altered to include other related costs and income. Fringe benefits, for example, might be added as a percentage to an instructor's salary. In a similar manner, the cost of monitors and technicians, if any, as well as maintenance and depreciation, might be treated as overhead and added to machine costs. On the income side, student fees might be added to tuition.

Thus far, little has been done to combat rising instructional costs except to advance tuition and fees. During the last decade (1959-1969), private colleges and universities have raised tuition and fees by over two and one half times the percentage increase in the consumer price index for the same period. This is a hardship on most families, and many educators are of the opinion that a ceiling is near. If so, an effective and carefully measured program of automated instruction might mean survival. □

Using the S-R Reinforcement Model

Robert E. Silverman
Contributing Editor

I have previously stated that behavior-science models can be a basis for a technology of instruction in that such models can assist in translating principles derived from laboratory studies of learning into principles of teaching (**Educational Technology** April 15, 1966 and October 15, 1967).

The purpose of this article is to depict how one model, the S-R reinforcement model, can be used in designing an instructional plan. The model will be described and then its use will be illustrated in terms of the problem of teaching ninth-grade students the metric system for measuring length.

THE MODEL

The S-R reinforcement model consists of a particular form of behavioral analysis in which behavior is represented in terms of the association between stimuli (S) and responses (R), and learning is represented in terms of the systematic changes in S-R associations that occur when reinforcements are appropriately correlated with responses. The term reinforcement refers to the events that strengthen responses.

A positive reinforcer is any event that increases the likelihood of the responses that lead to it. Food, money, praise, a smile, getting a "gadget" to work are all examples of possible positive reinforcers.

A negative reinforcer is any event whose termination will strengthen behavior. The reduction of pain or discomfort is negatively reinforcing. A person will generally learn to make responses that enable him to escape discomfort or the threat of discomfort. Thus, escape from the threat of punishment is negatively reinforcing.

It should be noted that the term reinforcement is a general one including in its meaning the concept of reward, for rewards are positive reinforcers.

The S-R reinforcement model leads to an analysis of instruction in terms of certain fundamental factors in learning. The model calls attention to responses, reinforcements and stimuli and in so doing it indicates three essentials for learning: **(1)** The learner must make the response he is to learn. He learns what he does. **(2)** The responses must be strengthened. Learning progresses as the responses in question are reinforced and increase in probability. **(3)** The responses should be put under the control of particular stimuli; these stimuli will set the occasion for the occurence of the responses.

It is of little value for a student to learn the name Napoleon Bonaparte unless he can give the response in the presence of such relevant stimuli as —"Who was the powerful Emperor of France during the first decade of the nineteenth century?" The question, in this case, is the stimulus that sets the occasion for the response.

The essential conditions of learning indicated by the model give rise to particular questions, and it is the answers to these questions that help in the solution of an instructional problem. The kinds of questions generated by the model are presented below. The questions are classified in terms of their relationship to response, reinforcement and stimulus factors.

Responses

1. What are the responses to be learned?

The identification of the responses is crucial if the teaching processes are to be effective. The learner acquires the behavior that happens to be occurring when reinforcement is given, whether or not this is the behavior that the teacher is trying to strengthen.

If many of the learner's responses are inappropriate, care must be taken to reinforce selectively only those responses that are deemed appropriate. The fact that the human is verbal and that much of his behavior is covert complicates the question, but it does not prevent its being answered. The best approach is to require as much overt activity as possible.

2. Are the responses to be learned already in the learner's repertoire of responses or are they novel and unfamiliar responses?

For example, if the student is to learn to identify and label a diagram of the human eye, he must be able to use the appropriate technical terms such as cornea, iris, lens, conjunctiva, retina, etc. Where the terms are unfamiliar, prior experience with them in the form of familiarization practice will be helpful.

The model does not directly indicate techniques for solving such problems as familiarization training. It serves more as a tool of analysis rather than a producer of techniques. However, the emphasis on response, reinforcement and stimulus does point the way to possible techniques, some of which will be discussed below.

3. What are the best ways to get the appropriate responses to occur?

A basic condition of teaching is to ensure the occurrence of the appropriate responses. Very often the appropriate responses are evoked by direct guidance or prompting, the so-called "tell-and-do" method. In some fashion, the learner is shown how to make the response.

For example, his hand may be guided by the teacher as he prints a letter, or he is given the problem with the answer and asked to copy it, or he is given the rules for solving the problem and then required to solve it, and so forth.

A less direct but sometimes more effective method of getting the responses to occur involves allowing the learner to respond freely in a setting designed to encourage the appropriate responses and selectively rewarding approximations of the correct responses as they occur.

For example, in teaching a child to say a new word such as "brother" the child is encouraged to make vocal responses. Each time he makes a response approximating the sound of "brother" he is rewarded. The standard for reward is gradually raised and by successive approximations the child is taught to say the word properly. Of course, the process can be shortened by providing the child with guidance in the form of a model to imitate. In that way the probability of his making appropriate vocal sounds is increased.

4. What responses might compete with the responses to be learned?

The model indicates that competition among responses will retard learning. If two or more responses share a situation, the likelihood of any one of them occuring is consequently reduced.

For example, an English-speaking person learning to speak French has in his repertoire many pronunciation responses that compete with correct French pronunciation. Such a person often must suppress certain well established responses in order to pronounce a word like "Saint-Cloud" in French. His initial tendency is to say "sant klaud" and it is only with difficulty he learns to substitute the correct French pronunciation "san klu."

5. What can be done to reduce the probability of competing responses?

A simple answer to this question is, prevent competing responses from occurring. This may be done by providing sufficient guidance to evoke only the appropriate responses and then selectively reinforcing these responses. In certain kinds of learning situations that is good advice. But very often, guidance is not sufficient, particularly when the competing responses are very strong.

When competing responses are strong, they must be extinguished and replaced by the appro-

priate responses. The process of extinction involves withholding reinforcement. The presentation of reinforcement makes responses more likely to occur, while the withholding of reinforcement extinguishes them, that is, makes them less likely to occur.

In the example above dealing with the pronunciation of Saint-Cloud, extinguishing the wrong responses would entail having the student respond to the printed words in such a way that each time he said "san klu" he would be rewarded, and each time he gave the English pronunciation, reward would be withheld.

Another approach would be to punish competing responses. For example, when Saint Cloud is mispronounced, the student is punished and when it is correctly pronounced he is rewarded. If punishment is to be an effective suppressor, it must be strong. However, strong punishment introduces undesirable factors into a learning situation, often making the situation aversive by evoking emotional responses which may in turn provide another source of competing responses.

Reinforcement

1. What reinforcers will effectively strengthen the responses to be learned?

The practical management of learning involves controlling reinforcing events, for these events play a critical role in determining whether or not a response will increase in frequency. While a major feature of the model is the principle of reinforcement, the model does not identify reinforcers for us. Many of these are well known and others can be identified by systematic observation.

We do know that praise, knowledge of having made a correct response, certain tangible items and particular symbols do prove to be effective reinforcers in a variety of teaching-learning situations.

The effectiveness of each of these may vary from situation to situation and from learner to learner, but in general, one of these or some combination will reinforce responses.

2. How can reinforcers be most effectively used?

The model does tell us how to use reinforcers effectively and how to increase the effectiveness of reinforcing events by identifying three factors:

(a) The Delay of Reinforcement. Reinforcers are most effective when they are given immediately. Learning will be grossly retarded, or will not occur at all, if the learner is not reinforced at the time he makes the correct response. If reinforcement is delayed, some responses other than the correct one may be reinforced.

Teaching machines and programmed instruction were developed to provide an effective means for the immediate presentation of reinforcement. One of the key features of programmed instruction is the immediate feedback given to the learner. If the feedback informs the learner that he is responding correctly it serves as positive reinforcement, in-

creasing the likelihood he will make that particular response again under the same circumstances.

(b) The Quantity of Reinforcement. The quantity factor is related to the question of motivation. The incentive value of a reinforcer depends on the learner's experience with the reinforcer in question. For a positive reinforcer to have a high incentive value, the learner must have had ample experience being reinforced by it and at the time of learning be deprived of it.

A small quantity of reward can be very effective if the learner has experienced such rewards and is now deprived of them, while a large reward can be ineffective if the learner has been satiated with the reward. Mild praise can be strongly reinforcing to a student whose failures have been outnumbering his successes, while high praise may be ineffective for a student who is constantly achieving honors.

(c) The Frequency and Schedule of Reinforcement. The frequency with which a response is reinforced determines, in part, how well the response will be learned. In the early stages of learning, every correct response should be immediately reinforced. However, as the responses gain strength they can be reinforced intermittently: Some of the correct responses are reinforced and others are not. When this procedure is carefully followed, it is possible to maintain responses at a high strength by reinforcing them occasionally. Intermittent reinforcement schedules generally lead to a high rate of responding once the response is well established. Furthermore, responses that have been maintained on an intermittent schedule, show greater resistance to extinc-tion than responses that have been continuously reinforced.

Stimuli

1. What stimuli are to control the responses? Another way to put this question is — What discriminations must the learner make in order to respond appropriately?

It is necessary to identify responses in order to teach them, and it is necessary to identify stimuli precisely in order to associate them with particular responses. If a learning task requires students to do something in response to an auditory signal, the characteristics of the signal must be considered and care must be taken to ensure that the signal is actually a stimulus. In other words, a signal is a stimulus only when it is apprehended. An auditory signal that is not heard does not stimulate a response; a visual cue that cannot be seen serves no stimulus function; a question that is not understood cannot stimulate the response of answering.

2. How should stimuli be associated with responses?

Teaching discriminations requires careful observation of the attention-provoking features of stimuli. The stimuli must capture the learner's attention if he is to learn to associate them with particular responses.

The actual association is carried out by pairing a particular stimulus with a response in the presence of some form of reinforcement. When this is done, the stimulus comes to set the occasion for the response, that is, it informs the learner that it is time to make a particular response and to be reinforced by doing so.

For example, a student learns to associate Pierre with North Dakota and Bismarck with South Dakota by first being reinforced for making the response "Pierre" to the stimulus, "What is the capital of North Dakota?" The question is the stimulus that sets the occasion for the response, and the correct response is, in turn, reinforced. An incorrect response, for example, "Bismarck," is not reinforced. The response of saying "Bismarck" to South Dakota is learned in a similar manner; it is reinforced in the presence of the question about the capital of South Dakota.

The key to discrimination learning involves the pairing of a stimulus with a response and seeing to it that the association of the particular stimulus and response leads to reinforcement. The stimulus in question is referred to as a discriminative stimulus. The question, "What is the capital of North Dakota?" is a discriminative stimulus for the response, "Pierre;" the question, "What is the speed of sound in air?" is a discriminative stimulus for the response, "1100 feet per second;" and so forth.

3. How can potentially interfering stimuli be controlled?

The best way to reduce interference from other stimuli is to arrange the conditions of learning in a setting that is as free as possible from distracting or interfering events. However, this may be difficult or impossible to do, particularly when the source of interference is related to the learning material itself.

When this is the case, it is necessary to increase the attention provoking properties of the relevant stimuli.

For example, in teaching a child to say "dee" when he sees the letter **d,** care must be taken to reduce interference from the letter **b**. One way to do this is to call attention to the differences between the two letters at the outset of discrimination training by showing the loop of the **d** in red and by exaggerating the size of the loop. The size and color prompts can then be gradually eliminated as the child learns to make the appropriate response "dee" to **d**. In the technical language of programmed instruction, this technique is referred to as "vanishing" or "fading" of prompts.

Techniques of establishing stimulus control have played a large role in the development of educational technology. The need for special visual media such as motion pictures and television, and for special auditory media such as tape recordings, records and the language laboratory systems is a function of the stimulus characteristics of the material to be learned.

The question of motivation

The S-R reinforcement model does not generate separate questions about the process of motivation,

but questions about motivation are considered in dealing with reinforcement. A learner must be sufficiently motivated to work for reinforcers.

In this sense, motivation is virtually equated with deprivation in the case of positive reinforcement, or with the presentation of aversive events in the case of negative reinforcement. A poorly motivated learner is simply one for whom few if any reinforcers are effective; a highly motivated learner is one for whom a particular reinforcer or a variety of reinforcers is effective.

Another way to state this is: It is difficult to teach an unmotivated student because he is not responsive to reinforcement, while it is easy to teach a motivated student, because he is responsive to reinforcement.

THE MODEL IN USE

Consider the problem of teaching ninth-grade students the units of length in the metric system of measurement. The analysis of this problem is shown below in terms of answers to the questions generated by the S-R reinforcement model. These questions are summarized in **Table 1** as questions of analysis and questions of implementation.

The analysis questions are dealt with first and then consideration is given to the implementation in terms of response, reinforcement and stimulus factors.

Analysis: responses

Responses to be learned. The responses to be learned include the following:

(a) Labelling responses. These include in terms of decimal equivalents the metric measures: millimeter (mm), centimeter (cm), decimeters (dm), meters (m), and kilometers (km), including the current spelling of the words and the correct usage of their abbreviations.

(b) Converting millimeters to centimeters, centimeters to decimeters, decimeters to meters, meters to kilometers; and converting centimeters to millimeters, decimeters to centimeters, etc.; and adding metric units, for example 3 mm plus 19 cm plus 6.3 m.

(c) Measuring length using a ruler 30 cm long, marked off in cm and mm. The measures are to be expressed in the appropriate whole unit with fractional amounts expressed in decimal terms, for example, 4.5 cm, or 6.8 m, or 3 mm.

(d) Converting each of the metric measures into the English system and vice versa. For example, convert 32 m into feet and convert 17 inches into cm.

Familiarity. Some responses are unfamiliar. Words like decimeter (dm) and kilometer (km) may require familiarization training.

Sources of Response Competition. The responses, one thousand to the stimulus kilo and one thousand**th** to the stimulus milli will compete with each other.

Analysis: reinforcement

The model does not identify reinforcers per se. It merely calls attention to the requirement that responses must be reinforced if they are to be strengthened. The implementation of reinforcement is handled by the model and is discussed below.

Analysis: stimuli

The relevant stimuli include the following:

(a) The words themselves and their abbreviations. Centimeter is a response, but it is also a stimulus. For example, "How many centimeters are there in an inch?" is a stimulus, setting the occasion for the response, "2.54 cm."

(b) Fractions or decimals such as 5/10 cm or .1 m

(c) scale readings on a metric ruler, for example

(d) English measures such as inch, foot, yard, mile.

Implementation:

(a) The Labelling Responses:

Familiarization of responses. A safe assumption is that some, if not all, of the words are unfamiliar and require familiarization training, often referred to as response training. This training consists of exposing the learner to written material in which he sees and reads these words in a meaningful context. For example, the learner may be given the following paragraph with instructions to read it and to try to answer the question that follows it:

Bill carefully measured the table and found it 78 centimeters (cm) wide and 2.3 meters (m) long. His friend, John, lived 1 kilometer (km) away and he did not wish to carry the table that distance only to find it would not fit through John's doorway. He telephoned John and was told the doorway measured 7.5 decimeters (dm) wide by 2,290 millimeters (mm) high.

Question: Would the table fit through John's doorway?

Hints: A decimeter (dm) is 10 centimeters (cm).
A meter (m) is 100 cm.
A millimeter (mm) is 1/1000 of a m.

Evoking the responses to be learned. The labelling responses may be initially evoked by means of prompts and then reinforced by arranging question-and-answer sequences using confirmation of correct responses (positive feedback) as the immediate reinforcer. For example, to teach the response **centimeter** the following item may be presented visually or auditorily:

Table 1

Questions Generated by the S-R Reinforcement Model of Teaching

RESPONSES

Analysis

1. What are the responses to be learned?

2. Are these novel or familiar to the learner?

5. What responses may compete?

Implementation

3. How is the learner to become familiar with the response?

4. How are the appropriate responses to be evoked?

6. How can response-competition be reduced?

REINFORCEMENT

Analysis

1. What reinforcers are likely to be effective?

Implementation

2. How are these reinforcers to be applied?

STIMULI

Analysis

1. What are the relevant stimuli?

Implementation

2. How shall they be associated with the appropriate responses?

3. How shall interfering stimuli be controlled?

A meter can be divided into 100 parts; each of these parts is called a **centi**meter. A cent is 1/100 of a dollar and a ....meter is 1/100 of a meter.

In the above item the response "centi" is prompted by the underlining of centimeter when the word is first presented, and by reference to cent. The reinforcing event is seeing or hearing the correct response and confirming that one's own response was correct.

Associating the relevant stimuli with the appropriate responses. To get the response **centimeter** to occur at a proper time in the proper context, it must be associated with relevant stimuli, for example, 1/100 of a meter or 10 millimeters, or .1 decimeter. The following item illustrates the procedure:

1/100 of a meter is a ...., and 1/100 of a dollar is a cent.

In the above item a prompt (cent) is still present to ensure the response centimeter in the presence of the stimulus 1/100 of a meter. When prompts are given, the correct response is easily forthcoming and consequently the confirmation of the correct response is less reinforcing than it would be for a more challenging question such as the following:

There are 100 .... in a meter.

The abbreviation for centimeter can be taught using essentially the same type of approach: evoke it using prompts, reinforce it, associate it with the relevant stimuli and reinforce the association. The following items illustrate how this could be done:

(1) The abbreviation for **centi**meter involves the c for centi and the m for meter. Give the abbreviation for centimeter.

(2) 3/100 of a meter is equal to 3 ...... (use abbreviation).

The reader will recognize the above items as examples of one of the programmed instruction methods, a method derived from the S-R reinforcement model.

The same general approach described above may be used to elicit the responses **decimeter** and **kilometer** and to associate them with the relevant controlling stimuli. However, a special problem arises in the case of teaching millimeter because of response competition between the responses one thousand to the stimulus kilo and the response one thousand**th** to the stimulus milli.

This response competition may be reduced by exaggerating or dramatizing the differences between the two responses, between the stimuli and between the stimulus-response associations.

The responses can be differentiated best by initially requiring that they be made in decimal form, for example, 1000 and .001. The two stimulus-response associations can be differentiated by giving them certain distinguishing characteristics.

For example, since kilo refers to the large unit, it may be shown in large block letters, KILO; and milli, because it refers to the small unit, may be shown in small letters, milli. The size of the letters is a prompt, enabling the learner to recognize that one calls for a large number and the other for a small number.

The purpose of such an artifice is to maximize the probability the learner will not confuse the two associations and make the wrong response to either stimulus. According to the model, the learner learns what he does, and if he makes errors, they will be learned and later have to be extinguished.

In teaching discriminations, it is useful to keep in mind the rule that learner errors are to be avoided. Where errors occur and are difficult to avoid, as might be the case in teaching the pronunciation of Saint-Cloud, steps must be taken to extinguish the competing responses.

(b) Converting Metric Units into Other Metric Units and Adding Metric Units:

The responses of converting metric units into other metric units and adding metric units are essentially the same as those involved in identifying the decimal equivalents of the metric units.

Once these decimal equivalents are learned, they can be used to mediate in the chain of responses required to convert or add units.

A student can quickly learn that a dm consists of 10 cm after he has learned that 1 mm is .1 cm, or that 1 cm is .01 m and 1 mm is .001 m. Of course, if the student cannot work with decimal numbers, he will not see the relationships. In this case, the teaching task would be a much larger one, beginning with instruction in fractions and decimals.

(c) Measuring Length:

The responses of measuring length are to be associated with the stimuli of the scale readings on a metric ruler. It will be assumed that the students are familiar with English-unit rulers, so no familiarization training is required.

The task entails making measurements by reading them from a metric scale to the nearest whole unit. This is effectively done in two stages: In the first stage, the student merely measures a number of lines comparing his measurements with those that are provided for feedback. In the second stage, more interesting tasks are used, and consequently the reinforcing effects of confirming correct responses is stronger.

A sample task might be the following:
Line A is 4.6 cm long. Guess the length of line B and write it here ....
Now measure line B to see how accurate your guess was.

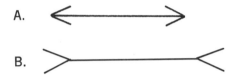

(d) Converting Metric Units into English Units and English into Metric:

Learning to convert metric units into English units is a straightforward association task. The metric units serve as stimuli and the English units as the responses. For example, the students are taught to give the response ".39 inches" to the stimulus, "How many inches are there in 1 cm?"

In this type of task, sequence can be important. The order in which the material is presented can be a source of interference, or, if properly used, it can be put to advantage.

In this conversion task, the optimal sequence would involve rank-ordering the responses from smallest to largest in the following manner: 1 cm = .39 inches, 1 m = 39.37 inches, and 1 km = .62 miles.

Learning the reverse conversion requires only one item: 1 inch = 2.54 cm.

There is nothing gained by requiring the student to memorize the metric equivalent for foot, yard, and mile.

Actually, this additional memorization would be disadvantageous, because the additional associations introduce a needless source of additional interference. The conversions for foot, yard, and mile are easily calculated once the student has learned the metric equivalent for an inch.

THE MODEL AND RETENTION AND TRANSFER OF LEARNING

The problems associated with teaching are interwoven with questions about the retention and trans-

fer of learning. Any model that purports to deal with learning must, if it is to prove useful, deal also with the conditions that affect retention and transfer.

In terms of the S-R reinforcement model, questions about retention become questions about the conditions that control and maintain responses. Since responses are put under the control of particular stimuli and the occurrence of the responses in the presence of these stimuli depends on reinforcement, our attention is directed to stimulus factors and reinforcement factors. These factors lead to three general principles relating to methods of increasing retention.

(1) Retention can be increased by using intermittent schedules of reinforcement to maintain the responses once they are learned.

For example, a response that is reinforced on an average of 7 out of 10 times after it is learned persists for a longer period after reinforcement has been terminated, than one which has been continuously reinforced, that is, every 10 out of 10 times.

(2) Retention is increased by increasing the number and variety of stimuli associated with a particular response. This may be done by having the learner relate what he is learning to other stimuli as well as those he is now learning. This procedure may be described as giving the material meaning. It also helps to have the learner practice the responses in a variety of settings so that they do not become limited to a particular setting. The more settings a response is associated with, the greater the chance that the response can be evoked in any setting.

(3) Retention is helped by seeing to it that no new responses are associated with the relevant stimuli between the time of learning and the time of retention testing. If a given stimulus has been associated with a particular response and then another response is paired with that stimulus, the chance of the first response occurring is reduced.

For example, if a student learning a list of state capitals has learned the response Columbus to the stimulus Ohio, and he later learns the response Cleveland to the same stimulus in a slightly different context, the two responses may compete when he is asked to name the capital city of Ohio. While one of the names will emerge, the probability of its being the correct one is reduced by the competition. The competition between the responses interferes with retention of the correct response.

The transfer of learning is critically influenced by the similarity between the learning task and the task to which transfer is being made. If task A is similar to task B in terms of the responses called for, then what is learned in B will transfer positively to B. The responses learned in A will assist in the performancé or the learning of B.

For example, learning the metric units of length will provide positive transfer to learning weight and volume, because the prefix responses have the same meaning: milli is 1/000 whether it precedes meter, gram or liter.

If task A is similar to B in terms of the stimuli, but the responses in the two tasks are different, then A will negatively influence (interfere with) B. For example, learning the French words for the parts of the body will transfer negatively to a task which requires learning the Italian words for these same parts. The stimuli are the same, but many of the responses are different.

THE MODEL AND TECHNOLOGY

An analysis of a teaching problem in terms of the S-R reinforcement model does not lead directly to the use of specific instructional techniques, nor does such an analysis necessarily suggest devices or specialized training aids. Techniques, aids and devices are developed in terms of answers to the questions raised by the language and mode of analysis of the model.

The model tells us to get the responses to occur. To do this effectively a device may be necessary. Devices are particularly useful in presenting prompts and in fading out prompts.

The model tells us to reinforce responses immediately and frequently. To do this we must have either a one to one teacher to student ratio or devise some techniques and/or devices. The reader will recognize the development of teaching machines and programmed instruction in these terms.

The model tells us to identify the relevant stimuli and to associate them with the appropriate responses. To do this, techniques of stimulus presentation are needed, and very often special devices, for example, films, television, recordings, mock-ups, and so forth play an important role.

Self-Instruction in Nursing Education: The Impact of Technology on Professional Curricula

Jerome P. Lysaught
Contributing Editor

There is general agreement among educators and health specialists that the profession of nursing is subjected to incredible pressures, both external and internal. In terms of providing the most fundamental health care to the sick, for example, nursing is caught in the midst of problems which it has not created, but which it cannot avoid. At the same moment when most manpower projections predict a deepening shortage in nursing personnel, the societal demand for extended health provision through Medicare and Medicaid has caused physicians and others to nominate nursing as the pivotal profession that could expand its role to take on tasks traditionally performed by the medical specialist.

In this situation, the very success of the health professions in combating disease and lengthening life expectancy has multiplied the difficulty of caring for the increased population that now requires their services.

Consider, for example, three trends that affect our need for nurses: the increasing number of new births, which represent a real explosion to nurses in obstetrical wards; the growth of a dramatic new field in geriatric nursing and institutional care for the aged as the span of life grows longer; and the newly emphasized concentration on preventive medicine and the inclusion of more and more families in health insurance plans — which raise their expectations and demand for professional care.

Because nursing represents the largest single body of professionals within the health field and the second best educated group in a general comparative sense, it is understandable that many observers look on nurses as the only present hope in what is otherwise an almost insoluble crisis. For example, in the past three years, there have been attempts to develop general pediatric competence among some nurses so that they can function as the primary examiner of children, doing the history-taking, general physical examination, and, indeed, making a fundamental judgment concerning "wellness" or "illness." Each of these activities is normally done by a medical specialist, but many pediatricians view the development of the nurse-pediatric specialist with approval and outright encouragement.

True, there are many problems, and there is far from universal acceptance of this new role and its parameters, but a start has been made. The same development can be seen in the return of the nurse-midwife. While there may be proportionally more questions and more reservations about this form of the nurse-clinician, there are many health professionals who see nurses as the natural group to assume such duties and roles in the face of sharply limited numbers of physicians and rapidly expanding numbers of consumers.

While changing the roles of the nurse may be an understandable and hopeful step toward solving

some of our health problems, it is not easy to accomplish. Nurses are historically a female profession, and their working pattern follows the normative behavior of American women. There are hundreds of thousands of "inactive" nurses, who are engaged in raising their children, caring for their families, managing households — or finding more satisfactory outlets for their energies than following the traditional role of the nurse. There is a great flow in and out of the active profession, resulting in many short and non-continuous periods of service for many individuals — and concomitant problems in re-orientation and re-education.

There is an increased competition for women among the traditional "female occupations" such as teaching and nursing, and the advent of new opportunities for women in business, sales, marketing, administration and public agencies. While definitive data are lacking, it is commonly accepted that the range of choice open to a girl at critical career points is far wider than a generation ago. Relatedly, the common experience with student attrition in nursing preparatory programs suggests that one out

of three entering students will drop out before graduation, and that a high percentage of those who complete their preparation will become inactive within one to three years after entering upon the work phase of their career.

As if these problems were not enough to daunt the most dedicated nurse educator, we must recognize the present flux within the institutions that provide professional instruction. There are, of course, several different paths available as entrees to the field. There are community college programs of two years' duration, hospital programs of three years' length, collegiate programs of four, and even graduate level preparatory programs that involve five or six years of formal preparation. All of these graduates (and there are, of course, many variations on the themes suggested above) qualify for professional admittance on the basis of passing the same examination for the Registered Nurse designation. If this sounds confusing, it is because it is! Moreover, the institutions themselves are changing drastically. Over the past 10 to 15 years, approximately half of the hospital schools of nursing have disappeared. Many closed, some consolidated, others linked hands with academic institutions. Simultaneously, the number of junior college programs in nursing has grown precipitately, frequently outstripping planning, facilities and resources.

Characteristically, schools of nursing face faculty shortages, lack of endowment, a scarcity of institutional support and an image that perhaps can be likened to the academic caricature of the old "normal school" that once represented professional education. Nursing must look forward to the challenges of increased minority representation in its ranks, with attendant educational problems, to the need for rethinking and refocusing its educational patterns, and to the necessity for amassing greater resources and wealth to meet all the other problems. One thing we can say without fear of contradiction is that there is enough work around to keep people usefully engaged over the next several years.

In confronting many of these vexing areas, nursing simply cannot command its own destiny. It must work in cooperation with other establishments and with the public (which is also to say with health consumers). There are some points, however, over which the nursing profession does exercise a great deal of control, and these may in the long run represent the most significant determinants toward attracting and holding persons to the profession. These "points" most certainly include the curriculum and the methods of instruction.

The changing nursing curriculum

With the many difficult problems that they must face, nurse educators have consciously emphasized — more than many other professionals — the need to examine the curriculum and plan effectively for student learning. One indication of this commitment is the requirement that institutions seeking accreditation by the National League for Nursing develop instructional objectives that specify in operational terms what students will do as a result of completing the learning sequence. The resulting activity among faculty members has dramatically brought out points of congruence and points of sharp disagreement. While each set of objectives is an admittedly incomplete and inadequate guide for institutional behavior, the process itself is the most important single ingredient in the refinement of the curriculum.

No less than the public, the nursing profession recognizes that there are differences among the graduates of the diverse preparatory programs. They share the vague feeling of uneasiness over two "nurses," one completing a two-year course, the other a five-year course, starting in the same hospital, doing the same work and receiving the same

compensation. Such a system, or non-system, offends reason.

Yet, to say there is something wrong is not to specify what is wrong — or how the wrong can be corrected. Unlike many educators who indulge in curriculum development on an individualistic basis, relying on each instructor to develop his own content and expecting the student to provide the "fit" among the several courses, nursing has placed its emphasis on institutional and faculty-wide involvement — with the conviction that, over time, there can be rational models developed for the differing institutions, models that reflect actual behavior differences expected among the graduates.

For example, there are several research studies underway to define and discriminate among the behaviors of nurse-practitioners at the "technical" and "professional" levels. Similarly, because the first distinction has some unfortunate semantic overtones, there are efforts to define behaviorally the activities of the nurse-generalist from those of the nurse-specialist. Still other nurse faculties are grappling with core curricula in community colleges and schools of allied health to determine the curricular interface between nurses and other health specialists — physicians, technologists, technicians, etc. At the very least, each of these efforts affords a single institution a clearer set of goals for directing their time and resources. Beyond that, it may yet result in a recognized "professional curriculum" that will provide a yardstick against which local institutions and course offerings may be measured.

Development of instructional systems

As important as the construction of learning objectives is to improved education, it is recognized by educational technologists as the first long step toward the development of an instructional system that can enhance the learning of individual students, contributing toward greater achievement and better efficiency.

In the face of the stated problems of nursing education — lack of qualified faculty, discouraging numbers of student dropouts and conspicuous differentiation in preparatory courses — it would seem eminently sound that an instructional system be developed that could invoke the known properties of individual participation and responsibility, required response behavior and prompt feedback of information to optimize the learning situation.

Short programmed sequences, well-written, with specified objectives and limited time requirements might well become the vital ingredient to the restructuring of nursing education. Not only could they be fitted into varying institutional patterns, but

Figure 1

Number of available para-medical self-instructional programs in the years 1965-1969.

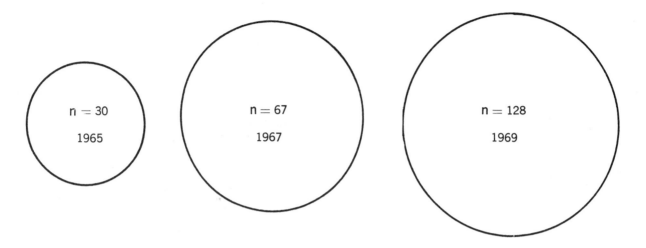

they could well represent initial instruction in preparatory institutions and needed refresher offerings in continuing education and return-to-work training.

It is a testimony to the serious intentions of nursing education that the preliminary work in developing objectives has been closely followed by an impressive number of developmental trials and research projects on the new instructional technologies. By any standard of comparison, nursing has moved as rapidly as any professional group in its attempts to define the advantages — and limitations—of individualized learning for its institutional goals.

While there are a large number of companion developments in educational television, audio-visual techniques and computer assisted learning, the remainder of this paper will be devoted to a discussion of the utilization of self-instructional programs in nursing education, since there is more definitive information available at this point on what has been done, what results have been obtained and what additional work is in progress.

The earliest known programs for the self-teaching of nursing subjects appeared in 1962. Perhaps the first project was that at the University of South Dakota, closely followed by those at Columbia University and the University of Rochester. For the most part, these were the beginning efforts of individual writers and researchers, and it was several years before larger institutional projects began to appear. Relatively early, however, the professional organizations provided encouragement and support to the fledgling programs, and the **American Journal of Nursing** started a continuing series of short programmed sequences in occasional issues of that magazine.

The full impact and pace of these developments can be shown in terms of statistical data compiled by the Rochester Clearinghouse on Self-Instructional Materials for Health Care Facilities. In **Figure 1,** we can compare the number of para-medical programs available over a four-year period from 1965 through 1969.

Certain explanatory comments must be made about these numbers. While the term para-medical is more inclusive than nursing, the programs included herein are ones that would be suitable for nursing instruction, although many would be of use in the teaching of medical technologists, practical nurses, x-ray technologists and others. Also, nurses were involved in the development and construction of many of the sequences that are not denoted exclusively for nursing education. In other words, most, if not all, of these programs have a functional role somewhere in the nursing curriculum. Moreover, it is obvious that there is a "better than arithmetic" rate of growth at work. The figure for 1969 is, of course, incomplete and will be enlarged before the end of the year. Finally, while the Clearinghouse has developed an extensive information gathering system, it is very likely that self-instructional sequences exist in various institutions that are not known or reported.

The programs included within this report span the entire range of professional learning. There are pre-clinical subjects like anatomy and physiology; there are clinical subjects like cardiac nursing and cancer treatment. There are cognitive areas like the knowledge of terminology, the understanding of drug dosage and the motor skill of operating an anesthesiology machine. There are the affective areas of handling grief and mourning, relating to a patient and analyzing reactions to treatment modalities. In short, there has been across-the-board development and experimentation.

Results obtained to date

Because nursing has concentrated on effecting changes in the instructional curriculum by exploiting the use of learning programs, not all of the testing has been done with the nicety of a psychometrician. On the other hand, there has usually been sufficient evidence to indicate that the program worked at least as well as more traditional methods — and occasionally in superior fashion. In any event, it represented a desired, viable alternative to the customary way of doing things.

At the University of Illinois, for example, Marilyn Bitzer[1] found that self-instructional materials on self-directed inquiry in medical-surgical nursing showed positive results when compared with lecture-discussion methods, although the differences were not of a significant magnitude. Hinsvark[2] found that the self-instructional approach was extremely useful in the teaching of specific manual skills in operating room nursing — such as threading surgical needles. Similar reports have come from Seedor[3], who used programs to teach asepsis; Job[4], whose field is the handling of patients with myocardial infarction; Roe[5] in nursing fundamentals; and Raine[6] in body fluids and electrolytes.

The list could be expanded, but perhaps one example of a controlled study from the developmental project at the University of Rochester could illustrate the general nature of the findings in nursing education on the use of self-instructional materials.

In the teaching of the basic course in fundamental nursing skills, the faculty was aware that a disproportionate amount of time was spent by the instructor in demonstrating a variety of skill procedures. Interviews and observations of the students showed that they varied markedly in their speed of learning and required performance to criterion level. Taught by conventional means, this was a classic instance in which instruction became paced to the slowest learner's pace — in turn, boring students who quickly mastered the technique. There was some apprehension on the part of the instructor, too, that over-practice on the part of many students might cause them to behave mechanically and overlook the pertinent scientific principles that should accompany the motor-skill learning.

Using the set of behavioral objectives drawn up for several of these procedures, the instructor developed for three selected skills a self-instructional package that consisted of a linear program-med sequence, an 8mm continuous loop film and a programmed laboratory exercise. Two evaluation techniques were simultaneously produced. The first was a skill checklist to be completed by the instructor on each student, the second a paper and pencil test on the background principles that underlay the procedure. The students were given complete individual freedom to determine use, sequencing and repetition of the materials in the package. This gave rise immediately to the first finding: students varied greatly in their unique learning patterns. Some students began with the program, proceeded to the film, then went through the laboratory exercise. Others worked in the opposite fashion. Some did not use all the materials. Some used only one part of the package. And at least one individual with relevant prior experience proceeded to the evaluation phase immediately.

In addition to emphasizing that even the "no instruction" group can achieve limited goals through general background knowledge and peer interaction, the data show no significant difference in achievement scores between the two instructional modalities. But here the non-significance of the comparison stops. **In terms of both teacher and student time, the self-instructional approach was far more efficient,** with the combined savings being used to classroom advantage in covering more areas than were formerly dealt with in the course.

Student reaction and motivation — at least as important a consideration in nursing education for the reasons suggested above — were extremely positive to the self-instructional approach. They felt that determining the rate and sequence of materials suited their own styles. They preferred self-correction to teacher intervention, and they reported that they felt more secure in their mastery of a given skill. Finally, they asked for the provision of more units based on this type of model.

In the field of medical education, where there are a goodly number of rigorously controlled and conducted studies on programmed instruction, the clearinghouse has analyzed more than 40 research reports. Almost two-thirds of them report significant learning effectiveness by programs in comparison to traditional methods, and almost one-third relatively equal success. Only one case is reported in which the self-instructional material was significantly less effective than conventional teaching. These figures are most useful to us because they encourage the development of more — and better — alternatives. While no comparable data have yet been obtained and analyzed for nursing education, there is little information to date to indicate that the proportions would be greatly different. But it is vital to emphasize the point that superiority is not the goal. Equality of results, while providing alternative solutions to real problems of instruction and learning, is the objective we are after.

Table 1

Mean Achievement Results of Conventional and Individualized Learning in Nursing Fundamentals

Procedure	Skill Test (Max. = 70)	Written Test (Max. = 15)
Conventional	58.3	13.0
Individualized	57.0	13.4
No Instruction	39.3	8.6

Summary and conclusion

Nursing education, because of the fierce challenges it faces and because of the very limited resources it can muster to face them, decided several years ago that the curriculum and learning areas were its most fruitful points of attack. By operationalizing its instructional goals, nursing is moving more rapidly than any other profession at this time toward an objective and rational statement of what a student nurse should do as a result of her education. In a companion effort, nursing educators have been at work for seven years taking units of those objectives and developing self-instructional materials for them. These currently include over 120 sequences of varying length and complexity.

Preliminary studies to date show a large number of applications of programming to different nursing areas and to the many different kinds of learning skills. While there is no large body of controlled experimentation that could satisfy the skeptic, there are a growing number of small studies that attest to the effectiveness and efficiency of self-learning techniques. When these findings are coalesced with companion efforts involving instructional television, audio-visual techniques and computer assisted instruction, it is likely that nursing will have the greater part of its professional curriculum systematized for student learning, and that new and worthwhile roles will become the characteristic feature of the nursing instructor.

No one can solve the problems of nursing single-handedly. The members of the profession have, however, demonstrated an unusual willingness to explore and develop curricular objectives and materials which are their own unique province, and by so doing, are manipulating those factors over which they do have control in order to enhance professional training.

In 10 years, nursing may well have become the model for American professional training; if this occurs, it will be due in large part to the successful development of systematic technology for individualized learning. □

References

1. Bitzer, Marilyn: Self-Directed Inquiry in Clinical Nursing Instruction by Means of the PLATO Simulated Laboratory. University of Illinois Coordinated Science Laboratory Report R-184, 1963.
2. Hinsvark, Inez G.: Programming Procedural Skills in the Operating Room. **Hospital Topics.** 41:55-58 (August) 1963.
3. Seedor, Marie M.: Programmed Instruction for a Unit on Asepsis. **Hospital Topics.** 41:50-5 (August) 1963.
4. Job, Florence K.: Programmed Instruction — A Tool for Staff Education Departments (mimeograph). Charleston: U.S. Naval Hospital, 1965.
5. Roe, A. K.: The Use of Learning Experiences (LEG) in the Associate Degree Nursing Program (mimeo). Fort Lauderdale, Fla.: Junior College of Broward County, 1968.
6. Raine, N. L.: An Experiment in Programmed Learning (Parts 1 and 2). **Nursing Times.** Vol. 62, No. 22, 23 (June) 1966.

An annotated bibliography of programs and papers on self-instruction in the para-medical fields is available from the Rochester Clearinghouse, River Campus Station, University of Rochester, Rochester, New York 14627.

114

An Example of a Mathematics Instructional Program for Disadvantaged Children

Jerome D. Kaplan

Within the past few years, considerable attention has been directed toward the education of inner-city children. Researchers and educators have tried to determine who the disadvantaged are, what their educational deficits are, and how these deficits may be overcome. It seems that most of the efforts of researchers and educators have been devoted to defining specific educational problems, preparing teachers who will teach in disadvantaged areas, and "enriching" classroom experiences. In providing enriching experiences for these children, teachers and researchers have no doubt created special instructional materials for disadvantaged children. But most of these materials, not highly publicized or published, are, consequently, not available for widespread use.

Language development has received the initial attention of researchers who are interested in the learning problems of the disadvantaged.

The purpose of this article is to describe a new method of teaching mathematics — a non-verbal program of instruction — that was designed and tested with first-grade children from a school in a disadvantaged area in New York City. Although other forms of programmatic material are available, there is no known completely non-verbal pro-gram designed to teach a specific set of objectives to disadvantaged children.

The program

One particular mathematical deficit that became obvious during a number of years of observing first-grade classes was the children's inability to perform simple additive and subtractive operations with zero. This observation was supported by means of informal testing. The problem can probably be attributed to such factors as:

1. A relative de-emphasis on the teaching of "0" when compared to the cardinal numbers 1 through 10.
2. General difficulty in comprehending the empty set.
3. Difficulty in providing examples for the empty set.

To offset the noted deficit, a non-verbal program of instruction using only multiple-choice responses was designed and pretested with members of the first-grade class cited above. The program follows the general form of a linear program, in which the student selects one of three responses. Immediately after responding, the student can confirm his choice by turning a page and comparing his response with the correct answer. In this program, only one frame appears on a page. The answer is identical to the question frame except that the

Jerome D. Kaplan is associate professor, Department of Mathematical Education, Teachers College, Columbia University.

Table 1

Sequence of Behavior in Program

1. Matches numerals to numerals
2. Matches numerals to numerals (0 only)
3. Matches objects to objects (1-5)
4. Matches objects to objects (6-9)
5. Matches objects to objects (0 only)
6. Matches objects to numerals (1-5)
7. Matches numerals to objects (1-5)
8. Matches numerals to objects (6-9)
9. Matches objects to numerals (6-9)
10. Matches numerals to objects (0 only)
11. Matches objects to numerals (0 only)
12. Matches objects (5 or less) with sums of sets of objects (using '+' and '=')
13. Matches numerals with unions of sets of objects
14. Matches unions of sets of objects with objects (five or less)
15. Matches unions of sets of objects with numerals (five or less)
16. Matches objects to unions of two sets of objects where one set is empty (sums less than 6)
17. Matches unions of two sets of objects where one set is empty to objects (sums less than 6)
18. Matches expression with numerals to union of two sets of objects

19. Matches expression with numerals to union of two sets of objects (empty set used)
20. Matches union of two sets of objects to expression with numerals
21. Matches union of two objects to expression with numerals (0 used)
22. Matches unions of two sets of objects where one set is empty to numerals
23. Matches numerals with unions of two sets of objects where one set is empty
24. Matches numeral to '0 + x' (x is a cardinal number from 1 to 9)
25. Matches '0 + x' to numeral
26. Matches numeral to 'x + 0'
27. Matches 'x + 0' to numeral
28. Matches numeral to '0 + x'
29. Matches numeral to solution of 'x + ... = x'
30. Matches solution of 'x + ... = x' to numeral
31. Matches numeral to solution of '......... + x = x'
32. Matches solution of '......... + x = x' to numeral
33. Matches numeral to solution of '0 + ... = x'
34. Matches solution of '0 + ... = x' to numeral
35. Matches numeral to solution of '......... + 0 = x'
36. Matches solution of '......... + 0 = x' to numeral

appropriate choice is indicated in the answer frame. A sample question frame follows:

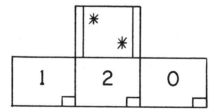

The entire program was presented in five small booklets, each containing about 30-35 frames (60-70 pages). The pages, which are 8½ by 5½ inches, were stapled together to form the booklets.

Prerequisite behaviors

Students were required to exhibit the following prerequisite behaviors before beginning the program:

1. Counts the objects in a set represented pictorially.
2. Identifies numerals from 1 to 9; given a written numeral, can state numeral verbally.
3. Associates numerals from 1 to 9 with appropriate sets of objects represented pictorially, and vice versa.
4. Chooses the set of objects which is equivalent to the union of two sets of objects.

Terminal behaviors

Desired terminal behaviors sought were:

1. Associates an empty set of objects with "0" and vice versa.
2. Chooses the correct answer for $x + 0 =$ .... from among three choices; also solves these equations:

$$0 + x = ...$$
$$........ + 0 = x$$
$$x + ... = x$$
$$0 + ... = x$$
$$........ + x = x$$

3. Solves $x + 0 = ...$
$0 + x = ...$ (x is a cardinal number, 0 to 9.)

Sequence of behaviors

To facilitate writing a program that would take the student from the prerequisite to the terminal behaviors, a sequence of behaviors was listed which served as a guide to the writing of actual frames (see **Table 1**). All of these behaviors are represented by one or more specific frames in the program.

Pretest/Posttest

A single test was designed for the purpose of pre- and post-testing. The 14 items of the test, designed to represent the terminal behaviors listed above, were administered individually. Two of the items required a verbal response from the child, while the remainder were multiple-choice.

The subjects were first-grade children from the school mentioned earlier. Only those children who indicated little mastery in the pretest went through the program and the requirement of prerequisite performance (see above). Because of this requirement, only six children qualified.

Results

Since a small number of children, six, participated in the testing phase, the results which appear in **Table 2** are only indicative. As the table indicates, the effect of the program was to raise the mean score of the test 6.3 points (45 percent). The degree of improvement ranged from an increase of 28 percent to 57 percent.

Table 2
Results of Trials

SUB-JECT	PRETEST		POSTTEST		PRE-POST TEST DIFFERENCES	
	# Correct	% Correct	# Correct	% Correct	# Correct	% Correct
A	5	36	9	64	4	28
B	4	28	9	64	5	36
C	6	43	12	85	6	43
D	7	50	14	100	7	50
E	6	43	14	100	8	57
F	6	43	14	100	8	57
MEAN	5.7	41.1	12	86	6.3	45

In terms of recorded error and observed delay in student response, the difficult frames were those which attempted to teach behaviors 12 to 15 in the sequence shown in **Table 1**. As any programmer knows, it is not always a single frame that is at fault, but often a sequence of frames that produces errors. In this case, changes in the stimulus-response form seemed to contribute to errors. For example, the transition from number-numeral matchings to translating a mathematical sentence and completing the sentence caused the greatest number of errors. Other changes in the form of the presentation also seemed to cause errors, indicating that psychological, as well as mathematical, issues were involved.

Observations and conclusions

All children worked for about 15 to 25 minutes in each booklet of the program. With only one subject, these were attention-span problems. One child would often ask extraneous questions after completing about five frames of each unit (average length: 32 frames). Considerable encouragement was required to "force" her through the program. All subjects at some time or other necessitated reassurance — particularly after making an error. One boy worked with considerable speed and accuracy through each unit, and when finished with a unit (after 15 minutes) would always ask for more work. As a reward, he was given a game with which to play.

Almost all children experienced difficulty in distinguishing between question and answer frames, since they were alike except for the answer which appeared in the answer frame. The format of this program, therefore, was often troublesome. For children, answers should be more readily available — on the same page perhaps — so that the student does not have to turn a page for confirmation. Page-turning should be simpler than the experimental version used here. Also, the booklets used did not lie flatly on the desk, creating some problems in writing and turning pages. While these small pieces of behavior may seem trivial, they are not when one is working with children who do not concentrate for very long.

Whereas a certain degree of success has certainly been demonstrated, it is not possible to project the use of programmed materials for full classroom use. Hawthorne-type effects may have been present: the presence of two adults in the testing situation cannot be minimized, nor can the individual administration of the tests and program to each child. The simplicity of the instructional material by which students can experience a high degree of success certainly contributed to the students' unusual attention span and their concentration. The absence of language may well have added to successful performance.

While the full scope of non-verbal programmed instruction has not been thoroughly investigated, certain tentative conclusions are possible concerning its use with disadvantaged children.

1. Programs can be used as supplementary materials. While they can certainly be used by the more advanced children in any class, they can also be used by the least advanced.

2. Crucial to the use of any instructional materials is the success which students experience. A program should start with simple frames that are very easy for all users. The sequence of frames that is employed should include a review of previously-taught material. A simple rule to follow would be: after each new concept that is taught, review that concept and the previous one.

3. The format should not intrude in any way upon a child's interaction with the material. Pages should be easy to turn; answers should be immediately accessible; and question-answer frames should be designed so as to prevent cheating. "Cheating" can be a problem with any population that uses programs. It is important for investigators to examine what causes cheating. Often it is brought about by frustration. In this experiment, for example, cheating occurred when a child was frustrated by a difficult frame or when he had made an error on the previous frame.

4. Multiple-choice frames are easier to answer than free-response items. Therefore, a program should lead from multiple-choice items to free-response frames.

5. The use of non-verbal programs to teach mathematics can be an aid to students who experience reading problems. The limitations of non-verbal programs are that explanations are not possible and vocabulary cannot be introduced. But for disadvantaged children with reading problems, the non-verbal mathematics program can be an excellent way to review and reinforce previously-taught skills and concepts.

6. Programmed instruction as a medium by which students interact with various stimuli (visual, auditory, tactile) will no doubt continue to provoke discussion. One of the striking by-products of this experiment is the knowledge that can be obtained about student performance. While observing students working through planned sequences which aim toward specific behavioral objectives, one can gain considerable information about students' learning behavior.

7. If a teacher becomes accustomed to managing a classroom not as a teacher-centered, but as a student-centered, experience, then programs, in their supplementary roles, can be quite useful. Designed and tested with a specific target population, programs will be available with which the teacher can "zero-in" on particular behavioral objectives. Thus, the teacher will be free to apply himself to real learning problems in mathematics.

□

References

Almy, Millie. **Young Children's Thinking.** New York: Teachers College Press, 1966.

Ausabel, David. Teaching Strategy for Culturally Deprived Pupils. **School Review,** Winter, 1963.

Dunkley, Melvyn. Some Number Concepts of Disadvantaged Children. **The Arithmetic Teacher,** May, 1965.

Kaplan, Jerome D. Programmed Instruction and the Culturally Disadvantaged. **New York State Mathematics Teachers Journal,** October, 1964.

May, Kenneth O. **Programmed Learning and Mathematical Education.** Mathematical Association of America, 1965.

Passy, Robert A. Socio-Economic Status and Mathematics Achievement. **The Arithmetic Teacher,** November, 1964.

Piaget, J. **The Child's Conception of Number.** London: Routledge and Kegan Paul, 1952.

Leiderman, Gloria, Chinn, William G. and Dunkley, Melvyn. **The Special Curriculum Project: Pilot Program in Mathematics Learning of Culturally Disadvantaged Primary School Children.** SMSG Reports, No. 2, Stanford: School Mathematics Study Group, 1966.

Wilkinson, Doxey. Prevailing and Needed Emphasis in Research in the Education of Disadvantaged Children and Youth. **Journal of Negro Education,** 33, 1964.

Williams, Alfred H. Mathematical Concepts, Skills and Abilities of Kindergarten Entrants. **The Arithmetic Teacher,** April, 1965.

Preparing Prisoners for College
Using Programmed Learning and Contingency Management

Mark Laurence Berman

Many persons who commit crimes do so because they lack alternative skills and behaviors. By providing such persons with alternatives to crime, their crime rate should be reduced.

A project sponsored by the Office of Economic Opportunity, entitled Newgate, is now underway at the State Correctional Institution at Bellefonte, Pennsylvania. The major objective of the project is to prepare inmates for college entrance. The major tools used to achieve this objective are programmed learning and contingency management.

Fifty inmates have been selected as students from among the seven thousand inmates in Pennsylvania committed to either the Pennsylvania Bureau of Corrections, Federal prison, or county jails. Most of the students are self-recommended. Following recommendation, potential Newgate students are screened by their institution. Those who

Mark Laurence Berman is assistant professor, College of Human Development, The Pennsylvania State University, University Park.

pass this screening are then interviewed by Newgate staff members, who rate each inmate as to his probability of succeeding in college, given the training he would receive in the project.

Inmates who receive high ratings are divided into Newgate students and control group by a random selection procedure. The Newgate students (i.e., the experimental group) and the control group are matched for such factors as educational background, length of sentence remaining, social adjustment and probability of success in college. A long-range follow-up study will compare the two groups on such measures as recidivism rate and educational attainment and income, in order to determine whether or not the Newgate project had any significant effect on the inmates.

Three categories of inmates constitute the Newgate student and the control groups. The first are those inmates who have either graduated from high school or who have recently passed the GED examination. The second category is composed of inmates who have completed ten or eleven years of school without having passed the GED examination. In the third category are inmates who have completed from six to nine years of school without having passed the GED examination.

Newgate students with a high school diploma or who have passed the GED examination are expected to qualify for college admission within one year from the date they join the project. Those who have completed 10 to 11 years of school, but who do not have the GED, are expected to qualify for college admission within 18 months of joining the project. Students with sixth to ninth grade background, and who have not passed the GED examination, are expected to qualify for college admission within 24 months of joining the project. Only inmates who are within two years of their minimum release date are considered for participation in the Newgate project.

Method

The Newgate educational system consists of four components: (1) Programmed materials covering 40 subject matters, including trigonometry, calculus, plane geometry, solid geometry, algebra, statistics, genetics, physiology, chemistry, physics, English grammar, reading comprehension, punctuation, spelling, Spanish, German, Russian, computer science, history, political science, sociology, geography and business administration. (2) Informal courses taught at the Institution by Newgate instructors. These courses include biology, English literature and composition, drama and social science. (3) College-credit courses taught at the Institution by Pennsylvania State University faculty. These courses include biological science, English and speech. (4) Individual tutoring and counseling provided by Newgate staff members, University students, University faculty and members of the local community.

A learning center, an instructional materials center and office space were constructed in the new education building at the Institution. Fifty oversize plywood carrels were built by inmate labor and placed in the learning center. Three large rooms are used for lecture and discussion, and a 125-seat auditorium is available for showing films or slides, and is equipped with Bunsen burner and wet sink for science demonstrations.

Ten Welch Auto-Tutors, eight Mast Programmed Readers and 32 Grolier Min-Max III devices make up the teaching machine complement of the project, though the majority of the programs do not require the use of machines. Record changers are available for use with the records which accompany the foreign language programs. All answers except those on the Welch programs are in written form and are permanently stored.

The contingency system awards points as a function of performance on the learning materials and in the classroom. For each frame which is answered correctly, the student earns one point. The points vary in trade value from three-quarters of a cent each for the Welch programs (which generally require more time per frame), to one-quarter cent each for all other programs. The points may be placed in the inmate's savings account for whatever future use, including financing of college, he wishes. They may be used to purchase items in the commissary, such as shoes, candy, or cigarettes. Points can be used to purchase books at one-half the list price, the project absorbing the remainder of the cost. In this way inmates can more readily acquire their own personal library, which will be of use to them in college.

Points are awarded differentially, according to the level of accuracy achieved.

Perfect (i.e., 100%) performance earns a bonus of 15% over the number of frames correct in a particular group (called a section) of frames. If the student achieves 95% accuracy on a section, he earns 10% more than the number of frames correct. If 90% accuracy is achieved, the student earns 5% more than the number of frames correct. Similarly, points are awarded for both pre- and posttest performance. On posttests, 100% accuracy earns 60 points; 95% accuracy earns 40 points; 90% accuracy earns 20 points. The points earned for posttest performance have the same value as points earned on the program itself.

In regard to pretests, 40 quarter-cent points (or 10 cents) are awarded for each pretest score of 90% or higher. If students score this high on the pretests, which are taken prior to beginning most of the programmed materials and individual sections within most programs, they are exempt from taking the particular material covered by the pretest. Points for high-level pretest performance are awarded to deter students from purposely doing poorly on the tests in order work on an unneeded program and gain points easily.

The payoff for posttest performance was set higher than that for performance on the programs for two reasons. First, posttests usually call for students to synthesize information and/or generalize from the information contained in the program. Second, cheating is possible on the non-machine programs, but it is unlikely that this will occur on the posttests, which are more closely monitored and for which no list of correct answers is available (at least to the student). Posttest scores are likely to be a more valid measure of performance. In keeping with this, payoffs are greater.

Finally, there are "student of the week" and "most-improved student" awards. The former, consisting of points worth $5.00, is granted to the student with the greatest accuracy on both programs and posttests during each week. The latter, consisting of points worth $2.00, is granted to the student with the greatest increase in accuracy on both program and posttests from one week to the next.

Student earnings generally range from $10.00 to $30.00 per month. Newgate is the students' job. They do no other work, spending 40 hours per week with the project. The weekly schedule of activities is as follows: 8:30 to 10:30 a.m. Monday through Friday, students work on programmed materials; 10:30 to 11:30 a.m. Monday through Friday, two instructor-taught courses, one of which meets on Monday, Wednesday and Friday, the other meeting on Tuesday, Thursday and Friday; 11:30 a.m. to 1 p.m. Monday through Friday, students eat lunch and stand for count before returning to the project; 1 to 3 p.m. Monday through Friday, students work on programmed materials; 3 to 3:30 p.m. Monday through Thursday, students have time to study in the classrooms (they may also study on their own at night and on weekends); 3 to 4 p.m. Friday, two half-hour instructor taught courses; 3:30 to 4:30 p.m. Monday through Thursday, two instructor-taught courses, one of which meets on Monday, Wednesday and Friday, the other on Tuesday, Thursday and Friday; 4:30 p.m., dinner and return to cells. College credit courses are taught to those students who are nearing college admission during the time of day they would usually be working on programmed materials.

The schedule was devised to provide a break from work on the programmed materials, and to give students exposure to information which is not available in programmed form. A drama course was placed at the end of the day on a three-times per week basis, in order to provide for an emotional outlet after an intellectually-taxing day.

The principle of successive approximation is used wherever feasible. Students do not move on to more demanding situations until they have demonstrated their ability to perform in less demanding situations. Therefore, students initially work only on programmed materials, which generate a high frequency of positive feedback and do not demand a great deal of them. After demonstrating proficiency, acquiring information, and having confidence in their learning ability built as a result of their work on the programmed materials, students then participate in the instructor-taught courses.

The instructor-taught courses are carried out on an informal basis, and have a two-fold purpose: (1) to provide information which is not available in programmed form; (2) to allow for a smoother transition from the self-instructional format, with its relatively few demands on the student, to the college format, in which the formal lecture-test cycle prevails. There is need for a transition step, then, from working on self-instructional materials at the correctional institution to functioning as a regular college student. This rationale is also behind the development of a half-way house set up on the Institution grounds for those students who are nearing their release and will soon be entering college. At this house, some restrictions are in effect; but, in general, students live in an environment which more closely approximates the campus scene.

Results

To date the academic performance of the Newgate students has been high. Accuracy on the programmed materials has generally been at approximately the 97% level. Posttest scores show an improvement, on the average, of 30% over pretest scores. All students are rapidly and efficiently moving through the materials, and are exhibiting self-confidence where little previously existed.

Overview

Inmates of correctional institutions typically lack (at least) two things: One, the confidence that they can succeed in the world-at-large. Two, the behaviors and knowledge to enable them to succeed. Programmed learning and contingency management are two approaches which can be very effective in developing both confidence and the skills necessary to succeed. □

A full outline of the Newgate program prerequisites and flow is available from the author.

Programmed Instruction and the Process Approach

Richard W. Burns
Contributing Editor

Programmed instruction serves two major roles in education: first it is a method of instruction; second it is a research tool. Programs can serve both of these functions in relation to the process approach to education. (See "The Practical Educational Technologist — The Process Approach," **Educational Technology**, May, 1969, pp. 54-57.)

The process approach to education is an exciting concept that needs much research to make it a reality. First, the processes on which to base curricular designs need to be identified and purified (elimination of duplication). Second, processes need to be described in behavioral terms. Third, educational events which will elicit the desired process behaviors need to be identified and described. Fourth, measurement situations and devices need to be developed for measuring processes. Fifth, the transfer values associated with processes need to be empirically substantiated. Sixth, curricular designs need to be established for implementing process learning. Seventh, processes need to be integrated into a general theory of learning. Eighth, age-grade learning of processes need to be developed into a pattern or sequence of learnable behaviors. Ninth, the process oriented curricular designs need to be tested.

How can programming contribute to the needed research? First, programming insists on viewing learning in terms of observable behaviors. After processes have been identified, they must be described in behavioral terms. A great deal of progress in behavioral description of specific objectives has been made in the interest of educational technology generally and programmed instruction in particular. (See "The Practical Educational Technologist — Behavioral Objectives — A Selected Bibliography," **Educational Technology**, April, 1969, pp. 57-58.) Second, programmed learning can serve as a tool to identify those learning events which will elicit various behaviors. As learners respond to key frames or sets of frames in a program, they in essence are leaving a record (written or recorded) which indicates progress toward or away from a desired behavior. Third, programmed learning can contribute to stimulus discrimination, which in all probability will be needed in learning complex behaviors, which include processes. Fourth, programmed learning has a discipline that is favorable to the development of educational designs which are of proven validity. That is to say, programmers know how to develop the software to be utilized by learners in acquiring stated behaviors.

The programming movement has been criticized as one which is overly pragmatic in its approach. Programmers, or perhaps more specifically behavioral analysts, have been accused of specifying thousands of behaviors which turn out to be acquired piecemeal with little apparent concern for the more complex behaviors, higher order principles, affective behaviors, and the interrelationships which exist in learning and between fields of learning.

Perhaps there is some truth to this criticism, although one should not expect the programming movement to solve all the problems which it might reasonably contribute to in a short period of time.

It should be of interest to the programming movement to investigate processes as they relate to education. Process behaviors integrated into software designs along with the development of other behaviors classifiable as knowledges, understandings and skills may be the answer to the critics.

The next article in this series will be "What Are Learning Products?"

Your reactions or comments to ideas expressed in this regular column are sought, as are any educational or classroom problems which you have.

Precision Teaching: A Useful Technology for Special Education Teachers

Robert N. Bradfield

For quite some time we have seen an ever increasing array of technological devices designed to enhance the teaching process in both special and "normal" classrooms.

We have seen variation upon variation of audio-visual aids, teaching machines and computerized systems designed to expedite the transmission of knowledge from the educational system to the child. Though there is probably no question that the classroom of the future will be a computerized one in which the child's educational development will be mediated through carefully planned and constructed programmed materials, at the present time there would appear to be several problems connected with such programming.

First, and possibly foremost in the minds of some, though a fiction if one thinks about it carefully, is *cost*. Our educational system is, as yet, unwilling to move to costly retooling until such time as the effectiveness of computerized programs has been proven more clearly, even though the cost over time may eventually prove to be far less if one bases the return on the amount of knowledge gained.

Second, we are still in the stage of simply storing information, at least in education. We do not have readily available computers which can make educational decisions based on the individual progress or functioning of a child. Educational programming is still in its infancy, and it must progress far beyond current levels before it can begin to approach its ultimate potential.

Finally, the range of programs which must be devised if we are to adhere to the concept of

Robert N. Bradfield is associate professor of education at San Francisco State College.

individualized instruction is so great that the problems of computerization are unquestionably multiplied. It becomes apparent that we not only have to teach children reading, writing and arithmetic, but that we are daily faced with a multitude of social behavior difficulties and needs as well. Special education provides an excellent example of such difficulties. In special programs, we face not only unique academic learning difficulties but frequently a wide range of social behavior learning requirements. We must teach Johnny to button his coat, and Mary to wash her hands. We must teach Billy to stop hitting and Kathy to stay in her seat so that learning may take place. We must teach Greg to respond differentially to sound and lip movement, and Jill to develop small-muscle skills. These and many more constitute the myriad of problems with which an advanced educational technology must cope. We now have the potential for just that kind of technology as a result of the development of the Precision Teaching method by Dr. Ogden Lindsley and others.

An adequately functioning and effective computer system requires at least two components: A language system which is consistent and which can be used and understood by all who work within the system (and hopefully by those who are outside the system) and a means of adding new information or feedback to its computation. Precision Teaching does this and much more. First, it provides a common language, a means of communication through which *all* those involved with the education of a given child may begin to communicate in precise and understandable terms. 2) It requires that we become definitively precise in our description of behaviors of concern, whether they be academic, social or physical. 3) It involves all aspects of the learning situation, including

123

environmental conditions and other stimulus variables, whether these stimuli be curricular materials or social conditions, as well as the consequences which may result from behavior. 4) It provides an ongoing, immediately available effect of any changes which may be attempted in order to modify the behaviors in question. 5) It allows us to make precise changes in specific parts of the learning environment, either antecedent or subsequent to the behavior of concern. 6) It allows us, in a very precise way, to do that which we have given lip service to for so long, to begin to "understand" the child and to let his *behavior* guide us in terms of our educational decisions. 7) It provides us with a system which is not simply imposed on a child and maintained by a teacher, but a system wherein the child can very quickly take over the responsibility for his own behavior management and learning and the maintenance of all records, thereby tremendously increasing the potential applicability of such a system.

Basically, there are four components to the Precision Teaching program. The first is a system of recording and charting data in such a way that one has a continuing, readily available record of behavioral changes which may be occurring. Specific behaviors may be either accelerated or decelerated. Lindsley has developed a six-cycle logarithmic chart which, in the opinion of this writer, has a potential never before available to educators. It combines the unique qualities of precise data recording of the widest possible frequency range (frequencies ranging from one behavior every thousand minutes to one thousand behaviors every minute may be recorded on the same chart) and simplicity (though initially formidable looking, it has been dramatically shown that third graders can readily learn and chart their own behavior rates without any difficulty whatsoever).

Not only does the chart allow one to record any behavior which is definable in terms of rate of occurrence, but it has also been "calendar synchronized" in order that, whether one is carrying on one project or a thousand, a visible time representation is provided, not only from the standpoint of the daily, weekly or monthly progression of individual behaviors, but also as a comparison of beginning and ending dates of different projects.

An example of this chart is shown in Figure 1. Just below the abscissa, or base of the chart, the caption "Successive Calendar Days" will be noted. Just above that it will be noted that vertical lines on the chart are numbered from zero to 140. Each of these 140 lines represents one calendar day, with every seventh line (darker lines) representing a Sunday. Along the top of the chart, running horizontally,

it will be noted that every fourth Sunday is marked with the numerals 4, 8, 12, 16 and 20, and above each of these numerals is a place for the day of the month and year. It can readily be seen, then, that the chart can be marked not only in terms of days of the week but in terms of weeks and months of the year in order that consistency of the time factor can be obtained in all projects in which Precision Teaching is attempted. Along the left ordinate or vertical axis of the chart, the caption "Movements per Minute" can be seen; and, just to the right of the caption, are numbers ranging from .001 to 1000. This numerical order allows one to represent visually the rate at which the specific behavior of concern is occurring. This rate is obtained by counting the frequency of occurrence of a specific behavior and dividing that frequency by the number of minutes during which counting was undertaken, hence "Movements per Minute." All data in Precision Teaching projects is graphed on a "Movements per Minute" basis. It will further be noted that from bottom to top there are six cycles on the chart, each a multiple of ten of the previous cycle. For example, .001 proceeding to .002 and so forth up to .01, at which time the count changes to .02, .03, etc. The use of the logarithmic chart system allows a proportional representation of data, and eliminates the distortion normally obtained from "ruler" type charts.

The second component of the Precision Teaching method is the requirement of precise "pinpointing" or defining of those behaviors which one may wish to alter. It must be remembered that all data within the precision management program are based on *rate*. Lindsley has defined "pinpointing behaviors" as "movements," and he feels that an adequate pinpoint must have two basic characteristics: 1) It must have a definable beginning and end, in other words, be a complete movement cycle. For example a "thumb sucking" movement would require that the thumb first be out of the mouth, then in the mouth, then out of the mouth in order to be a complete movement. 2) The pinpoint must pass the "dead man's test." If a dead man can do it, it can't be counted. Once behaviors of concern have been charted in this way it is possible to begin recording data in a precise and objective manner in order that we may obtain continued feedback with regard to the effect of any attempts which we might wish to make to alter that behavior.

It can therefore be seen that the two initial components of Precision Teaching involve the use of an extremely practical recording and common language system which allows both those directly involved in the project, and others as well, to quickly understand and recognize not only the purpose of the

Figure 1

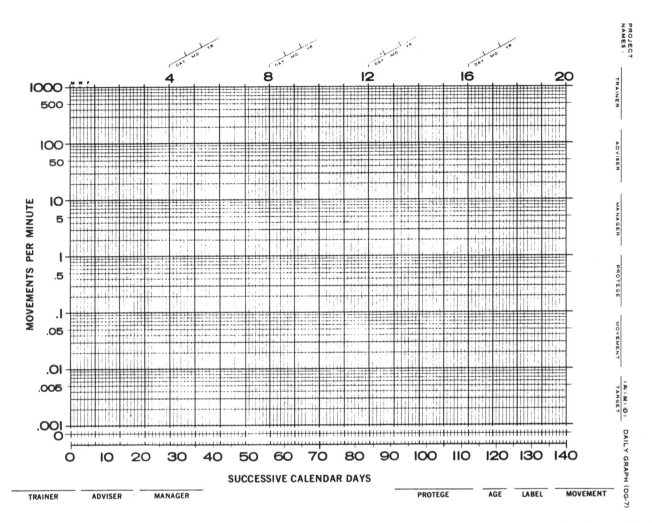

project but the progress of the individual. It brings into immediate focus both our successes and failures as teachers, and it requires that we begin to do something besides give lip service to the concept of individualized instruction. Examples of Precision Teaching projects follow:

Project Examples

One Precision Teaching project was initiated by a teacher in an attempt to decelerate the rate at which a 13-year-old boy tugged and pulled at her during the school day. During the week beginning Monday, October 28, 1969, this child, according to the chart kept by the teacher, was pulling and tugging at the teacher at a middle rate of four times every hundred minutes, with the rate accelerating during the week. On Monday, November 3, 1969, the teacher initiated a change in the project. She simply began turning her back on the child each time the behavior occurred. An immediate deceleration in the

behavior rate began to occur. At the end of a five-week period she had successfully decelerated this behavior rate from a middle rate of four times every 100 minutes to a middle of once every hundred minutes. In other words, she decreased the behavior by a divisor of four during this five-week period.

In another project, the teacher attempted to decelerate the rate at which a boy in her program was talking out during a specific 20 minutes of the school day. Initially this talk-out rate showed approximately one talk-out per minute. In this instance, again the teacher made one simple change at the beginning of the second week, keeping all other factors constant. Each time this child talked out, she called on *another* child with his hand raised. In a six-week period, this child's talk-out rate had decreased to zero. In this case, as in all projects, there was daily, visible feedback from the chart with regard to the effect of this change on the child's behavior.

A third example is a project in which the teacher wished to decelerate the inappropriate use of the pronouns "me" and "my" and increase the use of the pronoun "I." During the first week, or reference period, it was noted that the child inappropriately used these pronouns at a middle rate of two per minute, according to the teacher's chart. At the beginning of the second week, keeping all other variables constant, the teacher asked the child to count his own errors—and they kept a daily chart together. During the next five weeks, the child's error rate dropped from two per minute to one every two minutes. In other words, behavior frequency was divided by four. Unfortunately, this project had to be terminated at this time due to circumstances beyond the teacher's control.

Another example is that of an academic skills project designed to measure the effectiveness of a reading vocabulary building program with a young boy with a severe learning disability. In this case, the teacher felt that the child should attain a reading rate of approximately 30 words per minute on words which he had already been given before any new words were added. At the end of a three-week period, the child had attained this rate fairly consistently, and a change was initiated in which 10 new words were added to his list. As expected, his rate immediately dropped to approximately 10 words per minute with the addition of the new words and then gradually began to accelerate to the desired level. This is an excellent example of a curriculum project in which the teacher has allowed the *child's* behavior to determine when changes should be made in curriculum.

A final example is that of a project in which the precision charting procedure continually pointed to the *inadequacy* of the educational program, but was continually ignored. In this instance, a proficiency level of 9 to 10 problems per minute was indicative of readiness to proceed to a more difficult level of mathematics facts. Although there was some variation, this child, from the beginning of the project, was capable of attaining the required rate on single-digit addition facts. However, despite the evidence, the teacher continued for *six* weeks before making a change to a more difficult level. When this change was finally made (from one digit to two digit addition) there was *no* rate change, indicating that the child had already attained proficiency at this level. A careful examination of the child indicated that not only was he able to do addition facts at this level and much higher—he was also able to do subtraction, simple multiplication and simple division. This teacher had literally wasted everybody's time, and the child had simply learned *not* to learn for a period of almost two months. Had this teacher paid attention to her chart, this situation might have been remedied in a few days instead of months!

The IS-DOES Formula

An important component of the Precision Teaching method is the IS—DOES formula, in which Lindsley has attempted to include all of those environmental variables which might have an effect on the performance of an individual.

Not only are we far too imprecise in our designation of those variables which may affect the learning process, but even when we do attempt to become specific we too frequently mislabel these variables. Over and over again we refer to "stimuli" which do not stimulate, "rewards" which do not reward, punishment which does not punish, and so on.

If we are to fully understand learning and the uniqueness of the individuals who are part of the learning process, it is essential that we not only become more precise in identifying the components of that process, but also that we allow behavior itself to define the terms. Though we can never duplicate the rigor of a Skinnerian laboratory and maintain controls which would be ideal, we can, in the real world, at least approach such controls—if we try. The IS formula is intended to include all of the various kinds of things which exist in the individual's environment which *might* have an effect upon his behavior, while the DOES part of the formula is identical in structure except that it is composed of those events which have been identified as *having* an effect upon the pinpointed behavior.

Essentially there are five basic parts to the learning environment which are involved in the shaping or building of behavior. The IS formula is shown below:

PROGRAM/ANTECEDENT EVENT/MOVEMENT CYCLE/ARRANGEMENT/SUBSEQUENT EVENT

The PROGRAM portion of this formula includes all those things involved in the overall environmental setting, such as location, time of day, classroom seating arrangements, and so forth. An ANTECEDENT event includes all those factors which *might* result in the behavior or movement cycle and have an effect on the performance of that behavior, such as instructions, curriculum materials, demonstrations and so forth. The MOVEMENT cycle is the behavior which is being measured, while ARRANGEMENT stands for the numerical ratio between the movement and the subsequent event. For example, one might give one "M & M" candy for each problem correct, in which case the arrangement would be 1:1, or one hug or statement of praise for each ten problems correct, in which case the arrangement would be 1:10. Finally, SUBSEQUENT EVENTS are those events in the environment which *may* be the result of the movement cycle, and which *may* have an effect on the future occurrence of the movement, such as praise, grades, withdrawal of privileges, smiles, and so forth.

These terms provide a much more accurate initial description of the components of the learning situation. Until we are in the position to evaluate the *effects* of these components on the behavior, it can only be said that each component has the *potential* to change behavior, but has not yet demonstrated that it will do so. Once these components have *demonstrated* a behavioral function, we then have the DOES part of the formula. It is only then that PROGRAM components can be described as DISPOSITION COMPONENTS; ANTECEDENT event components can only then be described as STIMULI; MOVEMENT CYCLES can only then be defined as RESPONSES; ARRANGEMENT components can only then be defined as CONTINGENCIES; while SUBSEQUENT EVENT components can only then be described as CONSEQUENCES. We therefore see a change from the IS formula above to the DOES formula below:

DISPOSITION/STIMULUS
RESPONSE/CONTINGENCY/CONSEQUENCE

It may well be that through the development of the IS—DOES formula Lindsley has made a major contribution to education and psychology by reemphasizing the importance not only of precise behavioral definition, but also by calling attention to the fact that there are other equally important components in behavior modification procedures in addition to reinforcement. He has taken the emphasis off "M & M's" and placed it where it should be: on *the total learning process.*

The fourth and final component of the Precision Teaching system is the Behavior Bank. In this technology, as in many others, the computer has its appropriate place. The Behavior Bank is so designed that those who begin to use the Precision Teaching system may "deposit" effective projects in the bank and receive in return the privilege of withdrawing other projects at a later date, thereby making the experience of people in all parts of the world directly available to any member of the bank.

For example, Miss Jones is a depositor in the bank, and she has deposited a number of successful Precision Teaching projects which are credited to her account. In the course of teaching her special class, she runs up against a problem of head banging; and, despite a series of attempts to modify this head banging, she is unsuccessful. She may then, if she so desires, contact the computer bank for help. The computer will search out projects which have demonstrated effective procedures in modifying head banging behavior, making this resource available to Miss Jones. She therefore has readily available the expertise of successful behavior modifiers with specific reference to the exact behavior with which she is concerned. At the present time, the Behavior Bank contains over six thousand behavior projects, which is only a fraction of the eventual storage potential. In this case, then, the computer is used in a highly effective manner in that it stores *successful* procedures on a multitude of problems which can be made readily available to depositors in the bank in their efforts to help children.

We are long past the time when we can leave the emotional, social and academic education of children to chance. It has been pointed out far too frequently that children are over and over again exposed to a learning process which is not only painful but unproductive, at least unproductive in terms of those kinds of behaviors which we would like to build. Too frequently it is productive in terms of those very behaviors which we would like very much to get rid of. We assume learning when no learning is taking place and sadly have had no definitive ways of verifying whether or not such learning is occurring. It is high time that we begin to demand evidence that we are doing our jobs with children, not only children in general, but Johnny and Mary and Billy and Cathy. The Precision Teaching program provides at least a base for such proof and a means of evaluating what we are doing. It does not tell us what changes to make; that is left to the unique creative capabilities of each teacher. It does, however, provide that teacher with immediate feedback with regard to whether her "creativity" is resulting in a satisfactory product. As numerous writers have pointed out, failure to learn might be more appropriately called failure to teach. If we continue to avoid responsibility for assessing the effects of our teaching skills, particularly when adequate assessment techniques are available, then we are, indeed, the most immoral of practitioners. □

Editor's Note: Copies of the six-cycle chart illustrated in this article are available from Behavior Research Company, Box 3351, Kansas City, Kansas 66103.

Self-Growth and Self-Enhancement Through Technology

John Henry Martin

The fear that the introduction of new technology into education may dehumanize the process of learning is real. Accordingly, the subject, "Humanizing Education Through Technology," appears to be a contradiction. Adding more technology to a society which recently has become aware of shortcomings attributed to the consequences of technology must be viewed with skepticism. The impersonal world of engineered solutions which has run over human needs is one of the unhappy conditions of our times. Highways and airports have been built in conformance to limited criteria which have systematically omitted considerations of human comfort, conservation of ecological balance and the aesthetics of our landscape. By-product wastes from industrial production, sewage, garbage and combustion exhausts are all consequences of a myopic employment of technology. This recurrent pattern of a technology which creates a dehumanized society while serving some of that same society's wants is one source of anxiety about its greater intrusion into education.

Another source of concern with technology involves the assumption that the use of devices to usurp the human guidance of learning will impair or destroy those attributes of behavior which are derived from human interaction. For example, children reared in an emotionally constricted environment need the warmth and consideration of supportive teachers. Educational institutions must compensate for environmental deficits which afflict the personality development of children. Emotionally crippled children need special help in academic learning. Technology and its devices are seen in this context as being precisely the reverse of what such children need. Additionally, it is argued that children with such emasculated backgrounds, if exposed to more non-human experience or technologically contrived, vicarious simulations of life, will be reinforced in their withdrawals from human connections and in their inability to relate to the culture in self-productive and economically satisfying ways.

Why then do anything except take up arms against further technology in education? There are several important reasons. The first has to do with the nature of technology. Technology is more than its physical products; it is also a problem solving process of reasoning. That the process is only understood by most in terms of its artifacts ought not to conceal from us that it is also a pragmatic scientism—whether the old entrepreneurial inventor's thought probes or today's

more comprehensive processes of systems analysis and design. That the process in the past, and too frequently today, continues to exclude humanistic values from its goals and criteria does not mean that today's technology must continue to do so. I beg the question at this point of whether a profit-centered economy can require technology and its processes to be directed by values whose costs in profit terms may be higher than acquisitive capitalism can sustain. There is an argument here, but the compass of this brief statement precludes its examination. Nevertheless, human needs and a due regard for consequences can be incorporated as design requirements for judging any set of competitive solutions. What we have to learn to do as a society is to ask that the design criteria be enlarged to include social values, whether the problem involves automobile safety, Redwood forests or children in school. We cannot criticize the engineer for the omission of those values which his client has never included, if when the human goals were included, they were stated in rhetoric so fancy as to decorate the intent and not to determine it. Plastic flowers are not for smelling.

An example of narrow client thinking which has ignored human values has been the installation of centralized punch card techniques for recording the daily attendance of children in school. The compulsory attendance laws plus state-aid financial formulas long ago required each teacher to "keep a register" involving from one-half to two hours of manual labor each week. On a straight cost-effectiveness basis, simple punch card maintenance of a child attendance audit puts the teachers almost entirely out of the loop. What is being overlooked is that in addition to the legal and financial records needed, teachers' concerns for a sick child, the truant as a symptom of school or family malaise, and school attendance as an important element in the social maturation of children was built into the old manual process. Thus the old clerical imposition of the past compelled at least some attention to these important aspects of a child's life. What this narrow application of technology failed to do by omission, as it so often has in other areas, was to redesign the manual system into a more efficient process for keeping legal and financial accounts, while enhancing through feedback loops the information and the impetus for teachers to be professionally and compassionately concerned with absentee children. This issue is not earth-shaking. Teachers in the past who were essentially remote and indifferent to children were not made into surrogate mothers by being required to keep petty clerical records of children's attendance. Nor has the removal of the clerical task prevented the concerned teacher from continuing a devoted interest in children's welfare. What is illustrated is that the old system required a participation whose partial fall-out facilitated teachers' awareness of absences, illnesses, malingering, truancy, neglect and withdrawal as important elements of a child's life. The new system *unnecessarily* defined the task as the removal of a clerical burden, with the *presumption* that teachers would use the time more creatively. The task could have been defined by added criteria, requiring an information-gathering procedure—involving the school nurse,

John Henry Martin, formerly a superintendent of schools, is educational consultant and senior advisor, Reader's Digest Educational Division.

attendance or social worker, psychologist and the teacher into an efficient team on the alert for a child's behavior—important to those who would enhance his development. Once again we threw out too much baby with the clerical water.

What the example is designed to illustrate is that as we introduce the thought processes of technology into education, as program planning and budgeting become more commonplace, as systems teams undertake the modeling of new solutions to educational problems, we need to put into the process human welfare criteria as part of the original design requirements. *Education, particularly the education of children, does not need more efficient ways of being neglectful.* It critically needs the rational, disciplined analysis of technologists trained to include those attributes of systems which will enhance the human aspects of learning.

At this point, it is necessary to state what kinds of learning are likely to be improved by technology. That is, technology as conventionally thought of—as learning machines or devices. First, it is necessary to assert that machines are not likely to be employed successfully in the near future for teaching affective behavior. Although the instant play-back capability of television coupled with role-playing and sensitivity training holds great promise, children's personal growth in appreciation of one another, in generosity, in affection, in consideration, in the reduction of abuse, in the tolerance of genetic differences, in commitments to group welfare and civic responsibility are all behaviors which derive from social interaction. Social simulation and game playing have large potential contributions to make, but we are at the infancy of their adaptation to education. Of more current potential are those kinds of learning which can be described as individual. That is, those cognitive skills which are both acquired and employed in intellectual isolation. Among these are the old academic skills of reading and mathematics. The case for using technologically derived instruments and appropriately designed materials in these two areas is strong. The present productivity of the schools is inadequate; and in our cities, dealing with the children of the poor or foreign speaking, the results are abominable. From 50 to 75 percent of the children from such families are unable to read or compute effectively after six, eight and twelve years of schooling. Technology, *if seen as an activated model of learning theory*, can make a decisive difference.*

I believe that technology can make the difference as long as it is not used as a gadget representing a fragment of the learning act. Technology should free the teacher not only from the drudgery of classroom drill but also from the whole concept of pedagogy that calls for manipulation of children; for much learning is a private thing, and it can be individualized through the proper use of technology. Instruments for learning as defined here produce in the learner a sense of competency. With the rapid feedback of results, the child can discover and correct his own mistakes. He is thus freed as an individual from the lockstep process within a group.

Although learning with technology is largely tutorial in style, in a very private sense the learner feels that he is doing it himself. We all can recall the sense of exuberance with which a child says, "I do it myself," and similarly all mothers know the muscular determination of the spoon-fed infant to grasp the spoon with strange vigor in the early months of life. The three-year-old's determination to put on his own clothing is a symptom of an internal drive that education has ignored. A child in a learning environment responsive to him can and does achieve the same self-learning.

Implicit in the above is a shift from efforts to motivate learning based upon peer and sibling rivalry and social competition exploited by the school to learning energized by self-growth and self-enhancement. The act of learning produces an inner sense of well-being. The power of this experience to generate additional learning is the central dynamic change technology can bring to education.

But educational technology is merely a gadget, a fragmented tool, if it engages the child's senses only partially. It must embrace all his sensory capabilities and engage him in active participation. Consequently, technology, to be effective in the basics of education, must be multi-sensory in its capabilities.

Each of us attends to each experience with a unique mobilization of his senses. Some of us find it easier to see through our eyes while others see best by listening. Touch and grasp are of dominant importance to others, and labial learning is a common public display of our times.

At present we cannot predict differences in sensory styles from one child to the next. And if we could, there is reason to believe that we shouldn't. This much we know: whatever the dominance of one sense over the other, they are mutually supportive; and in learning, all are used. We can and do learn through the eye alone. We can and do learn through our ears. But we learn better—and in some cases we can only learn—if the learning environment, the technology, permits each of us to probe it with a sensory mix unique to itself.

A second major requirement of technology is that it be seen as a system whose behavior can be manipulated by the learner. *Learning is not a spectator sport:* the learner must do things. He must be involved. And the learning setting—the specialized environment called technology and its curriculum—must respond to the initiatives of the learner. The learner's capacity to intrude is a high requirement of all good education. In technology it makes the difference between learning systems and gadgetry, however complex.

An aspect of this participatory learning is the requirement that the learner's dominant role permit his random exploration of the material. He must be free to go forward, to reverse himself, to repeat in his own style within the broad frame of the program design. Self-pacing is certainly a great virtue of teaching machines. But when speaking of self-pacing one must not assume that speed is the dominant difference among learners.

*Much of what follows is adapted from an article by the author appearing in the *Saturday Review* (June 1969.)

This would ignore differences in human learning styles that involve the senses as well as every child's need for random exploration. This oversight stems in large part from a concept of programming largely linear in format. If material to be learned is structured in ladder rungs in a step-by-step fashion, then speed of learning becomes the dominant observable variable.

We have come a long way from this concept of ten years ago. Programming capability has grown as technological sophistication has increased. Unfortunately, it is necessary to be critical of the continued narrowness of the conceptual design of both the instructional software and of the technological delivery system as they have circumscribed each other. If the program is linear, if the responses of the learner are limited to simple yes-or-no or multiple-choice conventions, then the instrument may be a pushbutton machine and a weak version of what educational technology can and should be.

The seeming irrationality of the learner's probes (from moment to moment he closes his eyes in order to hear, tunes out the sound of the teacher or the television announcer while seemingly continuing to attend to that learning situation) is a complexity that technology and its programs must invite and not prevent.

When the learner is given control over these technologically structured pieces of the environment, he will pick and choose, move forward and backward, call for repetitions in a random, personalized fashion. It requires an arrogance equal to that of the pagan gods to assume that a curriculum programmed in conventional style will do more than constrict most learners. Every human being has a learning print as unique as his fingerprint.

Although this picture of the behavioral requirements of technology appears anarchic, structure enters the picture through an examination of the material, the subject, the skills and the concepts to be learned. Jerome Bruner, at Harvard, has made a major contribution to our thinking by pointing out that there is an internal integrity to human knowledge in many of its areas. Thus we bring the findings of students of linguistics and language to the teaching of reading to determine its internal structure, its phonetic base and, hence, the concepts and skills needed to derive meaning from silent speech in print.

A second area that brings reason to the instructional material programmed into the technology is our growing realization that words in print called textbooks are severely limited pedagogical instruments—with and without teachers. An example is the way we have used art and graphics. Despite the ancient Chinese injunction about the value of a picture, art and graphics have been used as after-the-fact, patched-on affairs.

The sound motion picture, 50 years old in entertainment and neglected educationally, showed us that the marriage of the human voice and other sounds with pictures and motion had a new efficacy in learning, despite its limitations due to its inability to permit the learner to get into the act. Now through a trilogy of graphics, text and sound, with as much pedagogical attention to each, and then to their interrelationships, a whole new organization of curricular materials is made possible by a new educational technology.

We are rediscovering the importance of exploration leading to inductive reasoning called discovery. J. McVicker Hunt has called this the match, the spark that closes the gap between the known and the unknown. [See *Ed Tech*, February, 1971.] This is the discovery process in learning. Our old reliance on the deductive process, in which rules are given and applications mandated, is still too much with us; and technology and its software should not prolong its excessive use.

How do we now examine the long and growing list of devices aimed at contributing to the relief of our major educational ills? We could catalogue overhead and filmstrip projectors, turntables and tape recorders, 16mm and Super 8mm projectors, broadcast and closed-circuit television, old-fashioned radio, light pencils and touch-sensitive surfaces, new fashioned audiovisual instruments, dial-access tapes and cassettes, the computer-based "Talking Typewriter," computer assisted instruction and the "Talking Page." We now need criteria based upon learning theory that will reveal the competitively established efficiency for these devices. Each will teach some things to some children. Because they differ in total cost, we must not assume they do not differ in effectiveness for particular kinds of learning. For example, a sound motion picture or television presentation of a dramatized situation is an extraordinarily effective means of having concepts understood and values learned by large groups. The same media have severe limitations if used to teach technical skills and certain dexterities.

Until we begin controlled research to delimit the behavioral parameters of kinds of technology most useful for certain learnings and for certain learners, we will continue our overgeneralized use of particular technologies. In the meantime, in the areas of greatest educational need, where present methods continue to do poorly, we need a technology that can respond affirmatively to such criteria as: 1) Does it involve many senses? 2) Does it permit the learner to get into the curriculum? 3) Does it make possible the braided trilogy of sound, text and pictures? 4) Does it bring freedom to the act of learning in the unique random style of each and every learner?

If it does, we have a learning system that can address itself to the present problems of education. Partial instrumentation will fragment the effectiveness of the handicapped learner.

Our schools have absorbed and exploited motivations and behaviors induced by middle-class child-rearing styles, which accent language growth, adult sanctions, peer and sibling rivalry, social conformity and competition. There is room for some doubt that children so raised and so educated are able to do more than verbalize the values of a humanistic society. For the large numbers of children in our society nurtured in homes differing from this model, who have not been successfully educated in our schools, the process produces social antagonisms, hostilities and negative self-appraisal. Hardly a source for optimism for the future of a society. Technology designed to match human learning behaviors must have an autonomy and dexterity of

Humanizing Education Through Technology: The View from an Ivory Foxhole

Leo E. Persselin

"The University may be a large, sometimes cold and seemingly unfeeling place—but let me assure you that you have not lost your identity, Number 17932."

behaviors that will induce learning in children as they are.

This is humanistic education at its best. Where the learner dominates the act of learning, where he measures his performance, where he modifies his acts as the result of his evaluation of the consequences, where he manipulates the materials of learning, and where he engages all his senses in his own style, then human growth is assured. Technology so seen, so designed and so functioning will make a contribution to education of children that will remove many present obstacles toward a more humanistic society.

Such instruments have begun to emerge. On the issue of humanizing education through technology, the present system's failure rate in the basic skills is producing large numbers of angry, alienated and unemployable youth. From their earliest encounter with a curriculum and teacher in the first grade to their premature departure, they are hourly taught that they are stupid, unteachable organisms, somehow organically different and defective. Learning instruments whose behavior has been engineered to be multi-sensory and whose software materials are harmonious to the best thinking in the subject fields of reading and mathematics are providing children with successful learning. A most important observation concerning the human consequences of technology-based learning is that the children involved grow in self-esteem, self-power and self-direction. A child's success in learning brings to him an internal euphoria of competence.

Alternatively, we have witnessed the many less-than-successful efforts to train the manual behavior of large numbers of teachers in order to optimize the learning of the basic academic skills. Those of us who have spent years attempting this task are not optimistic about this course of action. To optimize the behavior of a multi-sensory instrument as a delivery system for the skills of reading and mathematics holds, perhaps, the greatest current challenge to technology and education. The success of the effort will do a great deal to humanize both technology and education. □

Abram L. Sachar, chancellor of Brandeis University, has characterized the crisis which now besets education with the observation that "we are no longer in an ivory tower; rather we are in an ivory foxhole."[1]

A crucial aspect of this crisis has been the growing alienation of students and teachers alike from traditional educational systems. It is an alienation born of despair at what is felt to be an "impersonality" and "dehumanization" of the educational process, and fueled by what is viewed as a lack of relevance to the "real world" and to "human" values.

Is it possible to "humanize education through technology"? In order even to talk about the matter, we must first decide what we mean by "technology" and by "humanizing" education.

Do We Have Anything to Talk About?

Taking both of the terms in their narrowest sense, we may use "technology" simply to refer to the replacement of manpower with machine-power—or more specifically within an educational context, to the replacement of "teacher-power" with machine-power. "Humanizing" education, by contrast, may be restricted to the concept of the ideal tutorial relationship which exists between a master teacher and an individual student.

If this is what we mean by "technology" and "humanizing" education, we have nothing to talk about. "Technology" clearly means teaching by machine, and just as clearly, this is the antithesis of "human" instruction.

Within a broader context, however, "humanizing" education also may be interpreted as the enrichment of education by whatever means for realizing the individual's fullest human potential. This includes both student and teacher.

Again within the broader context, "technology" in education may refer to the use of both human and non-human resources for achieving maximum learning effectiveness. Within this context, we are no longer talking merely about using machines to teach. We are rather talking about an approach to education in which machines may or may not be used to make instruction at the same time more productive and less labor-intensive.

Leo E. Persselin is with the Dubnoff School for Educational Therapy, North Hollywood, California.

Within this context, "technology" and "humanizing" education are not incompatible. The technology we are talking about is not merely a technology of machines, concerned solely with the engineering of machines. It is rather a "technology of learning"—a *human technology* concerned with the *engineering of learning*.[2]

Essentially, educational technology may be defined in terms of three component elements:

1. *Programmed Learning.* Programmed learning means approaching the instructional requirements from the standpoint of what the learner needs, rather than what is most convenient for the teacher to provide. It implies teaching by clearly defined operational objectives rather than by intuition. It means achieving those objectives by the systematic application of scientifically established principles of learning.

Programmed learning does not necessarily mean teaching by machine, although it has opened some dramatic vistas for machine teaching. Nor does it necessarily imply individual instruction, although again, the discipline has vastly expanded opportunities for individualized learning. The principles of programmed learning may be applied in group instruction by a classroom teacher through a variety of techniques for contingency management, behavior modification and classroom "engineering."

Even in group applications, however, programmed learning means dealing with each learner as an individual. The accommodation of individual differences is central to the programmed learning concept.

2. *Mediated Instruction.* Mediated instruction encompasses the full range of non-human resources through which instruction might be conducted—all of the many forms of text, film and electronic technology which have been refined for educational use. But it does not exclude the human element in the instructional process. The ideal of mediated instruction is an optimum combination of the most effective machine and human resources which can be put together for achieving a given learning objective.[3]

Under any circumstance of mediated instruction, the teacher is present at least in recorded form. In individualized programmed learning through mediated instruction, all the characteristics of a classical tutorial relationship may be present: step-by-step instruction at the learner's own best pace; each step of instruction exactly the right size; active learner response; immediate feedback to the learner, reinforcing correct responses and providing remedial instruction for responses which are incorrect; and selection and presentation of subsequent steps based on the learner's preceding achievement.

Instructional systems which combine media with person-to-person interaction between student and teacher might assign functions to the teacher which are quite different from those of the conventional classroom. Whatever these functions may be, however, they remain both vital and indispensable.

3. *Educational Accountability.* Instructional systems based on concepts of programmed learning and which incorporate mediated instruction relieve the teacher of constantly improvising and performing primarily as a presenter of instruction. Instead, the teacher is freed to monitor and evaluate student accomplishment, to diagnose and prescribe for the solution of individual learning problems, to counsel and to motivate. In effect, the teacher's primary function shifts from that of instructor to educational manager.

The core concept in effective educational management is accountability. It is a concept which emphasizes output rather than input as the critical factor in evaluating the educational process. The most important measure of the instructional system becomes not how much money is put into the system, not how many degrees a teacher has, not how many hours and how hard the teacher works, and not how much material is "covered." It is very simply *how much the learner learns.* And learning achievement is measured in terms of *observable changes in the ability to perform.*

Individualized prescriptive instruction and ungraded critical-path learning programs impose stringent requirements for educational accountability. These requirements can be met, however, through teaching by objective and through the use of programmed procedures for tracking and evaluating individual learning achievement on a lesson-by-lesson, hour-by-hour and day-by-day basis. The feasibility for this in even the largest school system has been made possible by high-speed digital computers. The result is an instructional system in which educational output may be measured precisely, independently and objectively.

What Can Technology Do?

During the past three years, more than half of all the new public school buildings in the United States have been built on the open or modified-open plan.[4] These schools have burgeoned because their classrooms without walls contribute to the freedom and flexibility of instruction that technology makes possible. Rapid-access, computer-based data retrieval systems, TV- and film-based presentation systems, and methodologies for individualizing instruction in ungraded classrooms have made it possible to completely replace the "2 x 4 x 6" concept of the school system: 2 covers of a textbook; 4 walls of a classroom; 6 classes every day.

In these and other schools, technology is making it possible to offer courses which never before could be taught because of previously inadequate resources. Many of them are "enrichment" instruction in foreign languages, music, other creative arts and the humanities. Children are being taught to read in kindergarten. More complex subject matter is being offered in lower grades to students who have the opportunity to advance individually as fast as they are able to learn.

Advanced concepts in prescriptive instruction are creating whole new populations of learners—populations of all ages which in the past have been unreachable or unteachable: the physically and mentally handicapped, the culturally deprived and others with learning problems for whatever reason. The technology of precision teaching is making it possible to provide every learner with a "special" curriculum designed to meet his own "special" needs. As a result, today's category of "special education" might well disappear. Tomorrow, all education can become special.

Technology is completely reversing the traditional objective of audiovisual instruction—"bringing the world into the classroom" through the use of media. At best, this has provided only second-hand contact with the world—and, regrettably, second-hand education. Today's technology has demonstrated its potential for "bringing the learner into the world" for first-hand learning in real-life environments.[5]

Technology has demonstrated that the world can be turned into a global village where the individual may grow through first-hand experience in real-life locales. It has made possible educational systems which do not isolate students from the realities of life, but rather make them a part of life in ways which can give them greater human understanding. In so doing, it has demonstrated that the school can be the primary instrument not only for educating the "whole person," but also for interpreting the community to those who live in it, and for rebuilding the community to make it a better place in which to live.[6]

The Engineering of Learning: Closing the Process Gap

Machines do not solve problems. Only people solve problems. People may use machines as tools to help them solve problems. But if a tool is to be effective, the user must know how to use it properly. In effective technology, *product* and *process* are inseparable.

Despite the vast array of electro-mechanical hardware introduced onto the educational scene within the past dozen years, the technology of education has lagged far behind its potential because of what might be called a "process gap." Engineers have been more concerned with product than with process—with making machines rather than making machines serve human needs. This is why professional engineering and engineering education have had so little identification with educational technology in its broader context.

The "engineering of learning" concept is typically identified as a product of educational psychology. It is usually dated from B.F. Skinner's 1954 publication of "The Science of Learning and the Art of Teaching,"[7] in which programmed learning was first introduced to the general educational community.

The first published reference to a "systems" concept in education appeared in 1956, when James D. Finn, a professor of education, discussed an approach to audiovisual education analogous to the functional design of an airplane.[8]

Yet, as early as 1945—a decade before the works of Psychologist Skinner and Educationalist Finn—Engineer-Educator W.W. Charters already had noted that "the difference between engineering and education is one of degree rather than kind,"[9] and was proposing the application of engineering principles for restructuring and improving classroom curriculum.[10]

Without the engineer's understanding and command of process, the promise of educational technology cannot be fulfilled. But the need for the "how" of educational technology cannot be met either by profes-

"Computer—can you keep a secret?"

sional educators trying to be engineers or by professional engineers trying to be educators.

Clearly the answer lies in a truly professional collaboration between both educators and engineers.

Almost 70 years ago, in 1902, John Dewey envisioned a school system which would "provide at least part of the training which is necessary to keep the individual properly adjusted to a rapidly changing environment . . . it must provide means for bringing people and their ideas and beliefs together in such ways as will lessen friction and instability, and introduce deeper sympathy and wider understanding."

Educational technology can be the determining factor which will finally turn this vision into reality. □

References

1. Sachar, Abram L. The Future Is Not What It Used to Be. *The PTA Magazine*, September 1969, pp. 2-32.
2. Persselin, Leo E. Systems Implications for Secondary Education. *Journal of Secondary Education*, April 1969, *44* (4), pp. 159-66.
3. Persselin, Leo E. *An Approach to Systems Design in Audiovisual Instruction*, Ph.D. dissertation, University Microfilms Order No. 68-5878, University of Southern California, 1967. 609 p.
4. *Open-Space Schools Project Bulletin*, School Planning Laboratory, School of Education, Stanford University, March 1970, *1* (1). 7 p.
5. Ramo, Simon & Persselin, Leo E. Changing Functions of Urban Schools: The Role of Industry. *Educational Technology*, September 1970, *10* (9), pp. 58-60.
6. Morse, Tom. The Everywhere School. *School Management*, December 1969, *13* (12) pp. 39-45; The Anywhere School. *Ibid.*, pp. 46-55.
7. Skinner, B.F. The Science of Learning and the Art of Teaching. *Harvard Educational Review*, Spring 1954, *24*, pp. 86-97.
8. Finn, James D. AV Development and the Concept of Systems. *Teaching Tools*, Fall 1956, *3* (4), pp. 163-64.
9. Charters, W.W. Is There a Field of Educational Engineering? *Educational Research Bulletin*, February 1945.
10. Charters, W.W. Idea Men and Engineers in Education. *The Educational Forum*, May 1948.

Humane Benefits for Education: Some Directions in Technology

Donald E. Barnes

The word "benefits" appears in the title in its technical sense, as related to cost-analysis, and it suggests the theme of my argument: that technology's chief contributions to education will continue to take the form of adding alternatives for resolving cost-benefit dilemmas, that is, for improving cost-effectiveness of instruction. The main dilemma and a classic opportunity for technology, according to my proposition, takes the form of persistent tension between a finite supply of funds for education and steeply rising labor costs.

"We are in the very midst of the crisis of modern man," according to Erich Fromm.* "But there is hope—because there is a real possibility that man can reassert himself, and that he can make the technological society human," he concludes.

The remarks that follow are speculative by design and respond to the theme of the 1970 Vanderbilt Conference on "Humanizing Education Through Technology." At the outset, since many may be put on guard by the somewhat impalpable term, "humanizing," it seems fair to offer a definition of that and other key terms, including "technology" and "education," as used herein.

"Humaneness" and "humanizing" are employed for their reference to humanism and to the civilizing and ethical pursuits of mankind. Customarily, we use the word "humane" to describe the behavior and sentiments which set human beings apart from other animals. The idea of the dignity and worth of every human person ranks among the central themes in Western thought, and I would say that it is fundamental to the notion of "humane" activity. These meanings are associated with those goals in education which emphasize opportunity for full development of individual talent and the value of independent inquiry.

Technology consists of inventions and techniques for serving human demand. That definition goes far beyond the familiar characterization, "applied science," and discards the common assumption that humane activities and considerations are not involved. In my view technology embraces many of man's efforts to solve problems and improve his condition, especially through the development of products, in the broadest sense in which we speak of products, from the first conversion of sticks and bones into tools and weapons, through the invention of wheels, sails, wings and rockets, including along the way the development of slate and chalk, desks and chairs, buildings, classrooms, books and the whole constellation of electromagnetic products which offer so much promise as learning aids to students. Technology so defined pre-dates science, differs in aims and is independent of the methods of science, at least in large part. Yet in both realms there is a similar reliance upon aesthetics, and a premium upon original thought and creative endeavor; and both work similarly great influences upon what men believe and the ways in which men live.

For present purposes "education" refers simply to formal schooling, with emphasis on instruction in large public systems.

The proposal that I am advancing, namely, that technology will exert increasing influence on instruction and may do so with humane results, depends upon the operation of two powerful forces in American education. The periodic interaction of these factors seems to me to influence profoundly the history of technology in our schools.

The first force has to do with rising costs and limited resources. The expectation in recent years that the federal government would supply new money for schools in huge amounts may have obscured the likelihood to the contrary that society will divert only what it considers a reasonable proportion of its product to education, extraordinarily worthwhile as some of us may consider education to be. President Nixon's televised veto of last year's education bill dramatized that likelihood. According to Clark Kerr, education "already employs more people and uses more resources than any other major area of American society." *

John Gardner, as head of the National Urban Coalition, last year issued repeated warnings of critical scarcities of funds for the operation of American cities, and he named education as only one of numerous essential services likely to suffer. We are all too familiar with the reluctance of taxpayers in many jurisdictions to approve school bond issues; about 80 percent of the bond elections were lost in 1969. Rising costs seem to be leading to a serious decline, apparently just ahead, in the condition and in the very numbers of private colleges and universities. Sharp reductions occurred in both fiscal 1969 and 1970 in actual expenditures of the U.S. Office of Education. We tend to overestimate the contributions of the national government, anyway. NEA reports that federal sources provided only about 6.4 percent of total school revenue receipts in the 1969-70 school year.

The first force, then, builds up in the containment of expanding educational costs within relatively limited

---

* Fromm, Erich. *The Revolution of Hope*. Toward A Humanized Technology. New York: Harper & Row, 1968, p. 162

Donald E. Barnes is vice president of the Institute for Educational Development.

*Kerr, Clark. New Learning Looks Longer and Broader. *The New York Times*, January 12, 1970.

public budgets. Pressures of this kind now seem to be intensifying.

The second powerful force, which may interact soon with the former, is the often underestimated capability of technologists to improve cost-effectiveness in many instructional situations—not a decade hence, but now.

Ah, the great hopes and claims for technology only a few years ago: a carrel for every student; a new, electronic world for education; and mergers galore. But later it appeared that markets had been overestimated, and product applications were too distant in time, according to several companies interested in educational technology. Cost-effectiveness approaches to instruction seemed to yield unrealistic estimates and vague approximations. And so it was back to the classroom, close the door and resume the lecture.

Something like that, I suspect, describes the opinion in which technology for education is held at the moment by many and perhaps even most of the people professionally associated with education, an opinion which may be founded on major miscalculations.

In the meantime, technologists have designed and are testing much larger systems concepts for education, some of them with striking success. The individually prescribed instruction (IPI) systems of the Philadelphia regional education laboratory make a good example.

Rexford Tugwell has pointed out that technology "has its own laws" which, notably, "require that technology must be big." In fact, "It has to be comprehensive."*

A New "Generation"?

Engineers often describe products in terms of "generations." A second generation of electromagnetic technology for education probably is upon us already, and this one may be expected to offer numerous alternatives to the increasing costs of human labor. Such is the way with technology, time out of mind, and it seems unlikely that education will be exempt from that ancient economic tendency to replace expensive people with less expensive products. That process speaks to the very nature and purpose of technology. A hidden injunction seems to be involved, a moral imperative quite distinctly *humane* in character, to the effect that anything a machine can do as well as or better than human beings ought not to be done by the latter, anyway.

If I could plan the world my way, teachers and healers would receive the highest and best recognition which society can bestow, including pay for services. But that view of things has so few adherents that simply to maintain minimum levels of real compensation and to

gain reasonable working conditions, teachers have been obliged to seek the protections of collective bargaining.

The growth of trade-unionism among teachers, however successful, and the emergence of teacher strikes, however necessary for teachers' interests, in the long run may speed the advent and expand the impact of technology in education—for the very reason that such activities effectively increase the cost of human services. The interaction of the forces thus described tends to advance a relentless process which seems bent on replacement of some teachers by their own tools.

Replacement? One of the self-deceptions of educators—or is it the tendency to euphemism in sales approaches?—causes us to speak of "teacher *aids*" and "audiovisual *aids* to teaching." Through cost-effectiveness demonstrations, we shall come to know the successors to those products for what they will be, i.e., labor-saving devices. Despite the probability that the replacement procedure will consist largely of diversion of many potential teachers to pursuits other than education, teacher organizations may seek to resist instructional technology. That is suggested by the criticism, sometimes overstated, by union leaders and publications aimed at some of the performance contracting projects currently attempting to test claims of improved cost-effectiveness.

What Directions?

So much for the main outlines of my proposal. What directions for inquiry seem to follow? How can investigators isolate and measure humane benefits? Benefits scaled against what goals for education? What manner of human product could ever replace the gifted and consecrated teacher?

By one of those astounding coincidences which prove an argument, a major portion of the developmental effort in educational technology has been directed for some years toward individualizing instruction. The phrase covers numerous activities and objectives, of course; yet basically it has to do with a pupil studying and learning alone and at his own pace.

What values support this now well-recognized aim? What additional considerations could add humaneness? And what statements of value could guide the measuring of educational benefits?

One sure sign of humane values in the movement toward individualized study is the often repeated concern of its proponents for a fair learning opportunity for every child. The slow student should not be left behind, they say, and the children who are quick to learn must not be held back.

Another sign, and an exceedingly useful clue to the measurement of benefits, may be found in common statements about the nature of learning. Robert Glaser gave us the word "interface" several years ago to advance the idea that learning happens in the interface between the student and the material to be learned. It does not tend to happen through an intermediary. Presumed intercessors may even hinder and distract. "To teach" ought to be used only as an *intransitive* verb. People do not "teach" other people or "teach" a subject *to* other people, in the sense of putting

*Mayer, Milton *et al. On Liberty: Man Vs. the State.* Center for the Study of Democratic Institutions, Santa Barbara, 1969, p. 191.

knowledge into someone's head. Teachers manage learning environments, to be sure, but learning itself is a private act, like dreaming. Only the student can do it, and in some respects it is a wholly insular act.

"The requirement for learning is that the person who is to learn make an effort," observes Ralph Tyler. The learner's plight is solitary; another cannot make the effort for him. "If the child does not see in the school anything that he really wants to learn, . . . he just doesn't learn."*

Aristotle's dictum that men by nature desire to know supports the conclusion that children are eager to learn. It seems evident that they will manage to do so under a great variety of circumstances, and that the group pursuits of the traditional classroom often may not provide the most favorable circumstances.

All of those are statements of the sort that one would expect to find rather frequently used in connection with individualization of instruction through technology. They reflect values; they describe behavior; and they suggest many ways of measuring behavioral change. They show a prime concern for benefits to be realized by individual students. By the definition I have specified, they are *intensely humane.*

Such statements and concerns bear a categorical but unspecified relationship to two fundamental educational goals. Probably no other goal for education and no other achievement by students carry as much respect and approval among educators and large sections of the public as the summary qualification for the doctoral degree. Here is the ultimate end of formal education: it is the demonstrated *capability for independent inquiry.* It is surpassed in stature—which is to say in breadth of acceptance as well as rank—by only one aim for education, I would say, and that is encouragement of the voluntary practice of independent study after the end of formal schooling. Dewey said it for all, that the desired "result of the educative process is capacity for further education."

In these areas investigators may find improved assumptions for use in measuring benefits. Educational technology emphasizes—indeed, seems to concentrate upon the acceleration of—independent study; and hard upon the heels of that may follow independent inquiry. Is that really so? Could technology help our students toward the lifetime habit of private study? What are the linkages, if any, between individualized instruction and independent inquiry? Is it reasonable to expect that technology will directly and more efficiently assist the young in reaching levels of behavioral achievement answering the best standards applied to student performance by our oldest and highest educational institutions?

If so, then what better opportunities for technology and what more acceptably *humane* benefit could technology hope to bring to education? □

*Tyler, Ralph W. *et al. Agenda for the Nation.* Washington, D.C.: The Brookings Institution, 1969.